A Gathering of Evidence
Essays on William Faulkner's Intruder in the Dust

A Gathering of Evidence
Essays on William Faulkner's Intruder in the Dust

Edited by

MICHEL GRESSET

PATRICK SAMWAY, S.J.

SAINT JOSEPH'S UNIVERSITY PRESS
PHILADELPHIA, PENNSYLVANIA

FORDHAM UNIVERSITY PRESS
NEW YORK

Copyright © 2004 by Saint Joseph's University Press.
All rights reserved.
No part of this book may be used or reproduced
in any manner whatsoever without written permission.

Library of Congress Cataloging-in-Publication Data

A gathering of evidence : essays on William Faulkner's Intruder in the dust /
edited by Michel Gresset, Patrick Samway.
    p. cm.
  Includes bibliographical references.
  ISBN 0-916101-46-0 (alk. paper)
  1. Faulkner, William, 1897-1962. Intruder in the dust. I. Gresset, Michel.
II. Samway, Patrick H.
  PS3511.A86I534 2004
  813'.52--dc22
                          2004004372

Published by Saint Joseph's University Press
5600 City Avenue
Philadelphia, Pennsylvania 19131-1395
www.sju.edu/sjupress/

Saint Joseph's University Press is a member
of the Association of Jesuit University Presses

Cover photo: Hunter Cole

Table of Contents

List of Authors vii

Introduction ix

1   The Community in Action
    Cleanth Brooks 1

2   Man on the Margin: Lucas Beauchamp and
    the Limitations of Space
    Keith Clark 17

3   Eunice Habersham's Lessons in *Intruder in the Dust*
    Ikuko Fujihira 37

4   Teaching *Intruder in the Dust* Through Its Political and
    Historical Context"
    Robert W. Hamblin 57

5   Race Fantasies: The Filming of *Intruder in the Dust*
    Charles Hannon 75

6   Negotiating the National Voice in Faulkner's Late Work
    Joe Karaganis 97

7   Faulkner's Comic Narrative of Community
    Donald M. Kartiganer 131

8   Contextualizing Faulkner's *Intruder in the Dust*:
    Sherlock Holmes, Chick Mallison, Decolonization, and Change
    Richard C. Moreland 151

9   Man in the Middle: Faulkner and the Southern White Moderate
    Noel Polk 167

10 *Intruder in the Dust*: A Re-evaluation
    Patrick Samway, S.J. 189

11 Faulkner and the Post-Confederate
    Neil Schmitz 225

12 "The Sum of Your Ancestry":
    Cultural Context and *Intruder in the Dust*
    Evelyn Jaffe Schreiber 247

Permissions 259

LIST OF AUTHORS

Cleanth Brooks, author of *William Faulkner: The Yoknapatawpha Country*, among many notable works, was, before his death in 1994, Gray Professor of Rhetoric in the Department of English at Yale University.

Keith Clark, author of *Black Manhood in James Baldwin, Ernest J. Gaines, and August Wilson*, is Associate Professor of English and the Interim Director of the African American Studies at George Mason University.

Ikuko Fujihira, a member of the editorial board of *The Faulkner Journal of Japan* and author of *The Patchwork Quilt in Carnival Colors: Toni Morrison's Novels*, is Professor of American Literature at Chuo University.

Robert W. Hamblin, co-editor with Louis Daniel Brodsky of the five-volume *Faulkner: A Comprehensive Guide to the Brodsky Collection*, is Professor of English and Director of the Center for Faulkner Studies at Southeast Missouri State University.

Charles Hannon, author of *Faulkner and the Discourses of Culture*, is Associate Professor and Chairman of the Information Technology Leadership Program at Washington and Jefferson College in Pennsylvania.

Joe Karaganis, who received his Ph.D. in literature from Duke University, is a Program Officer for the Social Science Research Council in New York City.

Donald M. Kartiganer, author of *The Fragile Thread: The Meaning of Form in Faulkner's Novels*, is the Howry Professor of Faulkner Studies at the University of Mississippi.

Richard C. Moreland, author of *Faulkner and Modernism: Rereading and Rewriting*, is Professor of English at Louisiana State University.

Noel Polk, author of *Children of the Dark House: Text and Context in Faulkner* and editor of the novels of William Faulkner for the Library of America and Random House, is Professor of English and Director of Graduate Studies at University of Southern Mississippi.

Patrick Samway, S.J., who has written a book on the manuscripts and typescripts of Faulkner's *Intruder in the Dust* and also co-edited with Michel Gresset *Faulkner and Ideology: Perspectives from Paris*, is Professor of English at Saint Joseph's University in Philadelphia.

Neil Schmitz, author of *White Robe's Dilemma: Tribal History in American Literature*, is Professor of English at the University of Buffalo.

Evelyn Jaffe Schreiber, author of *Subversive Voices: Eroticizing the Other in William Faulkner and Toni Morrison*, is Associate Professor of English and Director of the Writing Center at George Washington University.

Introduction

With the publication in the summer 1999 issue of *The Virginia Quarterly Review* of "Lucas Beauchamp," which Patrick Samway, S.J., discovered in a long-forgotten file and which Faulkner had originally wanted excerpted from *Intruder in the Dust* (1948) and published as a short story (though it was never done during his lifetime), there has been renewed interest in this novel. Indeed, among the stars in the American literary firmament Faulkner's has remained consistently bright. Whatever litmus test one wants to use, Faulkner's fiction has always been recognized as among the very best ever written in the United States. And thus it is particularly fitting that a volume of 12 essays focusing exclusively on *Intruder in the Dust* be made available for the first time to students of Faulkner, of whatever stripe, who wish to appreciate this novel in different contexts and from a variety of perspectives. In short, this volume is a gathering of all sorts of methodological evidence for evaluating a novel that is, in itself, a detective story whose resolution depends upon securing appropriate legal evidence.

Toward the end of 1947, about four months before he started writing *Intruder in the Dust*, Faulkner was deeply involved in writing the horse race section of *A Fable* (1954), among whose principal characters are an elderly black man and two assistants (a white English groom and a teenage black boy)—characters not unlike those who would appear in *Intruder in the Dust*. By the end of January 1948, Faulkner's agent, Harold Ober, had received over 500 pages of the typescript of this large, incomplete novel. Although exhausted by writing *A Fable*, Faulkner still felt he had much more to do before it was finished.

As a change of pace and to renew his creative energies, Faulkner wrote Ober on February 1 that he had put aside writing *A Fable* and had already finished 60 pages of a draft of a short novel, what he called "a mystery-murder" whose theme concerned a "relationship between Negro and white, specifically or rather the premise being that the white people in the south, before the North or the govt. or anyone else, owe and must pay a responsibility to the Negro." As Faulkner began explaining the genesis of this new novel, he shifted the theme he had been dealing with in the horse race story; in *Intruder in the Dust* he wanted to develop the responsibility the white community toward the Negro.

Faulkner went on to compose two main drafts of this novel in a relatively short period of time. It is difficult to determine the exact pace at which Faulkner wrote *Intruder in the Dust*, though the typescript evidence indicates that he started off by writing approximately four pages a day. By February 22, he wrote to another of his agents, Robert Haas, that he had finished the first draft of his novel: "Am rewriting it now, a little more of a book than I thought at first so the rewrite will actually be the writing of it, which will take some time yet. I wont set a date; I'll just work at it." The second and final version would be more than twice the length of the first. By April 23, he had finished the novel and sent it to Haas, though he still had not resolved the word that would go before the phrase "in the Dust": "Cabal," "Masquerade," "Impostor," "Malfeasance," "Substitution," "Malaprop," "Malpractice," "Malaprop," or "Intruder."

Once the novel had been set in galley form, Random House sold the movie rights to M-G-M for $50,000, with Faulkner receiving $40,000 of this. Ironically, Faulkner began to know a sense of financial security, this time from a place that had often robbed him of emotional and creative security: Hollywood. When the novel was published in late September, Faulkner had proven that his creative juices had not abated, even though it had been six years since the publication of his last significant work, *Go Down, Moses*. *Intruder in the Dust* sold more copies in the first year (about 18,000) than any of his previous books.

The most likely source of the novel is *Come in at the Door* (1934) by William Campbell (alias March), a copy of which Father Samway saw in

1972 on the bookshelves of Faulkner's home, Rowan Oak, though he has no evidence that Faulkner had actually read this murder mystery, which depicts a white boy concerned with the death of an older man who is partially black. One should not discount, however, the potential influence of Mark Twain's *The Adventures of Huckleberry Finn* and *Tom Sawyer* or Charles Dickens's *Great Expectations*, as well as the lynching in the vicinity of Oxford, Mississippi, of Elwood Higginbotham, a black man and the confessed murderer of Glen Roberts, a white man, in September 1935; or the murder of Lawrence Marlor, also white, by Wilfred Jenkins, a black, in December 1936, or the lynching of Nelse Patton in 1908, as detailed by Charles Hannon in his essay in this volume. In addition, one might look to Faulkner's 1943 film script "Battle Cry," in which a young man from the South helps a black man who represents the ideals of his homeland. As is true with this film script, as well as *Intruder in the Dust* and other works of fiction by Faulkner, such as *The Reivers* (1962), which has a white boy-black man relationship or the horse race episode in *A Fable*, it is possible to see similar patterns emerge that serve as touchstones in appreciating significant dimensions of Faulkner's imaginative world.

Intruder in the Dust can be seen as the last panel of a triptych on race (with themes about black-white relationships that now seem outmoded), whose first expression is *Light in August* (1932) and whose second is *Go Down, Moses* (1942). It is an "unflinching portrait of racial injustice," as one critic called it in 1948, when it was first published. Faulkner the novelist (the novelist can theoretically be greater than the man, and it is important in this instance) had to create the Negro more than he received him ready made: we need only to look at *Sartoris* (1929) and to Simon Strother to find the best "Sambo" that William Faulkner could offer given the time, the region, and the cultural conditions of his upbringing in a small town, and to measure the progression from Simon Strother to Lucas Beauchamp. The novelist had come full circle from his delineation of Joe Christmas in *Light in August* (1932) and from the beginning of the creation of Lucas Beauchamp in *Go Down, Moses*.

Intruder in the Dust was received as Faulkner at his best by Eudora Welty, as she wrote in the Winter 1949 issue of *The Hudson Review*: "*Intruder* is marvelously funny....It doesn't follow that *Intruder*, short, funny, of simple outline, with its detective-story casing, is one of the less difficult of Faulkner's novels....Even the witty turns and the perfect neatness of plot look like the mark of a flash inspiration....As in all of Faulkner's work, the separate scenes leap up on their own...."—a view far different from that expressed by novelist Malcolm Lowry to Random House editor Albert Erskine (5 March 1949): "... with all its merits I keep thinking that it is only the first part of the second draft of a novel to be called *Intruder in the Dust*....It seems to be careless too, the writing sometimes almost frightening in its badness. Not that it is difficult exactly, but that I find myself often sinking through a quicksand of what is not even bebop without even a body at the bottom of it." It seems to us that most of the essays in this volume fall somewhere between the appraisals of Welty and Lowry, revealing a fictional complexity many readers have intuited but few have formally expressed.

It is good to remember that these 12 essays were written over a period of 40 years—the co-editors have decided to retain the original style and format of each essay—and thus reflect differing hermeneutical approaches, which, when taken together, can only but point to, and unravel, the novel's literary strengths and weaknesses. At least six of the essays (those of Keith Clark [1990], Robert W. Hamblin [2001], Joe Karaganis [1998], Noel Polk [1986], Neil Schmitz [1995], and Evelyn Jaffe Schreiber [2001]) deal with the race problem, treated in this novel for the most part as a "cultural code," as Evelyn Jaffe Schreiber termed it. While the second of these essays reminds us in historical terms who were the actors at the time, beginning with President Harry Truman and Faulkner's friend Hodding Carter, Keith Clark, relying on the discourse expressed by Houston A. Baker, among others, finds that Faulkner would not cut the cord between himself and the South's "cancerous racial history and a proclivity to confine the blackman to the space of a nigger." In his essay, Joe Karaganis notes that Gavin Stevens's voice was often equated with that of William Faulkner, and that what "most critics have reacted too negatively in *Intruder* is precisely this didactic ambition," or, to put it as did Noel Polk in his thoughtful and nuanced essay, "Stevens's shortcomings [make] us wary of accepting his words at face value." Faulkner would let the South set "Sambo" free in order to defend "both racial homogeneity and moral autonomy." What he had in mind in calling the Negro "Sambo" was the dated concept many white people had of the Negro (and it was "Post-Confederate," as Neil Schmitz put it in an essay that situates this novel within a panoply of other Southern fiction). As to Evelyn Jaffe Schreiber, she rightly stresses, citing the insights of non-American critics, that *"Intruder* is a novel about community awareness of the anachronistic ideology of white society."

As to the other six essays, Cleanth Brooks's (1963) and Father Samway's (1980) give overall, more comprehensive assessments—and in Father Samway's case based partially on the typescripts of the novel and its general structure—while the remaining four pick up rather specific approaches: Richard Moreland's article (1997) is devoted to an historical and ideological evaluation; Ikuko Fujihira's (2003) to a feminist approach of the novel through the character of Eunice Habersham, and Donald M. Kartiganer's (2003) to the novel's "comic form," reaching back as far as Menander and Greek comedy. Finally, Charles Hannon's (1995) looks at "The Filming of *Intruder in the Dust*" and how this provides a commentary on the original text itself. Whatever their approach, all the authors in this volume of essays seem to agree on one point: Although this novel is about the education of a young white boy, Chick Mallison, in a racially charged small Southern community, it is Lucas Beauchamp, a black man accused of murdering a white man, who emerges in many seemingly contradictory ways as an important literary figure.

Michel Gresset
Patrick Samway, S.J.

THE COMMUNITY IN ACTION

Cleanth Brooks

Intruder in the Dust represents a very curious mixture of literary excellence and faults. But its essential faults are not those that in the past have come in for rough handling by the critics. These latter tend to disappear, once the reader has put aside a few misconceptions. Such objections center around the character of Gavin Stevens and some of his talk on the race problem. It led Edmund Wilson, in his review of the book in *The New Yorker*, to treat the novel as "a kind of counter blast to the anti-lynching bill and to the civil rights plank of the Democratic platform," and other reviewers made much the same point.

Most readers find it impossible not to condescend to Gavin Stevens. They can scarcely be blamed, and in itself the condescension does no harm to the novel. What is of damaging consequence, however, is that many readers are quite certain that Faulkner admires Gavin Stevens, regards him as a kind of projected image of himself, and means to use him as his mouthpiece. But as the earlier chapters of this book should have made plain, Gavin Stevens occupies no privileged position in Faulkner's novels: sometimes he talks sense and sometimes he talks nonsense. Doubtless, what he says often represents what many Southerners think and what Faulkner himself—at one time or another—has thought. But Gavin is not presented as the sage and wise counselor of the community. His notions have to take their chances along with those of less "intellectual" characters.

A more cogent objection to this novel is the incoherence of the plot. *Intruder in the Dust* is another of Faulkner's flirtations with the detective novel. This is not to be held against it, of course; but the plot of a good detective story must justify its complications, and that of *Intruder* scarcely does so. When the excellent movie was made of the novel, the director very sensibly simplified the plot by reducing the number of times that Vinson Gowrie's grave was reopened.

Worse than the extravagances of the plot, however, is the incoherence of motivation and action. The murderer's motive for putting into the grave of his first victim, Vinson Gowrie, the body of Jake Montgomery, whom he has just killed, does not make entire sense. If the purpose was to remove the body of Vinson because it would not show the right kind of bullet hole, what is gained by substituting a body which will show no bullet hole at all, and one which is not even supposed to be in this grave? It would have made more sense to put Vinson back in his grave, and cart away the body of Jake. Was Crawford desperate and therefore foolish in doing what he did? Or was the action imposed upon Crawford by the author himself simply to complicate the plot?

When Crawford, from his hiding place, sees Miss Habersham, Charles Mallison, and Aleck dig up Jake's body and rebury it, and is therefore forced to dig up the body once more, this time he does leave the coffin empty. But why does he give Jake's body a hasty and therefore necessarily shallow burial elsewhere? Why doesn't he simply put the body of Jake Montgomery in the quicksand along with his brother Vinson's? That would have been quicker and easier, and apparently he was near enough to the quicksand portion of the creek to have done so.

Strangely enough, difficulties of this sort seem not to have troubled most readers of the novel; their objections lie, as I have said above, with Gavin Stevens. They feel that he talks too much and, worse than that, they cannot stomach what he says. This kind of reader comes to the novel with certain expectations and certain hostilities and irritabilities. In the charged atmosphere of today (and of 1948, when the novel appeared) such bias is to be expected. It becomes necessary, then, to remind the reader that *Intruder in the Dust* is a novel and not, in spite of Edmund

Wilson's comments,[1] a tract.

The surcharged atmosphere in which the novel has been read played all sorts of tricks on its reviewers. Elizabeth Hardwick, writing in the *Partisan Review*,[2] said that "the bare situation of the novel is brilliant," and went on to specify why: "an old Negro, Lucas Beauchamp, a man apart, 'not arrogant, not scornful, just intractable and composed,' *pretends* to be a murderer, wants to be innocently lynched, to add his own blood to the South's dishonor, as his last act of contempt for his oppressors." But Lucas Beauchamp does not pretend to be a murderer, and he has not the least desire to be lynched. He sends for a lawyer and tries to get a private detective. Though the situation looks black, he does not give up his case. To depend upon a boy's ability—not to mention his willingness—to check up on the bullet wound in a body now buried in an out-of-the-way cemetery is to rely on a forlorn hope, but Lucas does not dismiss it contemptuously. He plays it for what it is worth, and when the opportunity offers, he makes his appeal to the boy.

Other readers have not gone so far as to say that Lucas wants to be lynched, but they are so certain of his victimization that they are led to say that the community was determined to lynch him, whether or no. Irving Malin assumes that Lucas is to be lynched because he is "discovered one day standing next to the body of a white man. It does not matter," he says, "whether he is innocent or guilty."[3] But Mr. Malin is too eager to find against the community; even in New York City or Cleveland or Detroit, the presence of a man with a pistol that has just been fired, standing above the still-warm body of a man who has just been shot, affords a strong presumption of guilt. As for its not mattering to the community whether Lucas is innocent or guilty, that conclusion is contradicted by the events. Late in the novel Charles Mallison notes with scorn the speed with which the people in the crowded square slip away, once they find out that Lucas is not guilty. He observes bitterly: "They ran...there was nothing left for them to do but admit that they were wrong. So they ran home" (p. 197).

How did Lucas manage to get himself in the embarrassing position in which he stands, pistol in hand, over a still-warm corpse? Because, as we are to learn, Crawford Gowrie had concocted an elaborate plot to kill his brother Vinson and uses Lucas as a scapegoat. Lucas invariably carries his pistol with him every Saturday, just as he wears his good suit and hat; it is part of his holiday dress. Crawford Gowrie knows this and builds his scheme upon it. He sends a message asking Lucas to meet him near the store on this Saturday morning; and when they meet, he bets Lucas that he can't hit a stump fifteen feet away. Lucas fires his pistol, wins the bet, and is now holding a "hot" pistol. Crawford then asks Lucas to wait at this spot for a few minutes until Crawford can return with Workitt's receipt for the material that Lucas believes Crawford has stolen from Workitt. (Lucas had apparently threatened to report the theft to Workitt unless Crawford could prove that he had really paid for the material.) After Crawford has left Lucas, his brother Vinson comes up to Lucas (evidently having been sent by Crawford—this would have to be part of Crawford's plot). As Vinson stands beside Lucas, he is shot from a distance by Crawford. Hence it is that Lucas is discovered standing over the body of the slain man, holding a pistol from which a bullet has been recently fired.

Now we have every right to protest that such a plot is much too tricky and that a would-be murderer, less imaginative than Faulkner but more practical in the ways of crime, would have concocted some other way to stop the mouths of Vinson and Lucas, both of whom know that Crawford has been stealing lumber. But if the reader is going to accept the elaborate arrangement that will place Lucas apparently red-handed at the scene of the crime, he has little right to object if people in the community assume, as most people elsewhere would assume under the circumstances, that Lucas is the murderer. In any case, it is essential to our understanding of the novel for us to realize that when Gavin Stevens tells Lucas that he will take his case, he does so in spite of a presumption of Lucas' guilt that amounts almost to certainty. We must realize too that Charles Mallison, at the beginning, assumes that Lucas is guilty of murder.

At this point the figure of Lucas Beauchamp calls for a more careful look. We may be tempted to see in Lucas a champion of Negro rights.

In one important regard he is such a champion, but hardly in a programmatic sense. Lucas is basically a strong-minded individual with pride in himself, but his loyalty is not so much to his race as to his family. He is obviously very proud of being a McCaslin and he imitates very carefully the stance of his white ancestor, old Carothers McCaslin. Lucas, after all, is the same man whom we met in "The Fire and the Hearth." He is no would-be martyr; he is no crusader for civil rights; he is the tough and fearless old aristocrat who makes no concessions, who manages to keep his courage and his dignity under the most difficult of situations, and whose enforced passivity as prisoner is by no means to be confused with the courting of unjust punishment nor even the merely Stoical endurance of undeserved punishment. Lucas is an old man hustled into jail, an old man who has an incredible tale to tell and who is wise enough to know that it will be difficult to get anybody to listen to him, let alone believe him. This is the character that Faulkner renders so convincingly that even in his passivity he counts as a positive force throughout the novel.

Faulkner does emphasize the fact that many of Lucas' problems stem from the fact that he refuses to behave as the white community expects a Negro to. The author reconstructs for us what has gone on in the minds of the typical white men in this community: "We got to make him be a nigger first. He's got to admit he's a nigger. Then maybe we will accept him as he seems to intend to be accepted" (p. 18). It is interesting to see how Lucas handles himself in the face of this kind of truculence, especially when it becomes belligerently hostile.

One such incident occurs when Lucas, at the country store, encounters three young white men, the crew of a "nearby sawmill, all a little drunk." One of them says to Lucas: "You goddamn biggity stiff-necked stinking burrheaded Edmonds sonofabitch." Lucas replies: "I aint a Edmonds. I dont belong to these new folks. I belongs to the old lot. I'm a McCaslin" (p. 19). This is not precisely the soft answer that turneth away wrath, and it is not meant to be. The young ruffian at once threatens Lucas because of "that look" on his face, to which Lucas retorts: "Yes, I heard that idea before, and I notices that the folks that brings it up aint even Edmondses" (p. 19). The young white man snatches a club to bash in Lucas' head and is barely restrained by the proprietor's son. But Lucas refuses to run. He finally moves toward the door "without haste," and goes out calmly eating his gingersnaps. The terms of Lucas' retort are significant: they suppose his dignity not as a Negro but as a McCaslin; they involve not his race but his family. (They probably are, as such, the more infuriating to the underbred drunken white man. But we are concerned here with Lucas' conception of himself, not with that aspect of the matter.) Lucas is not consciously fighting for a cause. He is being himself, though in daring to be himself he undoubtedly promotes the cause.

Not the least important ingredient in Lucas is his patience, a patience which is tinged with philosophy and humor. A nice example occurs in the passage that closes chapter 3. Charles Mallison, having been fixed by the eye of this ancient mariner, is now getting ready to launch out on his insane quest to check the bullet hole in the buried body. He tries to get the last details about the cemetery from Lucas and then he explains to Lucas, almost frantically, that he can't possibly get back to town before midnight or one o'clock. Lucas quietly answers: "I'll try to wait."

The comment cannot be taken as merely "straight"—a declaration of Stoic submissiveness. Lucas is quite conscious of the grim humor of his statement. But it is no pert sarcasm either. Lucas' reply might very well qualify as one of Mr. William Empson's famous seven types of ambiguity. It can, and in the whole context must, mean several things: since all I can do is wait, I will try to shape my mind to that; my task (of waiting) will require more effort even than yours; I know that yours isn't going to be easy for you, but my waiting isn't going to be exactly easy for me either. We ought to be well enough acquainted with Lucas Beauchamp at this point to credit him with all of the possible meanings.

The way in which Charles Mallison incurred his obligation to Lucas is told in the opening chapter, with the account of the rabbit hunt and of the boy's falling into the icy creek, and the scene in Lucas' cabin in which the old man quietly exercises his authority, though with the courtesy of an old friend of the family. When Charles makes his *gaffe* of trying to pay Lucas for the meal that Molly has served him, Lucas disposes of the matter firmly but with calm and unruffled civility.

There follows the very sensitive handling of the white boy's sense of embarrassment at his faux pas, the sudden shift from shame to anger as he hears the rejected coins ring on the cabin floor, and then, as the weeks pass, the boy's bafflement and resentful frustration at the way in which the old man parries his every attempt to discharge the obligation. By countering each present sent by the boy with a present of his own, Lucas manages to keep the boy in his debt. Typical of Faulkner's sure touch is the way in which he handles the boy's sense of relief when one day Lucas meets him on the street and looks straight at him without recognition, seeming to have forgotten him completely. But later the boy learns that Lucas' wife has died not long before this encounter, and thinks with a kind of amazement: "He was grieving. You dont have to not be a nigger in order to grieve" (p. 25). So the boy has to make another test, and this time, when Lucas again passes him without a sign of recognition, the boy says to himself: "He didn't even fail to remember me this time. He didn't even know me," and experiences a sort of peace in believing that "it's over" and that he is now free of any debt to the old man, since Lucas has not "even bothered to forget me." But when the shocking news of Lucas' arrest for murder reaches him, the boy finds that Lucas has not forgotten him and that he is not at all free. His first impulse had been to evade responsibility by getting out of town, but he cannot really do this, and finally, in fascinated horror, he finds himself in the crowd watching Lucas being taken into the jail. He then realizes that Lucas is looking at him and addressing him directly: "You, young man. Tell your uncle I wants to see him" (p. 45).

Charles Mallison would, of course, have been unable to perform his mission without the aid of Miss Habersham. He had to have—though he did not then know it—her pickup truck, but he needs even more than that, her counsel and her moral backing. For reason and prudence are thoroughly on the side of his uncle, Gavin Stevens, who simply wants Lucas to get a fair trial and only such punishment as the law will properly mete out. The boy's former experiences with Lucas—and perhaps his present instincts—tell him that Lucas, in spite of his wildly improbable story, is innocent. But he is only sixteen, and too much is being asked of him; and so, without Miss Habersham's help, he could hardly have succeeded. In any case, he badly needs the confidence which an older person can instill. Miss Habersham herself is not at all at a loss. She can tell Charles: "Naturally [Lucas] wouldn't tell your uncle. He's a Negro and your uncle's a man" (p. 89). And again: "Lucas knew it would take a child—or an old woman like me: someone not concerned with probability, with evidence. Men like your uncle and Mr Hampton have had to be men too long, busy too long" (p. 89).

Charles would probably not have been able to carry out his mission successfully except for one other factor—a turn of events he could not have foreseen. The discovery that the body in Vinson Gowrie's grave was not that of Vinson at once disposed of difficulties that might well have wrecked Charles' attempt to rescue Lucas: the problem of getting the corpse into town and of bringing from the big city—in time to save Lucas—an expert capable of proving that the bullet that had killed Vinson could not have come from Lucas' gun. The discovery that the body of Jake Montgomery was lying in Vinson's grave immediately puts Lucas in the clear: there is to be no slow and perhaps difficult task of proving to the sheriff that Lucas is innocent. In this instance, Faulkner's having given a complicating twist to the plot makes for ultimate simplification of the story.

Once Charles has conveyed this surprising information to his uncle, his job is basically done, but not so with Miss Habersham's. For it turns out that Gavin, in spite of his earlier confidence that Lucas will be safe in the jail and that there will be no lynching, now, perhaps because he is at last conscious of the fact that Lucas is innocent, finds that he is not nearly so confident that there will not be a jail delivery. Accordingly, he makes his strange request of Miss Habersham. Deputies guarding the jail are "just men with guns....But if a woman, a lady, a white lady...." Miss Habersham understands him and agrees, though she puts a little barb into the lawyer as she does so: "So I'm to sit there on that staircase with my skirts spread or maybe better with my back against the balustrade and one foot propped against the wall of Mrs. Tubbs' kitchen while you men who never had time yesterday to ask that old nigger a few questions and so all he had last night was a boy, a child—" (p. 118). But Miss Habersham does not push her advantage further. She is eminently practical: she asks him to drive her home first so she can get her mending. If she is going to have to sit there at the jail all morning, she wants something to do with her hands. Otherwise, she points out, Mrs. Tubbs, the jailer's wife, "will think she has to talk to me" (p. 118).

Gavin Stevens is plainly puzzled at the turn of events. He is willing to admit his own moral bankruptcy: "it took an old woman and two children... to believe truth for no other reason than that it was truth, told by an old man in a fix deserving pity and belief, to someone capable of the pity even when none of them really believed him" (p. 126). Then bewilderment takes over, for he asks his nephew: "When did you really begin to believe him?...I want to know, you see. Maybe I'm not too old to learn either." But the boy tells him honestly, "I don't know."

Up to this point in the novel, the poor whites and the yeoman whites who live in Beat Four have been depicted as pitiless and vindictive. They constitute the basic threat to Lucas and to the law. When the sheriff and Gavin and Charles drive to the little country graveyard and prepare, now by daylight, to open the grave once more, old Mr. Gowie, the father of the dead man, comes out to challenge them. He answers fully to our expectation of what the head of the Gowie clan should look like and how he should act. Consequently it is a brilliant stroke on Faulkner's part to reveal to us—through the revelation to Charles—that old Mr. Gowrie is wracked with deeply human grief. Charles, watching the old man's face, "thought suddenly with amazement: *Why, he's grieving*: thinking how he had seen grief twice now in two years where he had not expected it or anyway anticipated it, where in a sense a heart capable of breaking had no business being: once in an old nigger who had just happened to outlive his old nigger wife and now in a violent foulmouthed godless old man who had happened to lose one of the six lazy idle violent more or less lawless...sons" (p. 161). The enlargement of the boy's sympathies thus works in two directions to include the chief of the lynchers-to-be as well as the man in danger of being lynched.

Because this novel has to do essentially with a young boy's growing up into manhood, and because, in any case, Lucas, by his situation, is prevented from taking very much action, much of the novel properly occupies itself with what is going on inside Charles Mallison's head—with his conflicts and discoveries and dubieties and decisions. The general parallel between this novel and *The Unvanquished* or "The Bear" is rather close. The tension in both cases is between a boy's ties with his community—his almost fierce identification with it—and his revulsion from what the community seems committed to do. Thus, from the very nature of the book, Charles Mallison's conflict of loyalties and his relation to his own community must come in for a prominent part. This is one of the justifications for the occurrence in this novel of the long tirades by his uncle, Gavin Stevens.

Gavin is the person who would naturally talk to the boy about the problems that are disturbing him, and the adult's notions about the community, the Negro, and the nature of the law and justice represent for the boy at once a resource and an impediment. It is against these that his own developing notions must contend and it is these views which he must accept, repudiate, or transcend. As for the merits of Gavin Stevens' theories as such, the reader who is interested in them may consult the discussion of them to be found in the Notes [of Brooks's book], page 420. But as far as the novel itself is concerned, they are subordinate to the main matter: Charles Mallison's development toward wider sympathies and a sharper ethical conscience.

The boy's attitude toward his homeland and toward the North, therefore, is of the first importance. The cosmopolitan reader may be surprised—and even appalled—at the notion that this Southern boy could see in his mind's eye the Northerners as consisting of "countless row on row of faces which resembled his face and spoke the same language he spoke and at times even answered to the same names he bore yet between whom and him and his there was no longer any real kinship and soon there would not even be any contact...because they would be too far asunder even to hear one another" (p. 152). But this vision is not an argument put forward by the author. It is simply a fact, part of a cultural situation that has to be taken into account.

So also with the observation that "every Southern boy fourteen years old" is capable of reliving the moment just before Pickett's charge at Gettysburg as if the issue had not been decided and its success were still a live possibility: "the guns are laid and ready in the woods and the furled flags are already loosened to break out and Pickett himself...[is] waiting for Longstreet to give the word and it's all in the balance" (p. 194). To call this passage "literary, flamboyant, historically ridiculous in terms of America today" is simply beside the point. As a matter of fact there were plenty of Southern boys in the 1940s who felt this way—and there are still some in the Mississippi of 1963. But in any case, to deny this belief to Charles Mallison is to remove one of the poles of his inner conflict and thus to misconceive the precise quality of his action. For it is just because the boy loves his native land and exults in its history that the threat of the lynching becomes for him something terrible: he sees the mob turning into one horrible face, "the composite Face of his native kind his native land, his people his blood his own with whom it had been his joy and pride and hope to be found worthy to present one united unbreakable front to the dark abyss" (p. 194).

It is because of his fierce patriotism and his resentment of the outlanders' eagerness to believe the worst that he feels so thoroughly betrayed by the action of his own people. They have been willing to believe Lucas a murderer, and now when they have found out that he is innocent, they rush home for fear that they may have to buy him "a package of tobacco" as a peace offering. Such is his bitter observation. But the bitterness is a function of his close tie to his people. Indeed, the whole experience, in which the boy meets a test of courage and experiences a deepening of his moral sensitivity, is conditioned by this tie. The particular experience that Faulkner describes is, apart from this tie, incomprehensible.

Much of the material that bears upon Charles' lover's quarrel with his community occurs in the tangled and difficult chapter 9. It is a lover's quarrel: this is how one has to describe Charles' jealous anxiety with regard to Jefferson. We are told of his "fierce desire that [his people] should be perfect because they were his and he was theirs, that furious intolerance of any one single jot or tittle less than absolute perfection—that furious almost instinctive leap and spring to defend them from anyone anywhere so that he might excoriate them himself without mercy since they were his own and he wanted no more save to stand with them unalterable and impregnable" (p. 209).

At the beginning of chapter 9, Charles and his uncle have just returned from the cemetery in Beat Four where the sheriff has opened the grave and confirmed the fact that Vinson Gowrie is not buried in it. Charles has now gone twenty-four hours without sleep, and the suspense about Lucas and the intolerable excitement of the night's foray are beginning to tell upon the boy. He feels "something hot and gritty inside his eyelids like a dust of ground glass" (p. 180). There is a tremendous compulsion to let go and slip off into forgetfulness, and yet he is too keyed up to be able to go to sleep. For one thing, he is very much concerned with how the town is going to take the discovery that they have made about Vinson Gowrie's murder.

Charles' thoughts, therefore, as they dominate chapter 9, are those of a person lightheaded from fatigue and lack of sleep, and the play of his thoughts occasionally takes on the quality of hallucination. Indeed, some of his reveries—for example, those on the spectacle of the crowd sweeping into the square and then later suddenly surging away from the jail and out of town—are tinged with more than a touch of hysteria. At one point Charles hears himself laughing and then discovers that the tears are pouring down his face. It is in this context that he has his vision of the Face, and later on, when he ruminates bitterly on the fact that the crowd seems to him to have fled, afraid to face the fact that they were wrong about Lucas, Charles has another vision, not of the Face but of "the back of a head, the composite one back of one Head one fragile mushfilled bulb indefensible as an egg yet terrible in its concorded unanimity rushing not at him but away" (p. 192).

Charles is appalled at the apparent unanimity with which the citizenry have acted, first in coming into the town to witness—he fears—a lynching, and then, with an equal unanimity, suddenly jumping into their cars and pouring out of the town square and into the roads leading to the country. The air of hallucination which this exodus takes on arises from the boy's fatigue and sleeplessness, but Charles' obsession with images of composite Faces and Heads reflects his basic concern: the notion of a community is dear to him. He does not think of himself as a member of a mere collection of people who happen to live in a place called Jefferson. Instead, he belongs to an organic society that shares basic assumptions. The proof of its organic unity is that its members can, without thinking or prior consultation, suddenly move together in a concordant action.

The tinge of hysteria comes out quite clearly when the tired boy, impatient to get home, is amused in spite of himself at the inability of his uncle to ease the family car into the solid stream of traffic flowing around the town square. Charles turns his thoughts to the plight of Miss Habersham and envisions her, now at the wheel of her light truck, trying to make her way to her house, not half a mile away, so that she can feed the chickens. He imagines Miss Habersham, since she is a practical woman, finally deciding to drive along *with* the traffic in the hope of finding a gap to turn through it, but, mile after mile, still carried along with it, until hours later she halts on a country backroad "among the crickets and treefrogs and lightningbugs and owls...and...at last a man in his nightshirt and unlaced shoes, carrying a lantern" (p. 189) answers her questions about how to get back to Jefferson.

Such flights of fancy mingle in this chapter with the more serious issues that lurk just below Charles' immediate consciousness. The serious concerns emerge quite clearly when the boy talks to his uncle about why the crowd poured back out of Jefferson as soon as it learned what had been found in the Beat Four cemetery. Charles insists that the members of the crowd ran to avoid admitting they had been wrong, but his uncle finds this a little too simple and proceeds to give his own explanation of the meaning of their unanimous flight. Gavin sees the crowd as something quite other than a mob: his shrewd surmise is that, in the first place, there were *too many* of them to constitute a lynching mob. Gavin evidently finds in the unanimity of the community something of hope rather than menace.

As an account of the importance of the community, this whole section of *Intruder in the Dust* ought to be compared with *Light in August*. The tone is different and the focus is different. Whereas in *Light in August* the community constitutes the necessary background of much of the action and gives that action its significance but is itself almost invisible, in *Intruder in the Dust* the meaning of the community is uppermost in the minds of Gavin and Charles and constitutes the chief topic of their speculation and dialogue. Whatever we may feel about Gavin's disquisition on the subject, the boy's sense of identity with his people and his desire to protect them from themselves is in itself eloquent.

Because *Intruder in the Dust* concerns Charles' coming of age morally, it is the boy who acts and makes the moral decisions. But Lucas, though limited to a passive role, is at the center of the process. He looms powerfully at the beginning of the novel, and at the end Faulkner has managed a fine exit for him. Charles and his uncle watch Lucas walking up the street on his way to the law office, and when Charles says: "He's coming up here," his uncle says: "Yes....To gloat" (p. 240). He says it good-humoredly, however, and he hastens to add that since Lucas is a gentleman, "he wont remind me to my face that I was wrong; he's just going to ask me how much he owes me as his lawyer." This turns out to be a sound prediction, but there is more to the confrontation than this. Lucas leaves with the honors of the field, and he is allowed the last word.

After Gavin has suggested to Lucas that he owes a debt to Miss Habersham and should take her some flowers, Lucas delivers the flowers and returns to the law office. Once more, he broaches the question: "I believe you got a little bill against me" (p. 244). But Gavin denies that Lucas owes him anything, and when Lucas proposes then to pay something to Charles, Gavin threatens to "have [them] both arrested, [Lucas] for corrupting a minor and [Charles] for practising law without a license." This is a bargaining maneuver which Lucas can appreciate and relish, and he more than rises to the occasion. There must have been at any rate some expenses;

he will at least pay the expenses. "Name your expenses," Lucas says, "at anything within reason and let's get this thing settled" (p. 245). So Gavin tells him about breaking his fountain pen while writing down some information given him by Lucas. It cost Gavin two dollars "to have a new point put in [the fountain pen]. You owe me two dollars." So Lucas opens his coin purse and carefully counts out two dollars, the last fifty cents in pennies, explaining: "I was aiming to take them to the bank but you can save me the trip. You want to count um?" (p. 246). Gavin says that he does indeed want them counted, but that since Lucas is doing the paying, he will have to do the counting. Lucas assures the lawyer that "it's fifty of them," but Gavin insists on the counting with: "This is business," and watches while Lucas puts the pennies on the desk and makes his tally. After shoving the fifty pennies across the desk, however, Lucas keeps his seat, and Gavin is forced to say, "Now what? What are you waiting for now?" And Lucas has, indeed, the last word: "My receipt" (p. 247).

The movie, "Intruder in the Dust," omitted this bargaining and money-counting scene. In place of it, the final shot showed Lucas moving away down the street as Gavin and his nephew watched from a window in the office. As they watched him, they talked about him, and their conversation made obvious their admiration for him as a man and their indebtedness to him for having given them a lesson in the need for keeping the moral conscience sensitive and alert. But it will be a very obtuse reader who fails to see the meaning as presented in the novel. The comedy of the bargaining, the insistence on treating the issue involved strictly as a matter of business, the counting out of every jot and tittle of the small payment, and, at the end, the business-like demand for a receipt—these are ways of avoiding any sentimental awkwardness. Lucas is well aware of what he owes to Gavin Stevens and what he owes to the boy. No one knows better than Lucas himself that what the boy has done cannot be repaid with money. It was Lucas, after all, who taught the boy that there are some things that one must not try to settle with a money payment. But the token payment in this instance, meticulously counted out, not for services rendered but "for expenses," is appropriate and even tactful. The handful of coins that, years before, dropped from Charles' hand onto the floor of Lucas' cabin, has at last been accepted by Lucas. And Lucas, in his turn now, puts on the office table his own handful of coins in token of a debt beyond payment. The comic mode turns out to be just the right solution of the problem. People who understand and feel affection for each other can turn the most serious matter into a joke, and may prefer the affectionate joke for expressing, without embarrassing sentimentality, the deepest kind of understanding.

Notes

1. "Faulkner's Reply to the Civil Rights Program," *New Yorker*, 24 (1948), 106, 109–12.
2. "Faulkner and the South Today," *Partisan Review*, 15 (1948), 1130–35.
3. *William Faulkner: An Interpretation* (Stanford University, Stanford University Press, 1957), p. 7

MAN ON THE MARGIN: LUCAS BEAUCHAMP AND THE LIMITATIONS OF SPACE

Keith Clark

While many people dismiss the blurbs on the dust jackets of novels as fatuous praise, I believe that William Faulkner's "praise" of Ralph Ellison's *Invisible Man* (1952) reveals something troubling about the man many consider our greatest literary artist. *Invisible Man*, says Faulkner, is exemplary because Ellison has "managed to stay away from being first a Negro, he is still first a writer." This comment suggests that "Negro" and "writer" exist symbiotically, the latter taking a necessary precedence over the former if artistic "success" is to be achieved.

I use this anecdote because it gets to the core of the problem underlying Faulkner's depiction of Lucas Beauchamp in both the short story "The Fire and the Hearth" (in *Go Down, Moses*) and the novel *Intruder in the Dust*. Indeed, many critics see Lucas as an improvement over Faulkner's previous portraits of black men[1]; Ellison himself lauded Faulkner's depiction of Lucas in *Intruder*. Other critics see Lucas as an extension of Faulkner's own personal feelings about the "race question," and many agree with Charles D. Peavy's assertion that *"Intruder in the Dust* represents Faulkner's strongest statement in his fiction regarding the racial crisis in the South" (50). In my treatment of Lucas in both "Fire" and *Intruder*, however, I approach Faulkner's protagonist not so much as an extension of the author's own views on race and racism, but instead as a character in the matrix of Faulkner's art. I agree strongly with Thadious

M. Davis's contention that "The real issue is whether Faulkner's black characters stand or fail on their own merit within the artistic context he has invented for them" (17–18). Indeed, attempting to determine whether or not Faulkner was a "racist" via his depiction of Lucas seems to me a moot point, for it presupposes that each work promulgates the writer's particular ideology—something that is abstract and amorphous.

Along the same lines, I feel it necessary to examine Lucas Beauchamp not in terms of the way Faulkner presents him within the context of the white Southern community, but the way he situates him in relation to a distinctly black one. Quite clearly, Lucas defines himself in terms of his white McCaslin heritage instead of his black lineage; of course, the paradox is that Lucas can never be integrated into the very family/community that he privileges. Faulkner further problematizes his text by presenting Lucas in a tenuous and even antagonistic relationship with other blacks. Why does Faulkner find it necessary not only to turn Lucas into an imitation *white* man, but also to place him at such odds with the people with whom he shares the common bond of race?

In "The Fire and the Hearth" not only is Lucas alienated in this way, but Faulkner reduces him and his fellow blacks to buffoons who can be saved only by the kindness of whites. As a "corrective," Faulkner creates a more "positive" portrait of Lucas in *Intruder in the Dust*: although he still insists on identifying himself in "white" terms, he is freed from the black-man-as-buffoon stereotype. Faulkner transforms him into a shrewd, intrepid man who stands up to his white oppressors. However, this "revision" renders an even more disturbing portrait.

Intruder in the Dust is even more fraudulent than "Fire" because Faulkner manipulates not only Lucas's physical and psychological place with respect to the black community, but also his narrative *space* as well—that is, the presence or absence of his *voice* in the text. Only when Lucas is both marginalized and silenced can he achieve what Faulkner considers a fundamental trait of black manhood—the ability to *endure*. The author transforms him from a character in the work into an abstraction called "Sambo," a psychological fetter of the racist South and an indelible part of its collective conscious. Taken together, then, the portraits in "The Fire and the Hearth" and *Intruder in the Dust* reveal a troubling paradox about the author's conception of his black male characters: not only must their "strength" and "humanity" be achieved by defining themselves in terms of the white community, but, more lamentably, these attributes must result either after distancing themselves from the black community or after severing their ties with it completely.

Clearly, Lucas's mixed heritage contributes to his dislocation and placelessness—what some might consider his status as a cultural orphan. On one level, then, by having Lucas question the boundaries separating black and white, Faulkner may have attempted to expose as artificial society's tendency to distinguish the world in such bifurcated terms. But even as prescient as Faulkner was, and even accepting "race" as a nebulous social construct, race—be it Euro-, Native-, or African-American in Faulkner's fictive universe—nevertheless signifies *difference*.[2] Indeed, in the South's racial hierarchies, Lucas is expected to maintain a very constricted *place* and by extension space. The author's inscriptions or signifiers notwithstanding, and despite the popular (dare I say politically *in*correct) inclination to see color as a superficial if not pejorative indicator of diverseness, the fact remains that a black man (Negro, Colored, African-American) accused of killing a white one in America faces a severe set of responses and consequences. I make this point about Lucas's blackness not unequivocally, for I recognize that novels such as *Light in August* and *Absalom, Absalom!* thrust all distinctions into disarray. But in "The Fire and the Hearth" and *Intruder in the Dust*, Lucas Beauchamp does not occupy the liminal position of a Joe Christmas or a Charles Bon; the shadings in the later works are more black than gray.

Craig Werner offers an instructive way of looking at the ways African-American authors such as Ernest J. Gaines, Gayl Jones, and William Melvin Kelley have "responded" to and "corrected" Faulkner's presentation of blacks. Werner draws on Robert Stepto's *From Behind the Veil: A Study of Afro-American Narrative* (1979), modifying Stepto's categories of Afro-American narratives in the creation of what Werner labels the "narrative of endurance." Werner feels that Faulkner severely limits his black characters by confining them to the long-suffering but enduring-black archetype. Specifically, he defines the narrative of endurance as being "static," as having a "temporal focus [that] is on the past or present rather than the future," and as defining the "black character in relationship to the Euro-American rather than the Afro-American community" (714). Werner further adds that this configuration produces a peculiarly "Euro-American 'black' hero," an "enduring saint" who is "physically enslaved but spiritually free" (714). While I basically agree with Werner's definition of the narrative of endurance, I would modify his category even further.

I feel that the *narrative of disassociation* gets closer to Faulkner's attitudes towards his black male characters. This delineation focuses more closely on the absence of black points of reference, and foregrounds the question of why Faulkner felt it necessary to estrange his black hero from family and community. I believe that concentrating on the black man's estrangement illuminates the main problem with Faulkner's few black male "heroes": he can never grant them their full humanity as unequivocally *black* men until he removes them from their own community and places them on the edges of a hostile white one. Clearly, in Faulkner's vision, the closer Lucas's ties to whiteness, the closer he comes to rightness and manhood. Thus, by the end of *Intruder in the Dust*, Lucas Beauchamp has not progressed at all: he began as a buffoon on the periphery of the black community, and he ends as a pariah, alienated completely from black folks, existing in a chasm between black and white, in deafening silence.

I wish to reiterate the importance of black *community* in my discussion. While "community" denotes a general connection between individuals, *communitas* conveys even firmer ties between people. A concept defined by anthropologist Victor W. Turner as "a relationship between concrete, historical idiosyncratic individuals" (131), the members of the *communitas*—unlike the more loosely connected community—are bound by more than mere physical space; they are linked more closely by psychological affinities resulting from a shared history. To help elucidate how this notion works vis à vis African-

American fictive discourse, I turn to Houston A. Baker's *Blues, Ideology, and Afro-American Literature*.

Baker delineates three basic stages of the "rites of the black (w)hole," which he posits as the black character's response to white society's "erasure" of him/ her—Americans' pernicious tendency to deny the very personhood of the black man and woman (153). The first stage involves the black character's withdrawal from the abnegating white community. Then, he subsequently renews his desire to (re)define self; in response to his *ahistoricity* in white America's eyes, he embarks on a journey to reclaim his own history. The process culminates with the character entering what Baker calls a "Black Expressive Community," which engenders wholeness and regeneration. Baker elaborates further on this newly-formed community, stipulating that it is "at the center of the black hole" and is "always conceived as 'marginal' because its members never 'return' to the affective and perceptual structures of an old, white dispensation" (154). Baker then demonstrates the way the "rite of the black (w)hole" works in Richard Wright's "Big Boy Leaves Home." The title character, after murdering a white man in self-defense, takes refuge in a kiln—a literal *hole* in the earth—and reemerges, newly rejuvenated and made *whole* through his interaction with another black character, who takes him North to freedom.

In Faulkner's fiction we see the antithesis of Baker's paradigm. Albeit splintered, a distinctly black "community" does exist, consisting of Lucas, Molly, Nat, and George Wilkins in "Fire," and Lucas, Molly, Aleck Sander, and his mother Paralee in *Intruder*. However, the fact that Lucas exists in such an antipathetic relationship to these individuals precludes *communitas*; concomitantly, Lucas's movement away from a black frame of reference to a white one marks an inversion of Baker's last stage, where the newly-liberated black character regains his sense of self through immersion into his "marginalized" but unequivocally black community.

In "The Fire and the Hearth" Lucas is both an "insider" and an "outsider" in relation to other blacks. While he maintains physical ties to Molly, Nat, and George, we do not see him as an integral part of this black configuration on a deeper, psychological level. While George E. Kent sometimes approaches hyperbole in condemning Faulkner's black characters, nevertheless he makes a salient observation that informs Faulkner's portrait of Lucas. In discussing Faulkner's flawed depiction of Dilsey Gibson in *The Sound and the Fury*, Kent adduces that "Faulkner, since he does not engage in the *otherness* of Dilsey—the complex relations to self and family which he would have to confront by taking a walk on a real black night from the big house to the cabin, and doing some sneaky listening there, is unable to give a sound analysis of her motivation, although her status as a major character demands it" (179-80; author's emphasis). In much the same way, Faulkner's depiction of Lucas suffers from the same topical (mis)treatment.

One aspect of Faulkner's characterization which complicates Lucas's "strong black manhood" is his relationship to his wife, Molly. Ostensibly, the relationship appears woefully underdeveloped: Faulkner assumes that because blacks possess the skill of "enduring" innately (e.g. the Gibson family), "strong" familial bonds result naturally. When Faulkner finally allows Lucas to take a step toward manhood—he requests that Zack Edmonds return Molly to him, and they subsequently engage in a physical confrontation—Lucas fails to execute his revenge as his gun "miss-fire[s]" (57). For Faulkner, Lucas's primary strength comes from standing up to a white man. However, the "miss-firing" of the gun implies Lucas's figurative castration; because the author insists that the black characters' interrelationships are unimportant, the defense of black womanhood becomes ancillary, subordinate to Lucas's interaction with whites.

Faulkner squanders an opportunity to portray a strong black male character able to challenge the racist white society which commodifies and de-sexes the black female, one that reduces her to either "whore" or "mammy."[3] From Faulkner's standpoint Lucas's killing Zack would constitute a breach of the unwritten Southern tenet which stipulates that black men simply do not kill white men under any circumstances. Furthermore, Lucas's failure to defend his wife's "honor" hints at what Minrose C. Gwin sees as Lucas's "feminine characteristics" in *Intruder in the Dust* (93); however, while Gwin sees the "feminine" Lucas as primarily positive within the context of the novel, I see his feminization as having primarily negative implications in the short story. One could further locate a sort of castration or de-sexing when Roth vehemently declares that Molly, not Lucas, will be allowed into his house, this decree following Lucas's participation in the ill-conceived divining machine scheme.

What distinguishes Lucas from a white character such as the doomed Thomas Sutpen is that Lucas could have exerted some control over his life. "Rich" by white standards, Lucas could demonstrate the extent of his manhood by further establishing not only the "house of Beauchamp" but also the "house of Wilkins" (daughter Nat and George Wilkins) as well. But again, Faulkner fails to examine the complexities of black family relationships and instead opts for the well-worn stereotype: the simple-minded black man who is ill-equipped for the rigors of heading a family and who therefore abandons his "house." Predictably, Lucas hastily agrees to "voce" (divorce) Molly after several decades of marriage. Not only is Lucas willing to forsake his wife, but he is complicit in the destruction of his daughter's home as well, exploiting George for purely selfish motives. Thus, Lucas becomes a caricature when juxtaposed with the tragic Sutpen, his machinations in comparison to Sutpen's dynastic concerns being far from tragic and closer to absurd.

To his discredit, Faulkner relies on facile stereotypes.[4] The author replaces the seriousness of Sutpen's quest for a design with something akin to burlesque and farce. The tragic possibilities of Lucas's plight—how personal avarice can lead to destruction of home and hearth—are undermined by acts of banality. For example, when Lucas's still and bootleg whiskey are discovered, the deputy reveals that Lucas was "standing there in his drawers and shirt-tail, hollering, 'Git the axe and bust it! Git the axe and bust it'" (65). Later, futilely searching for buried money with the divining machine, Lucas steals Roth Edmonds's mule, even though he can afford to buy one, and then concocts a scheme to avoid punishment (incidentally, George Wilkins exhibits obsequious, clownish behavior during this mindless mischief). While Lucas may be reminiscent of the trickster archetype of African-American literature (e.g., Charles W. Chesnutt's "Uncle Julius" in *The Conjure Woman*, 1899), his escapades differ because he "tricks" not to ensure his own survival, but instead to acquire excessive amounts of money. Indeed, this uncomic plot recalls Ellison's perceptive comment on American folklore, where "the Negro is reduced to a negative sign that usually appears in a comedy of the grotesque and the unacceptable" (48).

Considering that the presentation of the black male characters is informed by virulent perceptions of black people, Faulkner's depiction of Lucas's son-in-law, George Wilkins, is not surprising. Indeed, Lucas's portrayal is lessened further by his relationship with him. He virtually enslaves George, using him to hide stills, to run errands to the bank, and, most lamentably, to funnel money earmarked for Nat's stove and porch back into his own coffers. In elevating Lucas to the exalted status of black whiteman, Faulkner has simply grafted the role of "nigger" onto George in this transparent shifting of stereotypes from one character to another. Not only does Lucas's exploitation of George further taint him in relation to the black community, but it also detracts markedly from his role as a strong black male figure. To be sure, Lucas again mimics the behavior of his white literary ancestor Sutpen, who exploits the labor of *his* "wild niggers," and even the actions of Jason Compson, who delegates the well-being of a 33-year-old "idiot" to an adolescent black boy. Again, Faulkner's portrait of Lucas turns in on itself, sabotaged by the author's preoccupation with the black-man-as-incorrigible-fool myth; this time George Wilkins serves as the quintessential pantaloon in black.

In "The Fire and the Hearth" Faulkner weaves a mosaic that he would have the reader accept as evidence of Lucas Beauchamp's ability to act as a strong black man in the face of insurmountable obstacles. And, to be sure, the story abounds with instances of Lucas *gesturing* towards manhood: he goes through Zack Edmonds's front door; he "saves" himself and George from jail; he outsmarts the sleazy divining machine salesman; and in the end he proclaims "I'm going to be the man of this house" (121). But for all of Lucas's posturing, for all of his grand gestures, for all of his specious rhetoric on not being a "nigger but a man," Faulkner ultimately leaves us with a character so divorced from his culture and people that the acquisition of "manhood" becomes a pyrrhic victory, one unable to compensate for the peripheral space to which he is relegated. In conceiving *Intruder in the Dust*, Faulkner perhaps even recognized the fundamentally flawed portrait of Lucas in the short story, and the author may have seen himself as healing this deformed black man.

Faulkner articulates the seminal idea which spawned *Intruder in the Dust* in rather prosaic terms: "I've been thinking of a nigger in his cell…trying to solve his crime" (Blotner 1246). One way to look at *Intruder* and "Fire" *intertextually* might be to see the *Intruder* Lucas as a new and improved version of the "Fire" Lucas, as many critics agree with Erskine Peters's assertion that "[w]hen we encounter Lucas again in *Intruder in the Dust*, it is to Faulkner's artistic and moral credit that he develops the greater Lucas, not only sustaining that greatness without compromise but also rendering him as an exemplary force essential to the fulfillment of Faulkner's more mature vision of the Yoknapatawpha reality and its deliverance" (165). On the surface, the idea of the clown-man Lucas from "Fire" being transformed into the lawyer-sage of *Intruder* is a noble, even commendable one, perhaps signaling an attendant transformation in Faulkner's artistic conception of the "Negro."

In *Intruder* Faulkner *means* for Lucas to be a Herculean black *everyman*. The "new" Lucas refuses to call whites "mister"; he refuses money from the Huck Finnish Charles (Chick) Mallison, whom Lucas clothed and fed after the boy had fallen in the creek; when falsely accused of killing a white man (Vincent Gowrie), he refuses to tell his lawyer—and Chick's uncle—Gavin Stevens vital information because he sees that Stevens does not believe him; and finally, Lucas acts as his own attorney, engaging the services of both whites (Chick and Miss Eunice Habersham) and blacks (Aleck Sander, Chick's boyhood companion) to exonerate himself. It would appear that Faulkner's tortured portraitures of black men were being laid to rest, with this burgeoning picture of a black who was a *man* in every sense of the word.

However, I must reiterate my fundamental critique of Faulkner's depiction in "The Fire and the Hearth": in the "revised" *Intruder in the Dust*, the black man can only achieve full "manhood" by becoming a black superman who inhabits a space not merely on the outskirts of any identifiable black community, but a space completely *outside* of that community. In fact, even more so than in "The Fire and the Hearth," Lucas's status increases in direct proportion to how far he distances himself from other blacks. And not only does Lucas's limited communal *place* further blemish Faulkner's depiction, but his narrow *narrative space* reinforces his marginality. Faulkner pushes him to the periphery, rendering him not a voice in the text but instead an idea who is abstracted and filtered through the minds of Chick and Gavin. Instead of redeeming Lucas's deformed status, Faulkner further paralyzes him. Indeed, the marginalization now becomes *tripartite*: Lucas can never fully enter white society; he maintains *no* ties—not even perfunctory ones—to black people; and he is blotted out of the novel by the very person who controls his existence, William Faulkner. Contrary to what the author may have desired, *Intruder in the Dust* marks not an improvement on but a deterioration of Lucas Beauchamp.

Perhaps Walter Taylor's frank declaration cuts to the annoying problem which haunts Faulkner's characterization: "The problem was still how black Lucas was" (154). Just as he and Molly inhabited the same physical place but not a deeper, more binding space in "Fire," there is no semblance of *communitas* in their dealings with one another in *Intruder*. In fact, prior to Molly's death, the couple interacts in one acrimonious encounter: Lucas proudly informs Chick that Molly dislikes a portrait of her and Lucas because he made her remove her headrag: "I didn't want no field nigger picture in the house" (15). But this encounter works paradoxically, recalling the counterfeit "manhood" evident in the "miss-firing" episode in "Fire."

In Faulkner's discourse, the concept of "nigger" signifies debilitation, insidiousness, and dependence: at one point in "The Fire and the Hearth," when Lucas's role in making illegal whiskey is exposed,

Faulkner informs the reader that Lucas has fallen from the basically positive realm of "Negro" to the negative role of "nigger." Just as Lucas's "manhood" in "Fire" was a strange mixture of Negrophobia and pipe dreams of whiteness, he continues to internalize the very terms whites use to dehumanize blacks. To reject a picture of his wife in a headrag on the grounds that it perpetuates a demeaning "nigger" stereotype signals not a black character responding positively to his "erasure" by reclaiming his history, but instead it marks a repudiation of that history. Furthermore, in one of the few times that Faulkner grants Lucas language, it is disturbing that the author would have him use the "nigger" epithet in referring to his own wife, although Lucas does it indirectly. While the conjunctive issue of black womanhood proved troublesome in "The Fire and the Hearth," Faulkner eradicates this problem early in *Intruder*: he kills Molly off after the first chapter, along with shuttling daughter Nat and ne'r-do-well George Wilkins off to Detroit. Faulkner thus frees Lucas of the "niggerish" family that would thwart his quest for "dignity."

As if the erasure of Lucas's family were not enough, Faulkner continues to insist that the non-nuclear family, the black community, is the black man's bane and burden. Through Chick, Faulkner informs the reader that "Lucas was living alone in the house, solitary kinless and intractable, apparently not only without friends even in his own race but proud of it" (23). Apparently, Faulkner has severed Lucas's black ties in the name of emancipating him from "niggerdom." Even the black characters' epithet of address has changed, from "Uncle Lucas" in "Fire" to "Old Lucas" in *Intruder*; the former at least connotes kinship and community, while the new label conveys irascibility and derision. Other comments such as "I aint got no friends" (64) further suggest his alienation. Faulkner finally drives this point home in defining Lucas as an "old kinless friendless opinionated arrogant hardheaded intractable independent (insolent too) *Negro*" (79; emphasis added). Clearly, the author intends for Lucas's obdurate insistence on his *difference* to be a sign of strength, but instead it cements his position as a man on the margins.

While one might counter that Faulkner presents Lucas not as an exemplar of strength and manhood, but as a disfigured product of Southern racism, I contend that neither the novel's portrayal of any of its black characters nor authorial voice and point of view reflect such a level of textual self-reflection. Undeniably, the topical, socio-critical elements of the text are evident; as novelist Ann Petry observed in the 1940s, "The novel, like all other art, will always reflect the political, economic, and social structure of the period in which it was created" (32). But to see Faulkner as having gone a step further and critiquing Lucas's actions belies the discursive framework the novel establishes. On the contrary Lucas, as Faulkner configures him, transcends the sadomasochistic responses of a Joe Christmas. Nothing in the novel indicates that the author holds Lucas's self-imposed estrangement from other blacks up for the reader's ridicule and scorn. To reiterate Kent's point, had Faulkner delved more deeply into the ethos of black America in *Intruder in the Dust*, one might then argue that the narrative produces its black characters with a higher order of textual self-reflection. But rendering the blacks from whom Lucas estranges himself invisible does not reflect a novelist whose thinking goes beyond the generic rubric of social criticism; the novel, it seems to me, does not operate so complexly. Indeed, the book's outcome—a stoic black man saves himself from lynching by rejecting the corrosive violence used to oppress blacks—*celebrates* self-marginalization and individuality as means of surviving racism, even at the expense of wife, daughter, and community.

Intruder in the Dust abounds with episodes that could potentially free Lucas and his black counterparts from predictable stereotypes. However, Faulkner usually loses his capacity for more detailed analysis and opts for the hackneyed and the clichéd. In the character of Aleck Sander, Chick's young black companion who, along with Miss Habersham, carries out Lucas's order to dig up Vincent Gowrie's body to prove that his gun was not the murder weapon, Faulkner produces yet another opportunity to explore Lucas in a much broader human—that is, *non-white*—context. Aleck's participation in these nocturnal exploits should be seen in its proper historical context, as 16-year-old black boys did not generally assist cantankerous old black men accused of killing whites (as the Emmett Till tragedy reminds us, a black boy or man even perceived as stepping out of his designated "place" invited death).

Aleck's willingness to participate marks a courage seldom seen in Faulkner's fiction, as Lee Jenkins perceptively observes that the "integrity of Faulkner's attitude toward Sander is shown most conspicuously in the details of the grave-digging scene, in which we see Aleck performing in a quick, sure, and thoughtful way" (262). Recalling that *Intruder* might be a "revision" of "Fire," we might see Aleck as a revised version of the feckless George Wilkins, as Aleck's willingness to act contrasts sharply with George's fawning behavior. To a certain extent, Aleck's role even supersedes Chick's, since he has the most to lose.

Investing Aleck Sander with such a crucial role in Lucas's drama becomes the matrix for many possibilities in Faulkner's depiction of black male characters. Aleck's keen insight clearly links him to the old man, a connection which could put the few instances of black male bravery in a black historical context. However, in keeping within the parameters of the narrative of disassociation, Faulkner does not even allow Aleck and Lucas to meet, as he limits Lucas's mentorship role to educating Chick Mallison in an updated Huck-Nigger Jim saga. Again, we witness black men existing not in a context of cohesion and brotherhood, but instead in a world where they seldom come into contact with one another, confined to a role of "the Other."[5] As with the countless black boys in Faulkner's canon who maintain equality with their white companions until adolescence, Faulkner returns Aleck to a cozy, anachronistic black world—the author's standard milieu where black people eat peanuts and bananas and wear zoot pants. This is the final image Faulkner leaves us of the heretofore heroic boy on the threshold of manhood. Expectedly but regrettably, Faulkner's treatment of Aleck Sander is representative, for it elucidates most blatantly what I believe informs the portraits of all of Faulkner's black male characters: he allows them to reach the brink of manhood before he alienates them from their own people, or he returns them to their native environ, the halcyon world of "enduring," yet happy darkies.

The marginalization of the black male protagonist in the "white" text in and of itself might not be cause for special attention. Even though *Huckleberry Finn* examines the dehumanizing effects of slavery, the book's most resonant voice belongs to Huck, not Jim. Chick Mallison, the recipient of the "race" lesson in *Intruder in the Dust*, assumes a position similar to Huck's because Faulkner privileges him in terms of narrative space and point of view. But with Faulkner's attempted manumission of Lucas from the shackles of the one-dimensional black-man-as-buffoon stereotype comes a responsibility to abolish his *voicelessness* as well.

Lucas, as Faulkner intends him, represents the moral *center* of the text, for it is that complex dynamic of the South's treatment of blacks which spawns the novel's central action—the false but conceivable accusation that a black man killed a white one. Thus, as the character who sets the events of the novel in motion, it would seem that Lucas's centrality would be maintained throughout the book. However, Lucas's core position only magnifies his *narrative* marginalization, as he virtually disappears after the third chapter of an eleven-chapter book.

Lucas's invisibility and silence for the balance of the text almost make his contextual invisibility—the cramped space he inhabits outside the black community—seem secondary. While Faulkner intends for Lucas to be the glue that holds his artistic design together, the fact that he spends most of the book in confinement, both in the context of the action (he is in jail) and in terms of narrative space, creates yet further difficulties for the reader. Lucas's silence becomes stentorian, because his "impenetratable, intractable" mien haunts the text like Quentin Compson's shadow. Unfortunately, Faulkner requires Lucas be stripped of voice before he can assume the mantle of manhood. While Irving Howe accused Faulkner of not presenting an "articulate Negro who speaks for his people" (132) in his novels, I would counter that this is less the author's responsibility than to present one who *speaks* period. Howe's comment does, however, delineate one of the novel's major defects.

Faulkner not only cuts Lucas off from his own people, but he denies him a language and a voice through which he can communicate *his* story. Faulkner's presentation of the way characters perceive language is often overlooked in this novel, but comments such as Gavin Stevens's observation (revealed by Chick) about "how little vocabulary man really needed to get comfortably and even efficiently through his life" (47–48) take on more significance than they might first appear to have. As Stevens's comment suggests, the importance of language is diminished; perhaps Faulkner is even attacking the reliability of it here in much the same way he did in *As I Lay Dying*. With language presented in rather pejorative terms, Lucas's silencing would appear an ancillary issue.

Minrose Gwin downplays Lucas's absence of voice, commenting that "[t]hough Lucas's words are few, they are of utmost importance because they are articulations of individuation in a language the black voice has spoken in autobiography from the early slave narratives to the present" (93). Gwin's comment presupposes that there exists some link between Lucas's "few words" and a historically black experience. However, as Faulkner has presented him, Lucas has little or no conception of his history. On the contrary Faulkner has vehemently insisted on his *ahistoricity*—e.g., Lucas and Molly's disagreement over the headrag or, more significantly, Lucas's unfathomable arrogance in failing to comprehend the implications of a black man killing a white person in the South. Therefore, Lucas does not need language because he has no history to voice: he inhabits a cultural vacuum, hermetically sealed from both past and present, without a future.

If one were to accept Gavin Stevens's facile meditations on the insignificance of language, one would immediately question why he displays such verbal prowess. As I mentioned before, Lucas's victimization lies at the novel's core, establishing its key themes and breathing life into all of the characters. But Faulkner performs yet another peculiar act in creating his design: he shifts the narrative focus *away* from Lucas and *onto* lawyer Stevens, a man so divorced from Lucas's reality that he himself initially inhabited a marginal narrative space. Instead of playing Lucas's drama out to its *dénouement*, Faulkner asks the reader to suspend his or her disbelief, as the author not only foregrounds Gavin's voice, but allow him to abstract and objectify Lucas. Gavin will speak of him as "Sambo," the quintessential symbol of the black person's ability to "endure" in the tradition of Dilsey Gibson. I do not wish to argue the validity of equating Gavin's convoluted racial ideology with Faulkner's, although I will say that a cursory glance at the author's own "gradualistic" approach toward solving the "race problem" appears indistinguishable from Gavin's position.[6] What I see as a central problem is not Faulkner's use of Gavin as his mouthpiece, but why the author allows Gavin's voice to drown out not only Lucas's but Chick's as well. While Werner quite accurately talks about the "polyphonic approach" Faulkner takes toward treating race in *Absalom, Absalom!*, there is not only a dearth of other voices but a total absence of them in *Intruder*.

Although Gavin's bombastic rhetoric might superficially validate Gwin's assertion that "[t]alk is cheap" (95), I would argue that talk in African-American discourse is far more complex and meaningful. Dating back to slavery, blacks historically have been denied access to education, which may account for the reason African-American culture privileges the oral over the written. Indeed, language and voice have always held a special rhetorical significance; they have often been the only vehicles available for blacks to inscribe their (hi)stories. This may account for the myriad rhetorical dimensions of language in black literature and culture: the importance of the call and response trope, the intricacies of the black sermon, the linguistic significance of insult rituals ("signifying" and "playing the dozens"), and the seminal position the blues holds as a mode of expressing and transcending pain. That Faulkner cuts Lucas off from blacks in the text is one thing, but cutting him off from the conduit to attaining manhood—a voice for the expression of his own story—problemetizes an already problem-ridden text. Thus, Faulkner not only de-centers the text by figuratively killing off Lucas after chapter three, but he crucially de-voices his "strong" black protagonist, diminishing his booming presence to a faint whisper by the end of the novel.

Denigrating depictions of black men in literature, ultimately, transcend time and place: "And, as in the sixteenth century, the Moor in the *Poema de mio Cid* falls between extremes of the dehumanizing and the fanciful…" (Burshatin 119). The centuries notwithstanding, William Faulkner's version of the black male character—his "Moor"—remains equally dichotomous. Faulkner creates in Lucas Beauchamp a clown-cum-lawyer-cum-man, but the metamorphosis occurs at a great price. By the last two-thirds of *Intruder in the Dust* Faulkner has removed him to the periphery both in and out of the text, as I found myself having to scribble notes about the absent Lucas in the margins of the novel to remind myself that he was still its life-force. "Black manhood" in Faulkner's discourse becomes an oxymoron: as his "praise" for Ellison connotes, something in the artist's thinking would not allow him to cut the umbilical cord linking him to his native homeland—a South with a cancerous racial history and a proclivity to confine the blackman to the space of a nigger.

Notes

1. Lee Jenkins contends that Faulkner's depiction of blacks in *Intruder in the Dust* is a marked improvement, calling it "laudable" and a "significant departure from the caricatured and denigrated images of the blacks in his earlier work" (261). See also Charles H. Nilon's *Faulkner and the Negro*, a landmark in Faulkner scholarship as the first study devoted exclusively to Faulkner's "Negro"; Nilon generally praises Faulkner's depiction of Lucas as a step forward.
2. Houston A. Baker, Jr., relates an especially apropos anecdote in "Caliban's Triple Play," demonstrating how race and racism are so embedded in the American psyche. Driving in Philadelphia, Baker witnessed a "deranged, shabbily clad, fulminating white streetperson" spewing obscenities at passing motorists. When the streetperson sights the black motorist Baker, however, he "produced the standard 'Goddamned niggers! Niggers! Niggers!'" (*"Race," Writing, and Difference* 385). Baker's example illustrates how even the most indigent white person distinguishes black as other and inferior. While the Gowries may belong to the lower classes of Southern whites, Lucas's "placelessness" does not rescue him from the wrath of the white community when he is accused of killing Vincent; he is automatically designated a "nigger."
3. Walter Taylor makes a perceptive comment regarding the "asexual" quality of Molly: "The image of black womanhood revealed through Molly was one from which all eroticism had been censored, which focused itself solely on domesticity, and which suggested black women were childish to the point of helplessness" (143).
4. See Sundquist and Taylor.
5. Jenkins addresses the issue of Aleck Sander's "otherness"—the almost preter-

natural quality that distinguishes the "cerebral" white from the "mystic" black: "Aleck...has the ability to throw his tap stick at rabbits with an accuracy almost as great as Charles' ability to shoot a gun at them. This is the mysterious power of blacks, the thing that enables Aleck, when they are out at the graveyard digging, to be so helpful: he hears the mule coming down the hill two minutes before Charles and Miss Habersham hear and see it; he seems to have the ability to know instinctively what to do in a situation. Yet, for all Aleck's good qualities, they are still exotic, strange, and extrarational" (272).

6. Juxtaposing Gavin's rhetoric on how to eradicate racism in the South with Faulkner's personal beliefs illuminates their mutual ideologies. Gavin proclaims, "I am defending Sambo from the North and East and West—the outlanders who will fling him decades back not merely into injustice but into grief and agony and violence too by forcing on us laws based on the idea that man's injustice to man can be abolished overnight by police" (203-04). And in 1956 Faulkner asserted: "I have been on record opposing the forces in my native country which this present evil and trouble has [sic] grown. Now I must go on record opposing the forces outside the South which would use legal or police compulsion to eradicate the evil overnight" ("Letter" 51-52). Faulkner might have avoided this blurring of the art/artist distinction by granting Lucas a more dominant role in the latter part of the novel.

Works Cited

Baker, Houston A., Jr. *Blues, Ideology, and Afro-American Literature: A Vernacular Theory*. Chicago: U of Chicago P, 1984.

-----. "Caliban's Triple Play." *"Race," Writing, and Difference*. Ed. Henry Louis Gates, Jr. Chicago: U of Chicago P, 1986. 381-95.

Blotner, Joseph. *Faulkner: A Biography*. 2 vols. New York: Random House, 1974.

Burshatin, Israel. "The Moor in the Text: Metaphor, Emblem, and Silence." *"Race," Writing, and Difference*. Ed. Henry Louis Gates, Jr. Chicago: U of Chicago P, 1986. 117-37.

Davis, Thadious M. *Faulkner's "Negro": Art and the Southern Context*. Baton Rouge: Louisiana State UP, 1983.

Ellison, Ralph. *Shadow and Act*. New York: Vintage, 1964.

Faulkner, William. *Go Down, Moses*. New York: Random House, 1942.

-----. *Intruder in the Dust*. New York: Random House, 1948.

-----. "Letter to the North." *Life* 40 (Mar. 1956): 51-52.

Gwin, Minrose C. *The Feminine and Faulkner: Reading (Beyond) Sexual Difference*. Knoxville: U of Tennessee P, 1990.

Howe, Irving. *William Faulkner: A Critical Study*. 2nd ed. New York: Vintage, 1952.

Jenkins, Lee. *Faulkner and Black-White Relations: A Psychoanalytic Approach*. New York: Columbia UP, 1981.

Kent, George E. *Blackness and the Adventure of Western Culture*. Chicago: Third World P, 1972.

Nilon, Charles H. *Faulkner and the Negro*. New York: Citadel P, 1965.

Peavy, Charles D. *Go Slow, Now: Faulkner and the Race Question*. Eugene: U of Oregon P, 1971.
Peters, Erskine. *William Faulkner: The Yoknapatawpha World and Black Being*. Darby, PA: Norwood Editions, 1983.
Petry, Ann. "The Novel as Social Criticism." *The Writer's Book*. Ed. Helen Hull. New York: Harper, 1950. 32–39.
Sundquist, Eric J. *Faulkner: The House Divided*. Baltimore: Johns Hopkins UP, 1983.
Taylor, Walter. *Faulkner's Search for a South*. Urbana: U of Illinois P, 1983.
Turner, Victor W. *The Ritual Process: Structure and Anti-Structure*. Chicago: Aldine de Gruyter, 1969.
Werner, Craig. "Tell Old Pharaoh: The Afro-American Response to Faulkner." *Southern Review* 19 (1983): 711–35.

Eunice Habersham's Lessons in *Intruder in the Dust*

Ikuko Fujihira

> "I gonter tell you something to remember: anytime you wants to git something done, from hoeing out a crop to getting married, just get the womenfolks to working at it." (*GD,M*, 13)

Most critics will agree that *Intruder in the Dust* reveals the decline of William Faulkner's creative imagination. But during the Nagano interviews in the summer of 1955, Faulkner recommended that his Japanese audience read *Intruder in the Dust* first of all his novels, "because that deals with the problem which is most important not only in my country, but…important to all people" (*LG*, 166). Faulkner added that he profoundly believed his works "give a true picture of my part of America" (*LG*, 167). Did Faulkner, in his authoritative voice as the representative of American culture in Japan, want us to see the racial justice finally done to an innocent black man who narrowly escapes lynching by a violent mob in *Intruder in the Dust* as a true picture of the South? Whatever motive or reason Faulkner intended for his Japanese readers in the '50s, it now seems important to try a new reading of the novel in the wake of contemporary theories of feminism and post-colonialism.

Intruder in the Dust has not attracted as many scholars as have *The Sound and the Fury, Light in August,* or *Absalom, Absalom!* Among the few studies of the novel, I find Wesley Morris's and Jay Watson's remarkable essays to be especially stimulating. Morris discusses the representation of racial difference with a focus on Faulkner's language, while Watson pursues the character of Gavin Stevens in association with his act of storytelling.

Published six years after *Go Down, Moses, Intruder in the Dust*, dealing with the rigid racial code of the South, is apparently a *Bildungsroman* of a white Southern boy who grows up to revise/rewrite the deep-seated operation of race, gender, and family within a white-male-centered Southern culture. Unlike the lonely orphan-figures in Faulkner's major novels, Chick has a warm family with a very caring father and mother, along with fond memories of his grandparents. In addition, Faulkner gives the boy the Harvard-educated lawyer Gavin Stevens as his uncle, as well as two other powerful mentors: Miss Eunice Habersham, a white lady, and Lucas Beauchamp, a black man with white McCaslin blood. Faulkner scholars tend to focus their discussions of this novel on Gavin Stevens, Charles ("Chick") Mallison, or Lucas Beauchamp. I sometimes wonder why Miss Habersham's figure usually recedes into the background of even the most brilliant essays.

With a specific focus on Miss Habersham's persistent presence throughout the novel and Chick Mallison's growing awareness in his journey to become a responsible Southern male, this paper explores, first, the act of eating repeatedly mentioned in the novel and, second, Eunice Habersham's significant role as mentor for Chick Mallison, with a focus on her language of repetition. Finally, I will discuss the new sense of family developed in Chick's mind in parallel with the uncovering of a fratricide in the Gowrie family.

1. The Physical Act of Eating

The novel begins with Chick Mallison standing in front of the jail among the crowd waiting for the arrival of Lucas Beauchamp, arrested for the murder of Vinson Gowrie, a white man who is the youngest son of a violent outlaw family. Immediately, the story goes back four years to the episode of Chick's fall into a frozen creek and the subsequent hospitality he receives at Lucas's house. On that occasion, Chick is served the black man's "best" meal: "collard greens, a slice of sidemeat fried in flour, big flat pale heavy half-cooked biscuits, a glass of buttermilk" (13). These foods trigger the boy's first traumatic experience as a Southern white male. When Chick throws a few coins down on Lucas's bare floor as payment for the plate of greens and meat, Lucas angrily orders him to pick them up. In this way, Chick's paternalistic gesture in the Southern tradition is rejected by the black man who is its object. Since then, Chick has been obsessed with the image of the coins and the food he ate at Lucas's house. Lucas's behavior as a proud McCaslin descendant and not as a black man instantly and violently subverts Chick's commonsensical and secure understanding of the Southern value system, transmitted by his family and the community. Chick entirely agrees with the community's long-standing anger: *"We got to make him be a nigger first. He's got to admit he's a nigger. Then maybe we will accept him as he seems to intend to be accepted"* (18). In order to make Lucas a "nigger," Chick sends as Christmas gifts "four two-for-a-quarter cigars and the tumbler of snuff for his wife" and several months later, mails "the flowered imitation silk dress" (22) for Molly, Lucas's wife. At last Chick feels ease "because the rage was gone and all he could not forget was the grief and shame" (22). But four months after the dress was sent, Chick gets "a gallon bucket of fresh homemade sorghum molasses" (22) delivered ostentatiously by a white boy. Thus Lucas never surrenders to Chick and the game still continues after several exchanges of food and a dress. Four years after this shameful experience, Chick unexpectedly receives orders again from Lucas at the jail door: "You, young man....Tell your uncle I wants to see him" (45).

 Cleanth Brooks contends that the main part of *Intruder in the Dust* is about "Charles Mallison's development toward wider sympathies and a sharper ethical conscience" (289). Further, he admits Lucas's role as central in the process of the boy's moral development. Olga W. Vickery also has a high regard for Lucas's continued influence on Chick, who is educated "into virtue and human relationships" (135). After his uncle Gavin interviews Lucas as his lawyer at the jail, Chick and Lucas "looked at one another through the steel bars" (65). When they were leaving Lucas's cell, Chick "thought for a second that Lucas had spoken aloud. But he hadn't, he was making no sound: just looking at him with that mute patient urgency" (66). Before they look at each other through the bars, Lucas suggests that they send him "some tobacco" (65). Pressed by Lucas's urgent look, Chick goes back to the jail alone and talks with Lucas. "Tobacco" was Lucas's coded message for Chick to return to the jail, and the latter's acquiescence to this request marks the exact moment of Chick's involvement in Lucas's life and death struggle. In spite of his repeated assertion that "he was free" (23, 26, 27, 28, 30, 34, 42) from Lucas, Chick cannot liberate himself from Lucas's apparently business-like request, especially after he receives Lucas's implicit invitation to come back to the jail with the word "tobacco." Told by Lucas to go to the cemetery and dig up Vinson Gowrie's body to prove that he had not been shot with Lucas's forty-one Colt, Chick feels that he still owes Lucas for the food and hospitality four years before: "*So this is what that plate of meat and greens is going to cost me*" (68).

In this novel, Chick receives important lessons not just from Lucas's food but from the everyday act of eating at the dining table in his house. We sometimes see him sitting at a table and eating (33, *passim*). After Lucas's innocence was proved and the lynch-mob disappeared from the square, Chick "tried with no particular interest nor curiosity to compute how many days since he had sat down to a table to eat" (207). Chick comes to realize that the act of "eating has something to do with" his acceptance of the injustice and shame of the South. Then Chick remembers his uncle's words about the act of eating:

> ...man didn't necessarily eat his way through the world but by the act of eating and maybe only by that did he actually enter the world, get himself into the world: not through it but into it, burrowing into the world's teeming solidarity like a moth into wool by the physical act of chewing and swallowing the substance of its warp and woof and so making, translating into a part of himself and his memory, the whole history of man or maybe even relinquishing by mastication, abandoning, eating it into to be annealed, the proud vainglorious minuscule which he called his memory and

his self and his I-Am into that vast teeming anonymous solidarity of the world....(207)

Gavin interprets the act of eating as the medium through which human beings relinquish their memory and self into the solidarity of the world. When Chick ate Lucas's food four years before, he simply thought that he could pay for it with money and gifts and forget it forever. Instead, by eating the black man's food, Chick is imprisoned in the dilemma of his racial consciousness as a Southern white male.

The frozen creek accident brings forth another remarkable aspect of this novel, also presented in terms of physical experience. Before eating, Lucas tells Chick to "strip off" (11) the wet unionsuit to dry it. Eventually his naked body had to wear "the quilt like a cocoon, enclosed completely now in that unmistakable odor of Negroes" (11). Chick realizes that he had accepted the smell as part of his body and memory: "he had smelled it forever, he would smell it always; it was a part of his inescapable past, it was a rich part of his heritage as Southerner; he didn't even have to dismiss it, he just no longer smelled it at all as the pipe smoker long since never did smell at all the cold pipereek which is as much a part of his clothing as his buttons and buttonholes" (12). Thus Chick admits that he has naturally absorbed the smell of black people into his body and accepted it as part of his heritage as a Southerner.

In this incident, Chick, stripped of his own clothes, takes in black people's food and the smell of the quilt, making them part of his own body, self, and identity. Moreover, the incident gives Chick an opportunity to observe Lucas's outfit closely. Lucas wears "the gum boots and the faded overalls of a Negro but with a heavy gold watchchain looping across the bib of the overalls" (12). Later Lucas puts "a gold toothpick" into his mouth "such as his own grandfather had used" (12). In addition Lucas's hat was "a worn handmade beaver such as his grandfather had paid thirty and forty dollars apiece for" (12). Chick also sees "the gold-framed portrait-group on its gold easel" (14) in which Molly looks strange to Chick. He realizes why this is so: she is not wearing her headrag in the picture, obviously because Lucas doesn't want a "field nigger" picture in his house. Lucas's gold toothpick, his gold watchchain, and the gold-framed picture on its gold easel transgress his black identity in the South. Through the medium of his clothing and personal effects, Lucas ostensibly and bravely transgresses the border of racial difference and demonstrates his pride in the white blood inherited from his white grandfather, Carothers McCaslin.

Not limited to Lucas's outfit, Faulkner's descriptive efforts extend to detailed accounts of the clothing and physical characteristics of each character in this novel. Molly is "a tiny old almost doll-sized woman much darker than the man, in a shawl and an apron, her head bound in an immaculate white cloth on top of which sat a painted straw hat bearing some kind of ornament" (10). "One-armed Nub Gowrie" (79) is "a man in a wide pale hat and a clean faded blue shirt whose empty left sleeve was folded neatly back and pinned cuff to shoulder with a safetypin" (159). Above all, Chick frequently observes Miss Habersham's "plain cotton print dress and one of the round faintly dusty-looking black hats" (75).

However, what attracts Chick's attention more than Miss Habersham's print dress and hat is her acting power, her defiant voice, and her role as his mentor. She goes out to the cemetery with Chick and his "boy," Aleck Sander, and she sits at the entrance of the jail to guard Lucas from the lynch-mob. Miss Habersham's physical presence during Chick's expedition to the cemetery at midnight and then at the jail entrance all day provides Chick with lessons of life lived in real experiences rather than in abstract words.

In addition to the repeated scenes of cooking and eating (see also the breakfast scene at Sheriff Hampton's on pp. 107–14) in this episode of looking for the physical evidence of the bullet hole in the dead body, the repeated references to Miss Habersham's unchanging clothes and hat and detailed pictures of the other characters' outfits are deeply concerned with the central issue of the novel: "to bridge the gap between words and deeds by sustaining the parallel between them" (Vickery, 144). For Chick has to reconcile his education about manhood in the South, received in the form of language, with real experience; he has to decide what to accept or reject from the visible evidence that surrounds him, and finally redefine the Southern tradition in his own way.

2. Language of Repetition

Intruder in the Dust abounds with Chick's imaginative images. Chick pictures Lucas alone in the cell when Nub Gowrie comes to forcibly take him out to be lynched: "half a mile away the old kinless friendless opinionated arrogant hardheaded intractable independent (insolent too) Negro man alone in the cell" (78-79). Chick imagines how he could take a car and drive to the cemetery to dig up the grave by himself: "he could see himself reaching the church, the graveyard without effort nor even any great elapse of time; he could see himself singlehanded even having the body up and out still with no efforts, no pant and strain of muscles and lungs nor laceration of the shrinking sensibilities" (82). And Chick imagines himself having a conversation with Lucas: "thinking seeing hearing himself trying to explain that to Lucas too" (84). In his penetrating imagination, Chick is already independent of his uncle's view of Lucas as a black man who killed a white man by shooting him in the back.

The most attractive feature of the novel is Chick's free and vigorous exercise of his insight and imagination. Faulkner gives us a detailed picture of his consciousness at every stage of the effort he makes to grow into adulthood. The novel follows Chick's instinctive impulse to act to bridge the distance between his dreamy thinking and real experiences. In the process, his imaginative mind comes to accept a different discourse from the one he has learned to digest as a white Southern boy.

When he goes to see Lucas at the jail with his uncle, Chick still believes that Lucas is *"a nigger a murderer who shoots white people in the back and aint even sorry"* (66). But at the same time he perceives "that mute patient urgency" (66) in Lucas's eyes and goes back to the jail alone only to get new orders from the black man: to go out to the cemetery and look at Vinson's body (68-69). On his way back to Lucas's jail cell, Chick assumes: *"Maybe he will remind me of that goddamn plate of collards and sidemeat or maybe he'll even tell me I'm all he's got, and all that's left and that will be enough"* (68). Although Chick is still trapped in the nightmare of the food and the coins, he sees himself assuming a responsibility to save Lucas, if he were the only person available to Lucas in his crisis. However, "Lucas was not even asking him to believe anything; he was not even asking a favor, making no last desperate plea to his humanity and pity but was even going to pay him provided the price was not too high" (72). Therefore it is entirely his own sense of justice and responsibility that urges Chick to take Lucas's words seriously. Further, Chick instinctively knows that what is at stake is crucially "about the death by shameful violence of a man who would die not because he was a murderer but because his skin was black" (72). At this point, Chick's conscience as a white Mississippi boy is already becoming more balanced in terms of racial justice.

Meanwhile, Lucas relies on children's instincts rather than adults' common sense; Lucas's intuition warns him that Lawyer Stevens will never believe in his innocence. As a matter of fact, Gavin's theory of Vinson's murder is established unquestioningly upon circumstantial evidence: "Lucas was caught within two minutes after the shot, standing over the body with a recently-fired pistol in his pocket" (79). Chick repeatedly suggests to his uncle that Lucas may not be Vinson's murderer, by insistently objecting to his uncle's words: "Suppose it wasn't his pistol that killed him..." (79), "But suppose..." (80), or "But just suppose..." (80). However, what Chick has to hear is concealed in the simple repetition of this erroneous theory as it is repeated again and again in the same words:

> ...now he heard for the third time almost exactly what he had heard twice in twelve hours, and he marveled again at the paucity, the really almost standardized meagerness not of individual vocabularies but of Vocabulary itself, by means of which even man can live in vast droves and herds even in concrete warrens in comparative amity.... (80)

Chick's "marvel" at the "paucity" or "meagerness" of "Vocabulary" is already a sign of his growing critique of his uncle's philosophy of language: "he remembered his uncle saying once how little of vocabulary man really needed to get comfortably and even efficiently through his life, how not only in the individual but within his whole type and race and kind a few simple clichés served his few simple passions and needs and lusts" (47–48). Gavin's comment on language unquestionably has a negative connotation, though Gavin is unwittingly showing himself to be a good example of the meagerness of vocabulary, by repeating the same story in the same words that Chick had continually heard in the town. Chick is already departing from his uncle's adamant conviction about blacks and the paucity of vocabulary by proceeding to find a positive value in it. Wesley Morris discusses Stevens's observation on "Vocabulary" by expanding it to a commentary on language, specifically, "on the social functioning of language" (224).

> Its paucity or poverty is the very force of communal bonding, for it not only reduces language to a few phrases but, far more important, reduces familiar reality, what in this novel is called "fact" or "expectation," to comfortable predictability. (224)

Morris's comment above beautifully clarifies Gavin's point, but we should note more emphatically that Miss Habersham is the very factor that urges Chick to recognize this paucity of vocabulary as a positive force to tell the truth. She suddenly calls Chick's name when he was talking with Aleck Sander, his "boy," about the expedition to the cemetery to dig up Vinson Gowrie. Chick's unexpected conversation with Miss Habersham follows soon after his disappointing talk with his uncle Gavin, who refuses to change his opinion of the murder case, even though Chick earnestly appeals to him about the possibility of Lucas's innocence. In contrast to Gavin's incorrigible attitude toward the murder case based on the traditional Southern code of race, the conversation between Chick and Eunice Habersham reveals how the old lady's words are entirely dependent upon her own instincts, instead of relying on the prejudiced racial code of Mississippi.

> "He said it wasn't his pistol," he said.
> "So he didn't do it," she said, rapid still and with something even more than urgency in her voice now.
> "I don't know," he said. (87)

Miss Habersham's quick response to Chick's words is simply decisive and makes a sharp contrast with Uncle Gavin's lengthy speech in defense of the Southern tradition. This time it is Chick who repeats "I don't know" four times in his conversation with Miss Habersham (87–88). Moreover, Chick is frustrated as he cannot finish his sentence.

> "I just don't know. I still don't know. I'm just going out there...." He stopped, his voice died. There was an instant a second in which he even remembered he should have been wishing he could recall it, the last unfinished sentence. Though it was probably already too late and she had already done herself what little finishing the sentence needed....(88)

Chick's meeting with Miss Habersham at his home initiates him into a new territory of discourse which he had never explored. After a round of conversation about what Lucas said to Chick, we read an incredible passage in which Chick and the old lady become "indistinguishable" from each other and even switch parts by identifying their voices in the ensuing conversation.

> ...the two of them facing each other indistinguishable in the darkness across the tense and rapid murmur...the two of them not conspiratorial exactly but rather like two people who have irrevo-

cably accepted a gambit they are not at all certain they can cope with....(88)

Furthermore, Chick has to admit that "then he heard his own voice speaking in the same tone and pitch" (88), but it is Miss Habersham's voice that leads the conversation this time: "We don't even know it wasn't his pistol. He just said it wasn't" (88). Consequently, Chick is awakened to a positive interpretation of repetitive language, by listening to her voice.

> ...and now Miss Habersham in her turn repeating and paraphrasing and he thought how it was not really a paucity a meagerness of vocabulary, it was in the first place because the deliberate violent blotting out obliteration of a human life was itself so simple and so final that the verbiage which surrounded it enclosed it insulated it intact into the chronicle of man had of necessity to be simple and uncomplex too, repetitive, almost monotonous even; and in the second place, vaster than that, adumbrating that, because what Miss Habersham paraphrased was simple truth, not even fact and so there was not needed a great deal of diversification and originality to express it because truth was universal, it had to be universal to be truth....(89)

Through Miss Habersham's way of speaking, Chick realizes that repetitive language can tell the simple truth. Close to the end of the novel, when she knows that Crawford Gowrie, Vinson's brother and his real murderer, put his own brother's body in quicksand, she repeats three times, "He put his brother in quicksand" (228, 231). Opposed to Uncle Gavin's eloquent descriptions of digging up of the two bodies, Miss Habersham's simple interruption of his speech through the repetition of this short sentence more eloquently testifies to the atrocious cruelty of Crawford's murder and disposal of the bodies of his own brother and fellow worker, Jake Montgomery.

Thus Chick finds a positive power in Miss Habersham's language rather than a negative one and revises Uncle Gavin's lesson on language. The sixteen-year-old boy moves on to find justice and responsibility in his journey to reach manhood as a Southern white male. As if immersing himself in Miss Habersham's language of repetition and paraphrasing, Chick mentions the disappearance of the mob to his mother and uncle, with repetitions of the same simple sentence, "They ran" (190, 191, 192, 196, 197). Finally he reaches his own conclusion about the lynch-mob: "They were running from themselves" (202), since they were ashamed of themselves.

Gavin is curious to discover the moment that Chick discerned Lucas's innocence and asks, "When did you really begin to believe him? When you opened the coffin, wasn't it?…When was it?" (126). With his reply, "I don't know," Chick realizes that he doesn't know if he ever believed Lucas: "Then it seemed to him that he had never really believed Lucas" (126). Chick remembers that he didn't decide to go dig up the grave simply because he was told to do so by Lucas. Instead, it was Miss Habersham who led Chick to make the expedition to the cemetery. He confesses that at first he had believed "he would have gone alone even if Aleck Sander had stuck to his refusal but it was only after Miss Habersham came around the house and spoke to him that he knew he was going to go through with it" (112). Chick admits that *"a woman a lady shouldn't have to do this"* (112), but he physically and spiritually owes to her the apparently impossible trip to the cemetery.

Thanks to Miss Habersham's brave support, Chick is convinced there is truth to the words of old Ephraim, Aleck Sander's grandfather, about women and children: "Young folks and womens, they aint cluttered. They can listen. But a middle-year man like your paw and your uncle, they cant listen. They aint got time. They're too busy with facks….If you ever needs to get anything done outside the common run, don't waste yo time on the menfolks; get the womens and children to working at it" (71–72). Chick reminds himself of those legendary words when Miss Habersham joins his and Aleck Sander's trip to the cemetery.

Chick paraphrases Ephraim's words as follows: "*If you got something outside the common run...don't waste your time on the menfolks; they works on what your uncle calls the rules and the cases. Get the women and the children at it; they works on the circumstances*" (112). The old black man's wisdom is repeated and paraphrased not only by Chick but also by Miss Habersham. She speculates: "Lucas knew it would take a child—or an old woman like me: someone not concerned with probability, with evidence. Men like your uncle and Mr Hampton have had to be men too long, busy too long" (89-90). We don't know if this speculation is her own or if she heard it from somebody else. But it is interesting that she detects the nature of Lucas's psychology in his dependence upon Chick instead of upon Lawyer Stevens. The similar words quoted as an epigraph at the beginning of this essay are a lesson for McCaslin Edmonds given by a McCaslin slave, Tomey's Turl, in "'Was," the first story of *Go Down, Moses*. Tomey's Turl, a slave at the McCaslin plantation, colludes with Miss Sophonsiba Beauchamp to win successful marriages for both of them: Miss Sophonsiba with Theophilus McCasin, and Tomey's Turl with Tennie, Hubert Beauchamp's slave. Since Tomey's Turl is Lucas Beauchamp's father, Lucas might have heard the lesson from his own father.

Gavin finally makes a concluding remark on Chick and Miss Habersham's feat: "It took an old woman and two children for that, to believe truth for no other reason than that it was truth, told by an old man in a fix deserving pity and belief, to someone capable of the pity even when none of them really believed him" (126). What is clear from these repeated lessons that originated with Tomey's Turl and Ephraim is that women and children can act outside the traditional rules and codes in the South by following their own instincts amid the consideration of particular circumstances. Chick confesses that "he now recognized the enormity of what he had blindly meddled with and that his first instinctive impulse...had been the right one" (137-38).

As Morris insightfully explains, Chick's blind meddling ironically leads him to open his eyes to "the minority discourse...marked by its special kind of poverty" which "articulates 'truth' as opposed to the 'facts' which blind them to the truth" (224). But this does not simply mean that Chick has entirely switched his discourse from the majority to that of the minority. Chick identifies himself with his uncle's voice during Gavin's speech on Southern homogeneity: "once more his uncle spoke at complete one with him and again without surprise he saw his thinking not be interrupted but merely swap one saddle for another" (153). Of course, as Jay Watson eloquently contends, "One moment...Chick marvels at his uncle's ability to traffic 'not in facts but long since beyond statistics into something far more moving because it was truth...,' yet later in the novel Chick can come down hard against 'his uncle's abnegant and rhetorical self-lacerating' [133]" (110–11). As we have seen, Chick becomes one with Miss Habersham when they go to the cemetery together. But he has not thrown away his "whole native land, his home—the dirt, the earth which...[is] still shaping him into not just a man but a specific man, not with just a man's passions and aspirations and beliefs but the specific passions and hopes and convictions and ways of thinking and acting of a specific kind and even race" (151). But at least Chick has found a small hole in the monolithic, rigid Southern tradition of race and gender relations, which is opened when he joins Miss Habersham's call to brave action and the language of truth.

3. Fratricide or Family Ties?

Cleanth Brooks comments that "Charles Mallison would...have been unable to perform his mission without the aid of Miss Habersham" (286). Chick desperately needs her pickup truck, but he needs "even more than that her counsel and her moral backing" (286). It is indisputable that, without Miss Habersham's positive commitment to digging up the grave, nobody could have saved Lucas from the lynch-mob. But why does she so passionately attempt to help Lucas out of his difficult situation?

Miss Habersham is described as "a kinless spinster of seventy living in the columned colonial house" (76) on the edge of town "with two Negro servants" (76). Miss Habersham has no remaining blood relations, but her strong sense of family survives as something more extended. Talking with her about Lucas's request, Chick remembers an episode about her: "old Molly, Lucas's wife…and Miss Habersham the same age, born in the same week and both suckled at Molly's mother's breast and grown up together almost inextricably like sisters, like twins" (87). Molly and Miss Habersham slept "in the same room, the white girl in the bed, the Negro girl on a cot at the foot of it almost until Molly and Lucas married" (87). Therefore, the motivation behind Miss Habersham's decisive action to rescue Lucas from his predicament is that she considers Lucas to be as close as a brother-in-law. The two black servants Miss Habersham lives with are Molly's brother and his wife: the wife "did the cooking while Miss Habersham and the man raised chickens and vegetables and peddled them about town from the pickup truck" (76). They seem to lead a communal life in the same house, equally distributing the work and household roles to make a living. She is "kinless" but she has a family; she takes action in order to save a family member.

It could be very illuminating to remind ourselves of Chick's keen observation that Miss Habersham's hat resembles his own grandmother's. Moreover, he repeats the same observation about her hat: "the hat which on anyone else wouldn't even have looked like a hat but on her as on his grandmother looked exactly right" (130). From the above description of Miss Habersham's hat, we realize that Chick's observation goes beyond the simple association of two old women from the same generation wearing similar clothes. It is the way they wear the hat that is important. By connecting Miss Habersham's hat with that of his grandmother in this fashion, Chick feels safely supported, as it were, by his own dearly loved family member.

As I have already quoted (from *ID*, 12) in Section 1, Lucas's beaver hat and gold toothpick also remind Chick of his grandfather. More than that, Chick associates Lucas's manner of speech with his grandfather's when he thanks Lucas for the molasses: "Lucas had answered exactly as his grandfather himself might, only the words, the grammar any different: 'They turned out good this year. When I was making um

I remembered how a boy's always got a sweet tooth for good molasses'" (24). When Chick first notices Lucas's gold toothpick and his gorgeous beaver hat, he is shocked by what he reflexively considers to be Lucas's arrogance in imitating white men's clothes. But after hearing his own grandfather's speech in Lucas's words, Chick perceives a familial intimacy in his conversation with the black man. Consequently, Chick's family ties result in making Lucas's and Miss Habersham's lessons more effective simply because their clothing, accoutrements, and ways of speech resemble those of his grandparents.

When the murder turns out to be a case of fratricide within the Gowrie family, a deep-rooted mythical motif emerges in the novel concerning the family, one of the most important and lasting themes of the American novel. It is made clear that Vinson Gowrie was shot not with Lucas's forty-one Colt but with a German Luger automatic that Crawford Gowrie, Vinson's brother, obtained from Buddy McCallum in 1919 (178, 192). How can a brother kill his own brother? To answer this question, we might consider another: namely, is there any connection between the Gowrie family's violence and their womanless life? If we reflect on the highly significant roles played by women in Chick's education, the fact that "seven Gowrie men" lived "in the twenty-year womanless house" (219) emphasizes the violence and cruelty of the murder as contrasted with the useful lessons of love and trust that Chick's mother and Miss Habersham give him in the novel.

Chick Mallison is confused to see the mob dispersing quickly once they know that Vinson was killed by his own brother. More frustrating to Chick is Gavin's lecture on the simple moral precept: *"Thou shalt not kill"* (199). Furthermore, Gavin gives an extremely confounding interpretation of the mob's reaction to Crawford Gowrie, who killed his own brother: "They repudiated him. If they have lynched him they would have taken only his life. What they really did was worse: they deprived him to the full extent of their capacity of his citizenship in man" (202). Does Gavin suggest thereby that the mob could have taken Lucas's, a black man's, life by lynching without hesitation because it was impossible to take away a "citizenship in man" that was never granted to him in the first place? Gavin abhors the fratricide committed in the Gowrie family, but would it not also have been a fratricide to lynch Lucas? Jay Watson admires Morris's observation about "the inability of white Yoknapatawphans to see a lynching as a fratricide—to see a black man as a brother" (137). Furthermore, Crawford's careless atrocity shocks both Gavin and Miss Habersham. As has been already quoted, Miss Habersham emphatically repeats her outrage against Crawford's murder and burial of the bodies: "He put his brother in quicksand" (230–31). Gavin also makes a harsh comment on fratricide and quicksand: "That moment may come to anyone when simply nothing remains to be done with your brother or husband or uncle or cousin or mother-in-law except destroy them. But you don't put them in quicksand" (231).

To go back to the essential question, to ask "Is a lynching not a fratricide?" is to ask if Lucas is a brother to white people in the South. How much is Lucas respected, for example, by Gavin and Miss Habersham? The following conversation confirms their opposite attitudes toward Lucas. When they are discussing what Crawford did to his own brother, and the possible aftermath of the dreadful murder, Gavin tells Miss Habersham not to worry.

> "I'm not worrying," Miss Habersham said.
> "Of course not," his uncle said. "Because I know Hope Hampton—"
> "Yes," Miss Habersham said. "I know Lucas Beauchamp." (234)

As is clear from this conversation, Gavin believes in Sheriff Hampton, while Miss Habersham believes in her black brother Lucas. Gavin believes a white man cemented within the power structure of the South, while Miss Habersham trusts someone who is a member of her black family.

Miss Habersham, who is named "Miss Worsham" in the title story of *Go Down, Moses*, tries her best in order to help Mollie (Molly is spelled "Mollie" in the story) get the body of her executed grandson,

Samuel Worsham ("Butch") Beauchamp, back home. She explains her relation to Mollie to Gavin Stevens: "Mollie and I were born in the same month. We grew up together as sisters would" (*GD,M*, 357), which we hear from Chick's memory in *Intruder in the Dust*. When Stevens visits Miss Worsham's house to talk about Butch's funeral, Miss Worsham's servant, Hamp Worsham, his wife, and Mollie are singing a spiritual. They keep singing without bothering to stop at Stevens's arrival. Stevens cannot remain there and hurriedly runs from the house. He feels that he is almost suffocated by their singing; their minority discourse repeats the same phrase and line, "Sold my Benjamin" and "Sold him in Egypt." Gavin feels excluded from this minority discourse and thinks in panic: "*I will be outside....Then there will be air, space, breath*" (*GD,M*, 362). When Stevens apologizes to Miss Worsham for his visit, she says, "It's our grief" (363). Thus she does not invite Gavin into their ceremony of singing. Their singing space closes the white man out, with Miss Worsham's family tightly stuck together in their own grief. In this story as well, Miss Worsham, a white lady, believes that she and her black servants are a family.

It might be a little presumptuous to interpret *Intruder in the Dust* as a story of a young boy surrounded by supportive family members, juxtaposed against the motherless sons of the Gowrie family. But Chick once mentions that "he happened not to be an orphan" (138). We find Chick to be an entirely new boy character for Faulkner; for example, he is different from Quentin Compson or Isaac McCaslin, who also go through the pains of growth in their teens, just because he has a healthy and caring family.

Thanks to a family education by his parents, Uncle Gavin, Miss Habersham, and Lucas Beauchamp, Chick's imagination sees far beyond Gavin's and the community's wisdom. Gavin's speeches on "Sambo" (149–50), "homogeneity" (153–56), and "outlander" (215–17) mainly follow the discourse of difference: divisions between black and white, and divisions between the North and the South. But Chick seeks to transgress the boundary of difference and reach other people's domains. Thus Chick is ready to share Lucas's grief and shame: *"Because they always have me and Aleck Sander and Miss Habersham, not to mention Uncle Gavin and a sworn badge-wearing sheriff"* (209). He suddenly realizes that "they were his and he was theirs" (209). Chick does not exclude from his family powerful white people such as Lawyer Stevens or Sheriff Hampton. Thus Chick finally accepts other people's "injustice and outrage and dishonor and shame" (206) as his own: "he wanted no more save to stand with them unalterable and impregnable: one shame if shame must be, one expiation since expiation must surely be but above all one unalterable durable impregnable one: one people one heart one land" (209–10). Inside Chick's idealized family region, nobody kills his brother and nobody is lynched for any reason.

Chick's idealistic idea of "one people one heart one land" is shaped through a dialogue with Uncle Gavin's traditional white male discourse as well as through Miss Habersham's lessons in the minority discourse. In the process, the boy is driven to reconcile abstract language with real experiences. Therefore Chick's efforts, if successful, will settle the anxiety of Addie Bundren's dichotomy of words and doing: "words go straight up in a thin line, quick and harmless, and how terribly doing goes along the earth, clinging to it, so that after a while the two lines are too far apart for the same person to straddle from one to the other" (*AILD*, 173). As we have seen, far from Addie's frustration, Chick happily straddles the gap between "words" and "doing" by easily swapping from "one saddle to another" (153).

Works Cited

Brooks, Cleanth. *William Faulkner: The Yoknapatawpha Country*. New Haven: Yale UP, 1963.
Faulkner, William. *As I Lay Dying*. New York: Vintage International, 1990. Abbreviated as *AILD*.
-----. *Go Down, Moses*. New York: Vintage International, 1990. Abbreviated as *GD,M*.
-----. *Intruder in the Dust*. New York: Random House, 1948. Abbreviated as *ID*.
Meriwether, James B. and Michael Millgate. Eds. *Lion in the Garden: Interviews with William Faulkner: 1926–1962*. New York: Random House, 1968. Abbreviated as *LG*.
Morris, Wesley and Barbara Alverson Morris. *Reading Faulkner*. Madison: U of

Wisconsin P, 1989.
Vickery, Olga W. *The Novels of William Faulkner: A Critical Interpretation*. Baton Rouge: Louisiana State UP, 1959.
Watson, Jay. *Forensic Fictions: The Lawyer Figure in Faulkner*. Athens and London: U of Georgia P, 1993.

TEACHING *INTRUDER IN THE DUST* THROUGH ITS POLITICAL AND HISTORICAL CONTEXT

Robert W. Hamblin

Intruder in the Dust not only is one of Faulkner's most enjoyable and accessible texts, but it also provides one of the few instances in which Faulkner's fiction comments directly upon a contemporary political situation. This latter point is not insignificant, since many of today's students know very little about the history of racial segregation in the South and the degree to which that tradition became a divisive issue in the 1948 presidential campaign. Examining the political and historical context of *Intruder in the Dust* enables students to reflect on the manner in which a great modern writer blends fiction and fact to create a work of literature that, in keeping with the classical definition of art, both "delights" and "instructs."

I begin the study of *Intruder in the Dust* by leading a class discussion based on a close reading of chapters 1 and 2, which I believe represent one of the most discerning treatments of race in all of Faulkner. There we note how a twelve-year-old white boy (whom we subsequently learn is named Charles ["Chick"] Mallison[1]) has incurred a debt of obligation to Lucas Beauchamp, a Negro. This indebtedness has resulted from Lucas's charitable acts of rescuing the boy from an icy creek, taking the boy home with him, drying his clothes, and feeding him dinner. With a quick reference to the deconstructionist notion of binary oppositions, in this case the *privileged* and *unprivileged* terms of *white* and *black*, I ask the class to identify the ways Faulkner inverts the traditional racial hierarchy and to analyze how and why this inversion creates such profound embarrassment and shame in the young boy.

Students quickly note that at the start of the rabbit hunt Chick and his two black companions assume for that time and place the expected roles of their respective races: Chick leads the way and carries a gun, while the Negroes follow, armed with tapsticks. But Chick's fall into the creek upsets (both literally and symbolically) this traditional order, as the image of Chick lying helpless at the feet of the towering Lucas makes clear. From this point on the white boy is subjected to a series of commands by a Negro. "Come on to my house," Lucas says (7), and now Chick follows rather than leads. Chick would prefer to go to his white relative's house, but he finds "that he could no more imagine himself contradicting the man striding on ahead of him than he could his grandfather...because like his grandfather the man striding ahead of him was simply incapable of conceiving himself by a child contradicted and defied" (8). In other words, Chick recognizes that Lucas requires their relationship to be that of man and boy, not black and white. Inside Lucas's house Chick is ordered to strip naked and, while his clothes are being dried, to wrap himself in a quilt belonging to the Beauchamps. These actions, too, are symbolic, as Chick is stripped of his "whiteness" and made to take on the "blackness" that he has been taught all his life to scorn. Sometimes an alert reader will comment on the death and rebirth imagery that Faulkner employs in the description of Chick's being "enveloped in the quilt like a cocoon, enclosed completely now in that unmistakable odor of Negroes" (11). The reversal of roles is completed when Chick is required to eat the "nigger food" (13) that Lucas's wife Molly has prepared for him.[2]

Now floundering in a strange and confusing environment (for which a near-drowning is a very appropriate symbol), Chick seeks to reclaim the advantage he has lost. Thus he attempts to relegate Lucas to the traditional role of subservience by attempting to pay the Negro for his trouble. When Lucas, recognizing and declining the gambit, refuses payment, Chick drops the money to the floor. After Chick has refused to pick up the coins, Lucas orders Chick's black companions to return the money to the white youngster. Finally outside the house again, Chick seeks to rid himself of the symbol of his shame by throwing the coins into the creek, though he recognizes that "Lucas had beat him" (17).

For the next four years, unable to shake the feeling that his defeat at the hands of Lucas has "debased not merely his manhood but his whole race too" (21), Chick struggles to free himself from his obligation to Lucas, hoping by so doing, of course, to reassert the canceled order of his old familiar world. A game of one-upmanship now ensues. Chick sends Lucas and Molly a Christmas present of cigars and snuff, and he mails Molly a new dress—only to have Lucas reciprocate by sending a white boy on a mule to deliver a gallon of molasses to Chick. Now Chick is more frustrated than ever, "because this time Lucas had commanded a white hand to pick up his money and give it back to him" (23). Recognizing that Lucas will never allow him to repay the debt, Chick can only hope that in time the Negro will forget him. Until such time, the youngster reasons, his shame, and that of his race, will continue. Thus Chick plots to meet Lucas on the street, anxiously awaiting the day when he can pass his benefactor and encounter no sign of recognition. Finally, three years after the creek episode, Chick is persuaded that his hope of escape has finally been realized: "Lucas looked up and once more looked straight into his eyes for perhaps a quarter of a minute and then away....*It's over. That was all* because he was free, the man who for three years had obsessed his life waking and sleeping too had walked out of it" (25–26). Chick's freedom, however, is an illusion. Lucas has not forgotten, and he still controls the game, as the boy learns a year later. When Lucas is brought to the Jefferson jail accused of murdering a white man, he turns immediately to Chick for help, commanding him in the same manner he had on the day of the mishap at the creek: "You, young man," Lucas says. "Tell your uncle I wants to see him" (45).

Most students have no difficulty in defining the basic conflict between Chick and Lucas. While generally not agreeing with Chick's attitude, students understand the powerful social forces that require a young white Southerner immersed in the racist traditions of his society to feel compelled, with other white Jeffersonians, "to make a nigger out of [Lucas] once in his life anyway" (32). And today's students, who are well informed of civil rights issues concerning racial minorities, women, and gays, can certainly identify with Lucas's insistence upon equality and dignity. But I want students to see that Faulkner depicts, from the very beginning, the conflict between Chick and Lucas as a very complex issue. I ask them to identify ways that Chick and Lucas defy the respective stereotypes of white racist and black confrontationist.

Several significant points surface during this part of the discussion. Concerning Chick, students note, for example, the close friendship that exists between the white boy and his black playmate, Aleck Sander—a friendship that is symbolized, in ironic contrast to Chick's behavior in Lucas's house, by the meals they have shared together, "the food tasting the same to each" (12). Students also notice that Chick, observing Lucas, is reminded of his own grandfather, and that, after watching Lucas's response to the death of Molly, he realizes that "You don't have to not be a nigger in order to grieve" (25). Occasionally a student may even call attention to Chick's precocious observation that the smell that he has typically associated with Negroes might not be, after all, "the odor of a race nor even actually of poverty but perhaps of a condition: an idea: a belief" (11).

Similar contradictions exist in the characterization of Lucas. While Lucas is initially perceived as a militant black victim of white racism, the students quickly realize that Lucas, a descendant of old Carothers McCaslin, is part-white. What are the implications, I ask, of the fact that Lucas insists on thinking of himself as "white," while the community is determined to define him as "black"?[3] And what are readers to make of Lucas's pomposity, arrogance, and self-pride? These are qualities that are generally held to be defects, whatever the race of the individual who exhibits them. What I want students to see is that in his initial presentations of both Chick and Lucas Faulkner has refused to oversimplify the issue of race or character. Through the reversal of roles, by making Chick partly "black" and Lucas partly "white," and by simultaneously showing both with serious character flaws, Faulkner has inverted the binary oppositions and, in so doing, has blurred the standard assumptions that will be challenged even more strongly as the novel progresses.

At this point I interrupt the discussion of the novel for a side excursion into the political and historical context of the work. I initiate this part of our study by citing an incident from Faulkner's life recorded by Ben Wasson in *Count No 'Count: Flashbacks to Faulkner*. As Wasson recalls, in late February 1948, when Faulkner was engaged in the composition of *Intruder in they Dust*, he entertained at Rowan Oak an individual whom he greatly admired and respected—Hodding Carter, the publisher-editor of the influential Greenville *Delta Democrat-Times*. The outspoken Carter, who had been awarded a Pulitzer Prize in 1946 for his editorials condemning racial injustice and inequality, was one of most controversial Mississippians of his day (162–63).

Carter had traveled to Oxford in the company of Wasson, another Greenville resident who was Faulkner's friend from college days and for a time thereafter his literary agent. According to Wasson, the three men spent most of their day together drinking toddies, but they also talked about politics and Faulkner's novel in progress. Specifically, Wasson notes, Faulkner and Carter discussed "the burning question of the moment: 'Shall the South integrate or remain segregated?'" (162–63). Wasson does not record Faulkner and Carter's actual conversation that February day at Rowan Oak on "the burning question" of desegregation, but, as my students quickly discover, it is relatively easy to reconstruct the political context—and perhaps even something of the substance—of their remarks. It is even easier to document Faulkner's support of Carter's position. Shortly after Carter's visit to Rowan Oak, Faulkner included the following characterization of the newspaperman in a letter to Robert Haas, one of Faulkner's Random House editors: "[Carter's] name is familiar to you, probably: lecturer, liberal, champion of Negro injustice though no radical, no communist despite Bilbo and Rankin" (Blotner 264). Then, just days before the 1948 presidential election Faulkner told an interviewer: "I'd be a Dixiecrat myself if they hadn't hollered 'nigger.' I'm a States' Rights man. Hodding Carter's a good man, and he's right when he says the solution of the Negro problem belongs to the South" (Meriwether and Millgate 60).

With Wasson's question of integration versus segregation and Faulkner's stated preference for Carter and states' rights over Bilbo and the Dixiecrats before us, the students and I head for the library, where I challenge them to reconstruct, as best they can, the various attitudes that were being expressed for and against desegregation, particularly in the South, at the time Faulkner was writing *Intruder in the Dust*. The more knowledgeable students quickly lead the others through a search of the periodicals section, where they scan newspaper and magazine articles of the period. Their out-of-class assignment for the next class session is to continue this general search, adding book searches to their perusal of the periodical literature.

Back in the library for the next class meeting, I organize the students into small research groups and assign each group a specific topic that ideally has already surfaced in their previous search: President Truman's stand on civil rights, the reactions of the Dixiecrats to the president's proposals, and the contrasting opinions of Hodding Carter and Theodore G. Bilbo. At the next class meeting each group is asked to present the results of its research to the entire class. Following are brief summaries of the type of information that they present—information that I want the students to know before we resume our discussion of *Intruder in the Dust*.

1. President Truman's stand on civil rights. Just days before Wasson and Carter drove from Greenville to Oxford to visit with Faulkner, Truman had become the first American president in history to send to Congress a legislative package dealing solely with the issue of civil rights.[4] Truman's proposals were based on the recommendations of the President's Committee on Civil Rights, published as *To Secure These Rights* the previous October. This report, which examined the hardships experienced by a number of minority groups but particularly Southern blacks, blamed segregation for the conditions of poverty, violence, and discrimination that continued to deny the Negro both freedom and socioeconomic advancement. While the report did not go so far as to recommend that segregation be made illegal, it did identify Jim Crow laws as the principal cause for the plight of blacks and argued that so long as the "separate but equal" concept prevailed, inequality and injustice would remain. The report called upon the federal government to pursue a course of active intervention to ensure the civil rights of black citizens. Specifically, the President's Committee endorsed such measures as the passage of anti-poll tax and anti-lynching legislation, the immediate desegregation of the armed forces and other government agencies, the creation of a Fair Employment Practices Committee (FEPC) and a permanent commission on civil rights, and the prohibition of Jim Crow in interstate transportation. The committee even recommended that federal aid be denied to states that did not comply with the proposed measures.

2. The Dixiecrat response to the president's proposals. The Southern, states' rights wing of the Democratic Party, popularly known as Dixiecrats, recognized, rightly, that the president's general position on civil rights, if enacted into legislation, would change the racial, social, and political character of the South forever.[5] Such anxiety was especially acute in states that had the largest black populations. Disgruntled Democrats in those states, under the direction of Governor Fielding Wright of Mississippi, Governor Strom Thurmond of South Carolina, Governor Frank Dixon of Alabama, and political boss Leander Perez of Louisiana, sought to organize a grassroots opposition to the liberal leadership of the national party and, if necessary, pursue an independent course.

Shortly after President Truman sent his historic civil rights package to Congress, the Southern Governors' Conference convened in Wakulla Springs, Florida. The pressing item on the agenda was what should be the South's response to the president's and the nation's reforming zeal. Most of the governors present, believing that Truman could not win his party's nomination—and certainly not the election—without the support of the South, favored lobbying the national Democratic party to defeat or modify the civil rights package. Such was the view of the influential Thurmond. But Wright argued for a more radical approach: he wanted the Southern states to disassociate themselves from the Democratic party.

In early May, Wright hosted a conference for the dissident Southerners in Jackson. At that meeting the Dixiecrats agreed to meet again in Birmingham in July if the Truman wing of the Democratic party prevailed at the Philadelphia convention. Truman, of course, did secure the Democratic nomination in Philadelphia; and two days later, at the rump convention in Birmingham, some 6,000 disaffected Southerners unanimously selected an alternate ticket of Governor Thurmond for president and Wright for vice-president. In the November election this ticket would carry four states—South Carolina, Mississippi, Alabama, and Louisiana. The remaining Southern states, holding to their longtime tradition, voted for the national party's ticket of Truman and Alben Barkley. Further demonstrating that from the beginning race had been the chief factor in the Southern revolt, predictably the strongest Dixiecrat showing in the election came in the states that had the largest black populations: in Faulkner's Mississippi with 87 percent of the vote, in Alabama with 80 percent, and in South Carolina with 72 percent.

3. Hodding Carter's views. Carter's views on all these matters—and thus presumably the opinions he shared with Faulkner at Rowan Oak—are easy to ascertain. Carter's prize-winning first novel, *The Winds of Fear* (1944), had dramatized the rising fears and the violent reactions of Southern whites to the increasingly militant demands of Southern blacks and their Northern supporters. In the characterization of Alan Mabry, however, Carter demonstrated that some Southerners supported racial tolerance and a break with Jim Crow tradition. If *The Winds of Fear* was Carter's attempt to help Northern readers understand the thoughts and feelings of both the reactionary and moderate white Southerners, the editorials he wrote for the *Delta Democrat-Times* were attempts to get his fellow Southerners to look at their traditions and institutions in relation to broader issues of national policy and constitutional law.

As coincidence would have it, at the time of his visit with Faulkner, Carter was probably already at work on an essay expressing his personal views for the *New York Times Magazine*. That essay, entitled "The Civil

Rights Issue as Seen in the South," would be published less than a month later, on March 21, 1948.[6]

In that essay Carter presented the views of both "the average white Southerner" and the "Southern liberals" toward President Truman's civil rights proposal. To the first of these the president's program was nothing less than "a politically motivated and all-out offensive against the conglomerate of laws, customs and attitudes which gives expression to the doctrine of white supremacy" (15), which, according to Carter, was "the most persistent concept that has come down to us from our Western European predecessor" (54). To this group of Southerners, by far the majority of the white population, the proposed reform program represented "an attempt by a coalition of Communists, Northern Negroes, and self-seeking Northern Democrats to end abruptly segregation of any kind in the South and to replace local and state self-government with Federal domination" (15).

Carter acknowledged that the opposition of the reactionary Southerners to federal legislative and judicial mandates was both illogical and futile; but in the present political climate of the South, Carter argued, emotion was a far stronger motivation than reason. "The truth is," Carter explained, "that the South is afraid that its old racial pattern is going, and going too fast" (15). From such fear came the Southerner's anger, frustration, and "an undeniable desire to hit back somehow" (52). The political counteraction of the Dixiecrats, despite the heavy odds against its success, seemed to offer the only available weapon to use in the struggle.

The liberal white Southerners, whom Carter characterized as "a small and relatively voiceless minority" (15), were highly suspicious of the political motivations of the Dixiecrats; but they shared with their reactionary kinsmen a distrust of federal intervention. Moreover, while these individuals had rejected the political and economic tenets of the doctrine of white supremacy, most of them were still unwilling to accept the "social equality" (52) that would come with integration. Even the most liberal of the liberals, Carter pointed out, tended to be "gradualists" (53) who believed that any meaningful and lasting reform must come over an extended period of time and must be the result of Southern initiative rather than outside compulsion.

Carter concluded his essay with an alarmingly pessimistic view of the situation. The voices of the moderates and pragmatists (among whom Carter counted a significant number of Southern blacks) were being drowned out by extremists represented, on the one hand, by the Grand Dragon of the Ku Klux Klan, who predicted bloodshed if the proposed civil rights legislation was enacted, and, on the other, by Northern black revolutionaries like P. L. Praddis, editor of the *Pittsburgh Courier*, who equated Winston Churchill (because of Great Britain's policy in South Africa) with Hitler and Mussolini. Such incendiary positions, added to the long-standing (and, Carter feared, possibly ineradicable) antipathy between the white and black races, created a complex problem that defied easy and immediate solution. When and if a solution did come, Carter argued, it would be "unrelated and largely impervious to legislation" and would be effected by the South itself, "gradually and with the consent and participation of the white Southerners" (55).

4. Theodore G. Bilbo's views. How liberal in his day was Hodding Carter can best be understood by placing his views beside those espoused by the white supremacist Theodore G. Bilbo. One of the most popular politicians Mississippi has ever produced, Bilbo was elected to one term as lieutenant governor, two terms as governor, and three terms as U.S. senator. His book, *Take Your Choice: Separation or Mongrelization*,[7] was published just ten months before Faulkner began work on *Intruder in the Dust*. Originally presented as a patriotic effort to save American civilization from destruction, Bilbo's book today impresses most readers as clearly and irrefutably one of the most racist statements in all of American history.

Bilbo begins by claiming that "the Negro problem" (5), as he calls it, represents as huge a threat to the survival of white America as the recently concluded war with Germany and Japan. Recalling the end of that war, Bilbo notes: "Personally, the writer of this book would rather see his race and his civilization blotted out with the atomic bomb than to see it slowly but surely destroyed in the maelstrom of miscegenation, interbreeding, intermarriage, and mongrelization" ("Preface"). According to Bilbo, there is only one alternative to such interrelationships: the complete and permanent separation of the two races. Bilbo argues that the ideal way to achieve this goal would be to return all American Negroes to Africa, which he had sought to implement by introducing his "Greater Liberia Act" in the U.S. Senate in 1939; but, that effort having failed, the responsibility now falls to the white Southerner to resist the demands of reformers and maintain all patterns of social segregation.

Bilbo's harshest words are for those who would remove the traditional social barriers that have been erected between the two races. He pillories Eleanor Roosevelt and the Fair Employment Practices Committee for promoting integration in the nation's capital.

> By orders issued at the top, all partitions have been torn out in order to compel the whites and blacks to eat together in the same rooms and at the same tables. Negro wash basins and toilets have been wrecked or removed in order to compel whites and Negroes to use the same wash basins, the same towels, and the same toilet facilities. Hundreds of complaints have come to my office from white girls who are now forced to stand and wait patiently until the odoriferous females of the Negro race have finished their toilets in closets formerly used and occupied by white girls only. (124)

Other individuals and organizations whom Bilbo lambasts for supporting social equality between the races include A. Philip Randolph, W.E.B. DuBois, Richard Wright, Lillian Smith, Wendell Wilkie, Henry A. Wallace, the National Association for the Advancement of Colored People, the Southern Conference for Human Welfare, the United Council of Church Women, and the Communist Party of America.

Predictably some of Bilbo's most vitriolic attacks are hurled at individuals who promote school integration. He devotes an entire chapter of his book to lambasting "The Springfield Plan," an early experiment with desegregation implemented by John Granrud, superintendent of schools in Springfield, Massachusetts. Bilbo vehemently disagrees with Granrud's contention that segregation in American schools is "destructive of our concepts of democracy and our theory of the equality of all peoples and all races" (187). Bilbo also castigates A. Ritchie Low, a Vermont minister, for sponsoring summer visitation of black children from Harlem with white families in New England.

> Hundreds of Negro children from Harlem who had been exposed to life in this slum section with all the vices connected therewith have been placed in white homes throughout New England to "live, eat, and sleep" with white children. What possible good could come from such an experiment?...Any white man, minister or layman, who would promote such a program certainly is either totally misinformed or has no regard for the integrity of his race. (189–90)

In Bilbo's view, there can be no compromise on the issue of race:

> If we sit with Negroes at our tables, if we attend social functions with them as our social equals, if we disregard segregation in all other relations, is it then possible that we maintain it fixedly in the marriage of the South's Saxon sons and daughters? The answer must be "No." By the absolute denial of social equality to the Negro, the barriers between the races are firm and strong. But if the middle wall of the social partition should be broken down, then the mingling of the tides of life would surely begin. (55)

Despite the pressures exerted from both without and within, Bilbo argues, the white South will never surrender its position on this matter.

> The South stands for blood, for the preservation of the blood of the white race. We shall not relax in any way whatsoever the social barriers which have been erected to maintain the purity of that blood....There is not enough power in all the world, not in all the mechanized armies of the Allies and the Axis, including the atomic bomb, which could now force white Southerners to abandon the policy of the social segregation of the white and black races. (58–59)

As students quickly discover, such views as the ones cited here clearly demonstrate just how entrenched and rabid were the prejudices with which Southern moderates like Hodding Carter (and Faulkner) had to contend.

Supplied with this background information, the class is asked to turn its attention again to the text of *Intruder in the Dust*. I begin this phase of our discussion by first telling the students that Faulkner described the novel as "a mystery story plus a little sociology and psychology" (Blotner 267) and then asking them to align the major characters of the novel with the various attitudes toward race that have surfaced in their investigation of the cultural and political context of the novel. Some of these links are fairly obvious: the students have no doubt that the Gowries and their Beat Four cohorts voted for Bilbo, and they recognize Gavin Stevens's preachments on politics and race in chapters 7, 9, and 10 as remarkably similar to the views of Hodding Carter.[8] Students find frequent allusions to President Truman's civil rights proposals in Stevens's speeches (for example, the references to "lynch-rope," "legislation," and "the simple ratification by votes of a printed paragraph" [155] are probably allusion to *To Secure These Rights*), but they note that most such references are negative in tone, and they find no character who can be said clearly to identify with the position of a "Northern liberal." Some try to force Miss Habersham into this role; others, more persuasively, argue that Lucas's confrontational behavior best conveys the "Northern" stance; still others point to the

Chick at the end of the book, as opposed to the Chick of the beginning. But the final consensus is that Faulkner has intentionally devalued this viewpoint in his text. "What are readers to make of this fact?" I ask. The students eventually conclude (correctly, I believe) that Faulkner's implied position is one marked by a strong degree of defensiveness and rationalization. A moderate, not a liberal, and a gradualist, Faulkner, like Stevens/Carter, impresses students as a constitutional states'-righter, one who is deeply distrustful of Northern intervention and genuinely persuaded that "the Negro question" is the South's problem and one that can be solved only over a long period of time. Non-interference, expiation, and gradualism—these are essentially Faulkner's views on the race question.[9] Some of my students (not all white, by the way) agree with Faulkner on the issue, while others (not all black) strongly disagree.

Only now am I ready to lead the class in a close examination of the initiation of Chick Mallison, whom I take to be the protagonist of the novel. The class has already noted, in its discussion of the opening chapters of the book, how Chick initially shares many of the racial attitudes and prejudices of his society. At this stage of the narrative, significantly, Chick is closely identified with his mother, who in her overly protective behavior and unwillingness to grant him freedom and independence is associated with "that nightraddled dragonregion of fears and terrors in which women—mothers anyway—seemed from choice to dwell" (32). As the novel progresses, however, Chick gradually but steadily moves beyond her reach and control, entering a strange and forbidden world in which he allows his actions to be directed by a black man. This latter behavior is so radical (at least for a white Mississippi boy in 1948) that it can only be described as a type of rebirth:

> It would be some time yet before he would realise how far he had come: a provincial Mississippian, a child who when the sun set this same day had appeared to be...still a swaddled unwitting infant in the long tradition of his native land—or for that matter a witless foetus itself struggling...blind and

insentient and not even yet awaked in the simple
painless convulsion of emergence. (96–97)

It does not escape the students' notice that this emergence culminates in an act of social rebellion—an act that is even more startling because of the young age of the perpetrator. "So, by the end of the novel, where are we to place Chick on the political spectrum we identified earlier?" I ask the students. All place him somewhere left of center; some are even inclined to see in him the making of a "liberal." "If he were old enough to vote," I inquire, "would he vote for Truman?"[10] The students are always uncertain of the answer to this hypothetical question, although recently a student with a keen sense of Southern history responded, "Probably not, but when he's in his twenties he might vote for John Kennedy and support Martin Luther King." I agree, partly because I know a sizable number of actual Mississippians of Chick's generation whose political views evolved precisely in such a direction.

I conclude the study of *Intruder in the Dust* by asking the class to discuss the meaning of the title. Students immediately associate the title with the act of gravedigging by Chick, Aleck, and Miss Habersham; as Gavin says, "You violated a white grave to save a nigger" (242). But I want students to move beyond this literal level of the story to see that what Chick, Aleck, and Miss Habersham unearth and expose in this novel is not merely a corpse but the outworn and outdated stereotypes perpetuated by the Jim Crow South. In this regard they are "intruders" in a far greater realm than a rural cemetery; what they violate is the "dust" of Southern tradition.[11] And in the Mississippi of 1948, a Mississippi still largely under the control of the Bilbos and the Dixiecrats, rather than moderates like Hodding Carter and William Faulkner, this violation of tradition was a far greater crime than digging up a grave.

Notes

1. The fact that Chick is nameless in the early pages of the novel reinforces his lack of individual identity and his dependence upon his culture's mores and traditions.

2. The act of eating is a dominant motif in this work, serving, as the extended passage on page 207 reveals, as a symbol of the rite of initiation. If time permits, the instructor might discuss Faulkner's use of this symbol in relation to the sacrament of the Holy Communion.
3. Here a brief discussion of miscegenation and the "one-drop [of blood] rule" may be required, but hopefully the end result will be a recognition that Lucas's color—white, black, or mixed—is immaterial: that ultimately, as both Lucas and (I think) Faulkner's text make clear, in a lawful and democratic society all individuals are equal and justice must be color-blind.
4. For a detailed discussion of President Truman's position see William C. Berman, *The Politics of Civil Rights in the Truman Administration* (Columbus: Ohio State University Press, 1970), 79-135.
5. See Robert Garson, *The Democratic Party and the Politics of Sectionalism, 1941-1948* (Baton Rouge: Louisiana State University Press, 1974), 281-314.
6. For a broader treatment of Carter's views on civil rights see John T. Kneebone, "Liberal on the Levee: Hodding Carter, 1944-1954," *Journal of Mississippi History*, 49 (1987):153-62.
7. The conflict between Bilbo and Carter is treated in Garry Boulard, "'The Man' Versus 'The Quisling': Theodore Bilbo, Hodding Carter, and the 1946 Democratic Party," *Journal of Mississippi History*, 51 (1989):201-17.
8. Richard Gray's recent book, *The Life of William Faulkner: A Critical Biography* (Oxford: Blackwell, 1994), perpetuates the mistaken notion that the Gavin Stevens of *Intruder* is modeled on Phil Stone (23). Stevens, like Stone, is a lawyer; but Stone's ideas on race were closer to Bilbo's than to Carter's and Faulkner's.
9. If students want to pursue this matter, I point them to Faulkner's later essays, such as "On Fear: The South in Labor" and "If I Were a Negro," both printed in *Essays, Speeches and Public Letters by William Faulkner*, ed. James B. Meriwether.
10. I once commented to Jimmy Faulkner, Faulkner's nephew, "I would dearly like to know how Faulkner voted in the 1948 presidential election." Jimmy replied, "He probably didn't even vote."
11. Occasionally a student will quarrel with this interpretation by pointing out that Faulkner's title employs the singular rather than the plural form of "Intruder." If one wants to make much of this fact, then, as some classes conclude, the "intruder in the dust" may well be Lucas Beauchamp, since his behavior is the catalyst for all the actions of the novel.

BIBLIOGRAPHY

Berman, William C. *The Politics of Civil Rights in the Truman Administration.* Columbus: Ohio State University Press, 1970.

Bilbo, Theodore G. *Take Your Choice. Separation or Mongrelization.* Poplarville, Miss.: Dream House Publishing Company, 1947.

Blotner, Joseph, ed. *Selected Letters of William Faulkner.* New York: Random House, 1977.

Boulard, Garry. "'The Man' Versus 'The Quisling': Theodore Bilbo, Hodding Carter, and the 1946 Democratic Party." *Journal of Mississippi History* 51 (1989): 201–17.

Carter, Hodding. "The Civil Rights Issue as Seen in the South." *New York Times Magazine* 21 March 1948: 15ff.

------, *The Winds of Fear*. New York: Farrar and Rinehart, 1944.

Faulkner, William. *Intruder in the Dust* 1948. New York: Vintage, 1972.

Garson, Robert. *The Democratic Party and the Politics of Sectionalism, 1941–1948*. Baton Rouge: Louisiana State University Press, 1974.

Meriwether, James B., ed. *Essays, Speeches and Public Letters by William Faulkner*. New York: Random House, 1965.

-----, and Michael Millgate, eds. *Lion in the Garden: Interviews with William Faulkner, 1916–1962*. New York: Random House, 1968.

Wasson, Ben. *Count No 'Count. Flashbacks to Faulkner*. Jackson: University Press of Mississippi, 1983.

RACE FANTASIES: THE FILMING OF *INTRUDER IN THE DUST*

Charles Hannon

I first visited Oxford, Mississippi, in June of 1991, to examine Oxford's city and county courtrooms, and to consider how the formal construction of the law in Faulkner's hometown might inform the writer's career-long interest in that most official of cultural discourses. While there, I learned to distinguish between the law as a prediscursive body of rules and regulations, and the law as one of several "delivery systems" that mediate the individual subject's imaginary relation to the Symbolic Order of culture. The manner in which apparatuses such as law, literature, newspapers, and film produce a particular reality for their audiences became especially clear after I finished reading Faulkner's murder mystery *Intruder in the Dust*, viewed Clarence Brown's film adaptation (thanks to the Center for the Study of Southern Culture), and attempted to learn more about the context of Faulkner's story about lynching narrowly averted by researching what the local paper, the *Oxford Eagle*, had reported of two events: the actual 1908 lynching of Nelse Patton for the alleged murder of a white woman named McMillin, and MGM's filming of Faulkner's story "on location" in the spring of 1949. I found very little on Nelse Patton in the *Oxford Eagle*: approximately two column-inches, six sentences in all, with the headline "Negro Lynched by Mob," and a short narrative in which Mr. McMillin, serving a jail sentence, sends Patton to deliver a message to his wife.[1] According to the story, Patton had "remained about the place," prompting Mrs. McMillin to attempt to frighten him away with a revolver. This allegedly led to Patton disarming Mrs. McMillin and then slitting her throat. I was struck by the absence of detail in this front-page story: for what crime had Mr. McMillin been jailed? What message did he send his wife? Why did he choose Patton to deliver the message? What witnesses were there to tell that Patton "remained about the place"? Why would he do this? How do we know Mrs. McMillin pulled a gun on Patton, or what her motives were? Why would Patton kill Mrs. McMillin? How was Patton captured? Who was in the lynch mob that took him from the jail? How did they overcome the jailers, or did they even have to? Finally, although this hardly exhausts the number of questions a motivated journalist might have pursued regarding the event, what had happened to Patton's body?[2]

Although I was puzzled at the time, the absence of these details made more sense after I understood the story's ideological function as a rehearsal of the dialectic of racial subject-formation, in which white Southern men are offered a position of superiority, what the narrator of *Intruder in the Dust* calls the "white man's high estate," over the black Other.[3] The Nelse Patton of the *Oxford Eagle* story was no longer an actual person, but the ideological figure of the Negro used throughout Southern history to "stitch up" inconsistencies within the fantasy-construction of white superiority.[4] As an ideological apparatus, the newspaper story had transformed the actual Nelse Patton into an object of erasure, delivering for its readers a particular version of reality in which clear racial divisions exist between blacks and whites. Yet the necessity of Patton's rhetorical transformation attests to a fundamental irrationality in the ideological system supported by the newspaper. To apply Slavoj Žižek's phrasing, the newspaper served as a support for the ideology of white supremacy, producing "an illusion which structures the effective, real social relations" of the segregated South, yet also masking some "insupportable, real, impossible kernel" which is inconsistent with the illusion.[5] Žižek's formulation of the process by which the Symbolic is mapped onto the unconscious is thus open to a concept of social antagonism, unlike the Althusserian instance of interpellation, which for Žižek "never fully succeeds": "there is always a residue, a left-over, a stain of traumatic irrationality and senselessness sticking to it."[6] As several readers of Faulkner have shown, his fiction is most critical of Southern racial ideology when it represents its irrationalities and internal inconsistencies, especially as these inflect individual subjectivity.[7] Quite often, this irrationality emerges in the form of a dialectic of dependence and disavowal: the white subject requires the presence of some black Other to supplement the fantasy of uncorrupted racial boundaries, yet hates this dependence and enters into any number of delusions in order to disavow it. The figure of the Negro in the *Oxford Eagle* story on Nelse Patton represents this kind of half-willed, half-unconscious delusion: it "stitches up" the inconsistencies in segregation ideology by rehearsing the sublation of white dependence upon the black Other that defines both lynching, as an extreme act of racial division and disavowal, and the everyday experiences of whites in a segregated society.

I will occasionally refer to the Nelse Patton story as I explore events surrounding the filming of *Intruder in the Dust* in the spring of 1949, which also strikes me as an episode of subject-formation, but one uniquely determined by alterations in the discourses of culture available to Southerners after World War II. My primary focus will be the elaboration of film as a vehicle for the fantasies of the South's dominant classes, where this function had previously been performed in the discourse of American historiography and in the legal rhetoric of manifest destiny.[8] Marxist analyses have long recognized film's capacity to create the illusion of mastery in the subjects it produces through the apparatus of the camera lens. This illusion reifies the relation between capital and labor, encouraging the spectator "to desire and possess a consumable space from his or her own perspective, a space in fact requiring the presence of 'an individual' for its lines (perspectival) to be justified."[9] While film's perpetuation of capitalist paradigms is an important consideration for any discussion of film and American culture, we need to recognize that in the segregated South, the same technology would reinforce regional assumptions about racial difference, which legitimated, for white Southerners, the practice of subordinating black experience to white.

Although theorists generally understand the illusion of mastery as it is created for audiences viewing a finished film, I will discuss it as a deferred object of desire analogous to the endlessly deferred moment of racial purity, which is the impossible object of desire in the segregationist fantasy. Following Žižek, I will seek the kernels of irrationality that always threaten to erupt within the field of ideology produced by such apparatuses as the novel, the camera, and the newspaper.

American historiography of the Civil War and Reconstruction is fraught with the dialectic of dependency and disavowal. In one example found throughout the literature, the Union's dependence upon black labor and black soldiers is disavowed through the perpetuation of proslavery stereotypes of the benevolent planter, the loyal slave, the evil carpetbagger, and the freedman quickly learning to miss the old days under slavery. Although revisionist historiographers such as W. E. B. Du Bois had corrected many of these misrepresentations by the late 1930s, by then they had become staples of American cinema, and remained so until at least the 1950s.[10] Not only did the first American films rewrite *Uncle Tom's Cabin* in the same proslavery vocabulary as the historiographers were then using to write American history, but America's first great film director, D. W. Griffith, who pioneered techniques of feature filmmaking still in use today, directed and produced the viciously racist *The Birth of a Nation* (1915), and this, along with its virtual remake *Gone with the Wind* (1939), cemented proslavery ideology in white America's cultural imaginary.[11] Recognizing how profitable these films had been, MGM marketed *Intruder in the Dust* as the third installment of a Southern trilogy beginning with *The Birth of a Nation* and *Gone with the Wind*.[12] Although Faulkner's narrative takes place in the late 1940s and not in the Reconstruction past, both it and Oxford's collaboration with MGM deploy the same dialectic of dependency and disavowal that these earlier films—and the discourse of New South historiography—had made available to white subjectivity.

For example, just as the Southern plantocracy and its avatars historically have disavowed their dependence upon black labor, whites in *Intruder in the Dust* ritually scorn their economic reliance upon blacks.

The novel registers this dependence in several places—not least in Lucas's annual payment of his property taxes—yet Faulkner's narrator describes "the whole white part of the county" driving into Jefferson to witness Lucas's lynching, travelling the new roads to the town's jail and courthouse, all of which, in their minds, "existed only by their sufferance and support" (143).[13] Moreover, each time Chick half-remembers something, he is recalling and then disavowing a similar example of dependence, as with the memory that Miss Habersham and Molly, Lucas's wife, had been "born in the same week and both suckled at Molly's mother's breast and grown up together almost inextricably like sisters, like twins" (86). When he first recalls this biography, we see that Chick has already learned to disavow its details: "here again something nagged at his mind his attention but already in the same second gone, not even dismissed: just gone" (76). This disavowal in the face of dependency predicates most of the violence performed or contemplated in the novel, and its essential role in the production of white subjectivity is always on the verge of exposure. Indeed, most of Chick's education in this *Bildungsroman* is tied to his exposure of the dialectic he temporarily has refused to activate with regard to Lucas's lynching. "[I]t seemed to him now," the narrator observes at one point, "that he was responsible for having brought into the light and glare of day something shocking and shameful out of the whole white foundation of the county" (135).

Chick's critical examination of the cultural and psychological processes that produce him as a Southern white male contrasts with anything Southern film audiences might have expected from Brown when he proposed to film Faulkner's novel in Oxford. As was the case with the earlier films by Griffith and Selznick, audiences would have expected Brown's film to reproduce these processes as essentially "real" and natural. They could rely upon film as an ideological apparatus, in other words, to reproduce and thereby support the effective relations of existence under segregation. The claim that Brown's film would represent the "real" Oxford was made repeatedly in the *Oxford Eagle* during Brown's filming. Of particular interest was the number of local buildings that would appear in the film, and the percentage of finished product that would be filmed on location. Speaking of the "substantial resemblance" between Faulkner's "word picture" and the environs of Oxford, one writer for the paper continued: "That 'substantiality' and the 'character' that is real in these real scenes is what Mr. Brown says he hopes to capture in this film, a reality which he could not simulate in Hollywood."[14] Some articles even spoke of the "Oxford Method" of filmmaking, claiming that the more a movie is filmed where the story "takes place," the more accurate it will be.

Our awareness of the strategies of exclusion that ideologically determined discourses such as newspapers, literature, and film rely upon to represent the "real" induces us to recognize, however, that the Oxford in Brown's film is a reflection of the white fantasy—in this case, the fantasy of a South whose black population is either erased, or subject to erasure at any moment. Chick ruminates throughout Faulkner's novel upon the "simple and uncomplex" vocabulary available to the people of Jefferson and Beat Four for "the deliberate violent blotting out obliteration of a human life"(88). Brown's film begins in the aftermath of this blotting out: "Where they all at?" the man looking for a shoe-shine boy asks in the film's earliest lines; "Seems to me I ain't seen one darkey in the road since yesterday." Jefferson's blacks are hiding: as Chick, Miss Habersham, and Aleck Sander travel that night to Caledonia Chapel, we see three scenes that Brown has inserted to emphasize black fear of white retributive violence. In one, a black woman covers her children with a bed cover; in another, three adults drink coffee in the dark; and in the third, a single man watches fearfully as the car and horse go by. The succession of these images amounts to an obsession in Brown's film with the power of whites to remove the town's black presence. Chick's father, similarly obsessed, uses a metaphor of sanitation as he cautions Chick to "stay home until this thing is cleaned up—over, finished, and done with." Finally, Brown's film represents the racially "cleansed" town in a celebratory atmosphere: while the townspeople wait for the Gowries to lynch Lucas, they game, flirt with one another, and generally enjoy the festive music broadcast over their heads.

Intruder's obsession with the power of whites to remove the black presence from a protected town square speaks volumes about the development of film as a discursive domain producing its audiences as racial subjects in the late 1940s. The sudden acceptance of Faulkner's story among his otherwise antagonistic neighbors suggests they are in need of some new apparatus to support the dialectic of white superiority which had sustained their vision of an Anglo-Saxon South since the days of Andrew Jackson. Cheryl Lester's thesis about black migration suggests one cause of this anxiety: migrating in droves since World War I, African Americans had been protesting the region's oppressive racial climate and asserting an agency denied them in white representations of the South and Southern history.[15] In this context, the man whose desperate search for some black Other opens Brown's film represents the white South's anxiety over black migration, which threatened the dialectical foundation of its racial identity. But Brown's film also creates the reassuring fiction that blacks would always be available, once empowered whites created the conditions for their reemergence. In this, it follows Faulkner's text rather closely: "they were still there," Faulkner's narrator repeatedly suggests, "they had not fled, you just didn't see them" (95). In the context of black migration, then, the filming of *Intruder* evoked a mass nostalgia over a South that no longer existed by 1949. As several film theorists have noted, film has this delusional capacity to "fix" a particular view as historical reality.[16] For the residents of Oxford, film could project a segregationist fantasy that excluded blacks from a protected white center, but maintained their availability as binary references in both the social and psychological construction of white racial identity.

As it came to represent the effective relations of whites and blacks under segregation, the filming of Faulkner's novel supported the everyday fantasies of white privilege. In fact, filming became a metonym for these relations, an "associated idea substituted" for segregation.[17] Implicitly, every moment of filming referred to a future moment of viewing the film in segregated movie houses across the South. But MGM's presence in Oxford represented segregation most fully when it exposed the daily inconveniences and irrationalities of a racially divided society. Juano Hernandez, like the character Lucas Beauchamp he portrayed, forced Brown and others to confront many of these irrationalities. Hernandez obviously required lodging while in Oxford, but law and custom prevented his housing with other white actors. The dilemma was resolved when prominent members of Oxford's African American community volunteered to house Hernandez and other black members of the MGM crew, but this solution only raised another difficulty, when Faulkner found he could not invite Hernandez to the cast party he hosted at Rowan Oak. As Joseph Blotner reports, "He was a fine actor and a cultivated man, but if they invited him they would have to include the Bankhead family [his hosts] as well, and they felt that they could not do that."[18] In addition to these high-profile instances, one can imagine the number of daily aggravations segregation created for Brown's film—a film Brown himself had championed as "the most eloquent statement of the true Southern viewpoint of racial relations and racial problems ever sent out over the nation."[19] The Chamber of Commerce, for instance, encountered difficulties casting local African Americans for the film's jail scene, because, as the *Oxford Eagle* reported, "The colored people don't appear to fancy being in the jail even in make believe.[20] Like the system of segregation itself, producing *Intruder in the Dust* as a support for segregation ideology gave Brown and the residents of Oxford daily opportunities to deny and disavow their dependence upon blacks.

One might think that the daily irrationalities of an ideological fantasy would eventually discredit it in the eyes of those experiencing them, but according to Žižek, they actually ensure its "unconditional authority" by simultaneously deferring and making real the object of desire.[21] Instead of discrediting the segregationist fantasy, each example of white dependence upon blacks makes the desired future moment of racial division and disavowal more real—the moment of viewing Brown's film in a segregated cinema house, for instance; or the moment of lynching, in the case of both Faulkner's characters and the mob that acted against Nelse Patton forty years earlier. Each time the promised moment of racial separation approaches, however, it immediately withdraws again as the impossible object of desire. *Plessy v. Fergusson's* one-drop [of blood] rule is an excellent example of this phenomenon, since it posited an impossible standard as the proof of racial purity and thus necessitated a truly absurd taxonomy of legal distinctions in order to support it. *Plessy* was by no means the first legal decision to promise and then endlessly defer the South's desired object of racial homogeneity. The Indian Removal Act of 1830 generated an array of similar legal technicalities as the basis of deciding who would count as an Indian for the purposes of removal and, later in the century, land allotment in the West. Since the early nineteenth century, Southern discourses of racial differentiation have tended to conflate Native Americans and African Americans as a single, threatening Other, because they have been motivated by a similar desire to remove racial Others from an imaginary white space. In the 1940s federal cooperation with the fictions of law and custom that segregated whites from other races in the South began to weaken, however. The unconstitutionality of Jim Crow laws received increased federal scrutiny in the 1940s, just as, according to Felix Cohen, there had run in federal Indian legislation since the 1930s "the motive of righting past wrongs inflicted upon a nearly helpless minority."[22] Again Oxford's taking up of Faulkner's story in the spring of 1949 can be seen in relation to anxieties caused by these contextual historical events, because both Faulkner's text and Brown's film offer the discourse of Native American removal as a way of cancelling Lucas's claim to a white ancestry and fixing him firmly in the position of the Other.

When we first see Lucas in *Go Down, Moses* (1942), he is hiding his still in an Indian burial mound so he can then tell the landowner, Carothers Edmonds, that George Wilkins, Lucas's aspiring son-in-law, is manufacturing on his property. Lucas's digging unsettles the mound and it collapses, covering him in dirt and pottery, and depositing in his hand a single gold coin. This coin symbolically connects Lucas with the South's racial Other of a hundred years earlier—the Cherokee of Georgia, and the Chocktaw and Chickasaw of northern Mississippi and with the desire for gold that motivated whites to dispossess Indians of their lands. In a crucial scene from *Intruder in the Dust*, the discourse of Indian removal again separates Lucas from the white South and marks him as essentially different. As Chick enters the sitting room of Lucas's home to dry off from his mishap at the creek, readers are presented with alternate frameworks for interpreting Lucas's racial identity. In one of these, Lucas is represented in a painting reminiscent of Grant Wood's *American Gothic*:

> ...there looked back at him again the calm intolerant face beneath the swaggering rake of the hat, a tieless starched collar clipped to a white starched shirt with a collarbutton shaped like a snake's head and almost as large...and beside him the tiny doll-like woman in another painted straw hat and a shawl. (14)

Nearby this portrait hangs a second framed image, a "lithograph of a three-year-old calendar in which Pocahontas in the quilled fringed buckskins of a Sioux or Chippewa chief stood against a balustrade of Italian marble" (10). In the revised American Gothic, Lucas's claim to both a white and a black identity is undercut by the permanence of the frame surrounding his relationship with his all-black wife, Molly. The threat posed by Lucas's dual heritage is thus contained within this frame. At the same time, the historical figure of Pocahontas and her actual role as a uniter of races are repudiated in the insistence upon essential difference which dominates the legend of Pocahontas, and its representation in the lithograph of Pocahontas wearing "quilled fringed buckskins." While the framing of the Italian balustrade does suggest her voyage across the Atlantic, it marks her as essentially different in the same way that the portrait frame marks Lucas. Moreover, the lithograph of Pocahontas erases both her life with colonist John Rolfe and her symbolic crossing of racial and cultural boundaries among the British. Significantly, Chick's contemplation of these images precedes his own attempt to instate an essential racial barrier between himself and Lucas, when he paternalistically offers Molly coins in return for what Lucas had intended as common decency.

In Brown's film, the lithograph presenting Pocahontas as a symbol of essential difference is replaced by a painting that represents Euro-American expansion in the nineteenth century. Although our view of the painting is obstructed by actors Claude Jarman Jr. and Juano Hernandez, we can just glimpse a team of horses pulling a covered wagon, and a scout on horseback with his back turned in a gesture that indicates his responsibility to protect the white pioneers from Indian attackers. Like the gold coin that drops into Lucas's hand in the Indian burial mound in *Go Down, Moses*, this painting subordinates Lucas's claim as a Southerner to the discourse of expansion and Euro-American domination of the continent. Moreover, just as each of these images placed in Lucas's home rehearses a particular fiction about America's European discovery and Euro-Americans' subsequent "manifest destiny," the scene acted out before them, Chick's demand that Lucas pick up the coins Chick has dropped on the floor, rehearses the ideology of white superiority, even in Lucas's own home.

In different but similarly motivated ways, then, Faulkner's novel and Brown's film modify nineteenth-century discourses of racial removal as they participate in the dialectic of dependency and disavowal that has sustained white identity in the South for nearly two hundred years. This dialectic relies upon a rhetoric of purity at the center and threat at the margins, and possibly Gavin Stevens's espousal of this rhetoric—his theory of a homogeneous South—will further explain Oxford's uncharacteristic sympathy with him in the spring of 1949. For Gavin, purity is evident in the ubiquity of Anglo-Saxon surnames, names like Workitt "that used to be Urquhart only the one that brought it to America and then Mississippi couldn't spell it" (146). This use of common names to prove the dominant culture's "pure" genealogy is echoed by a columnist in the *Oxford Eagle*, who, backing up Lafayette County's "historic contention that it is the most Anglo Saxon spot in the entire United States," notes that "among the hundreds of Oxford citizens who appear in 'Intruder in the Dust,' scarcely six non-Anglo-

Saxon names could be found!"[23] The Southerner's interest in supporting the ideal of pure origins is indicated by the final line of this writer's story: "the Anglo-Saxon blood has been kept intact down the years." For both Gavin and this nameless columnist, proper names signify racial purity, a quality invoked in any justification of white hegemony. As James Snead has observed, this is why Lucas's name is so disturbing to whites in *Intruder in the Dust*.[24] Already a sign of miscegenation whose physical presence repudiates the dominant culture's basic racial philosophy, Lucas is also very careful that people know the proper genealogical referent of his name: "I aint a Edmonds," Lucas corrects the sawmill lout who harasses him at the crossroads store, "I belongs to the old lot. I'm a McCaslin" (19). Lucas's presence thus denies Gavin and his community the right to tell themselves stories about the county's pure, Anglo-Saxon origins. In response, this community seeks to rewrite Lucas's white ancestry in Native American terms, and thus exclude him from their vision of an homogeneous Anglo-Saxon South.

This desire to remove Lucas from the protected center of the white South, evident in Faulkner's novel and Brown's film, suggests Southerners' anxieties in the late 1940s over their losses in the national debate over segregation, following Truman's desegregation of the military during World War II, and his party's reelection in 1948 despite, possibly because of, the civil rights plank in its campaign platform. If one could isolate a single event that launched this debate into the 1948 campaign it would be the skirmish that erupted at the Democratic nominating convention over the language of the civil rights plank.[25] The drafting committee at the convention had cooperated with Truman's campaign team in crafting a moderate civil rights statement, asserting the following: "We again call upon the Congress to exert its full authority to the limit of its constitutional powers to assure and protect these rights."[26] This ambiguous language was a concession to Southern Democrats, who could read it as a recognition of the limits of federal jurisdiction, and of the validity of the doctrine of states' rights. When minority drafts were put to a floor vote, however, this language was replaced by the following statement:

> We call upon Congress to support our President in guaranteeing these basic and fundamental rights: (1) the right of full and equal political participation, (2) the right to equal opportunity of employment, (3) the right of security of person, and (4) the right of equal treatment in the service and defense of our nation.[27]

Obviously, this language repudiated the doctrine of states' rights. As a consequence of its adoption, delegates from Southern states, including Mississippi and Alabama walked out of the Convention and on 17 July, dissatisfied Southern Democrats met in Birmingham, Alabama, to nominate Governor Strom Thurmond of South Carolina, and Governor Fielding L. Wright of Mississippi for President and Vice-President on a States' Rights ticket. In several Southern states, including Mississippi, this ticket was listed on the official ballot as the nomination of the Democratic Party.

One reason the story of Lucas's near-lynching in *Intruder in the Dust* should be read in relation to the Democratic split in 1948 is that this split was a culmination of Southern opposition to federal antilynching legislation throughout the first half of this century.[28] Although Strom Thurmond was himself considered a "liberal-minded" governor because he was known to pursue the perpetrators of lynching in his state, "he always opposed a federal antilynching law as an unconstitutional invasion of states' rights."[29] Southerners like Thurmond and Wright had always resisted this legislation because of the precedent it would set for federal intervention in the South, especially in matters relating to segregation. While desegregation was thus the paramount consideration of the States' Rights party, it had been articulated before World War I, primarily through opposition to federal antilynching legislation which amounted, for the Dixiecrats, to the unconstitutional extension of federal powers into state law enforcement. As Anne Goodwyn Jones notes in her contribution to this collection, much of the lobbying on behalf of antilynching legislation was done by members of the Association of Southern Women for the Prevention of Lynching.[30] How is the political activism of Southern women against the criminal actions of white men represented in Faulkner's novel? Like the transformation of African Americans into a rhetorical figure which is then always available as an object of erasure, the politically active woman is transformed by novel and film into the stereotype of the passive "kinless spinster" (75), always on the verge of political irrelevancy. "Good evening, sir," Chick says to Miss Habersham as he interrupts her conference with his uncle (74). She is in his blind spot, but even when he acknowledges her presence he simultaneously can forget her: "He had dismissed her; he had said 'Excuse me' and so evanished her not only from the room but the moment too" (77). Although Miss Habersham's role in freeing Lucas is crucial, the ludicrous scene at the jail in which she passively resists Crawford Gowrie's attack shows that Faulkner's text too is blind to the active role of women in the battle against lynching. The spinster-stereotype allows both the novel and the film to "stitch over" the ideologically inconsistent fact of "radical" Southern women with the socially acceptable image of a respectful white male (Crawford Gowrie!) bowing to the wishes of a venerable lady.

The South's opposition to the intrusion of outsiders into "regional" affairs is familiar to anyone who has studied civil rights history. It also formed initial responses to the idea of filming Faulkner's story on location, as Faulkner himself had related in a conversation quoted by Blotner: "people were saying, 'We don't want no one comin' into our town to make no movie about no lynchin'."[31] And in an article for the *Oxford Eagle* that looked back to early concerns about the "public relations problem" of bringing non-Southern black actors into Oxford, Phil Mullen writes, "just at the time, racial tension throughout the country had been inflamed by the politicians. That certain type of red-tinged racial extremist could have created incidents which would have done great harm."[32] Although the elections thus contributed to an atmosphere in Mississippi and in Oxford that was hostile to outsider commentary about racial relations, this atmosphere dissipated when

Brown and MGM pitched the idea to local merchants. Soon after Brown arrived in February 1949 to scout the area for filming in the spring, the local Chamber of Commerce met and voted to support Brown: the film would be "of great economic, cultural, and advertising value to Oxford," Chamber of Commerce President C. S. Haney claimed, as he pledged Oxford's full support.[33] Oxford's merchants overcame their initial reluctance because it made good business sense, but their decision combined economics with a concern for the region's national image, apparently convinced by Brown that the film could be "a great credit to Oxford and to the South."[34]

We could say that Oxford's merchants saw an opportunity for profit in Brown's proposal, and leave it at that. But I want finally to show how these merchants and professional men and women were also concerned that only a lower-class, bigoted view of race relations was reaching the North, and saw the presence of Hollywood's cameras as an opportunity to define the "real" South as primarily mercantile and middle-class. "Class" thus describes an additional category of removal outlined by the discursive arrangements of Faulkner's story in Oxford in 1949. It is distinguished from the nineteenth-century removal of Indians to the Western territories, and from the twentieth-century removal of both black-white interdependence and the political protests of Southern women from the "real" South, primarily in the degree to which the removal of lower-class whites necessitated the simultaneous refashioning of white Southernness. To be sure, the doctrine of a pure, Anglo-Saxon South is itself evidence of the dominant culture's self-constructions in relation to its underrepresented populations. But the process by which the white South was redefined as primarily middle class, merchant, and professional is unlike these earlier episodes of subject-formation because it involves the sacrifice of one whole class of whites in order to continue the illusion of a pure center threatened by hostile margins.

Unlike the Agrarians' touting of the poor yeomanry in the 1930s, or *Gone with the Wind*'s portrayal of aristocratic landowners, the people behind the filming of *Intruder in the Dust* celebrated a middle-class, professional identity for themselves and their region. In the premiere edition of the *Oxford Eagle*, the editors call attention to Oxford notes written by MGM publicist Barrett Kiesling and scattered throughout the nation's media. Most of these celebrate the realism of the film by noting, for example, its use of Oxford's own St. Peter's Episcopal Church, rather than a Hollywood set, in the opening scene. But the notes also stress the mercantile and professional image of Oxford that Brown's film would publicize across the country. "St. Peter's was built in 1851," one note reads; "It now joins the Lafayette County Jail, a college professor's home, a cotton farm, a dress shop, a drug store and a lawyer's office in the list of authentic settings which Brown used."[35] Moreover, an anecdote printed under these notes suggests how class image was a pervasive issue during Brown's filming. Brown, looking for a local resident to portray the proprietor of Fraser's Store, found George Galloway at his own general store and cast him on the spot:

> It disturbed him that director Brown had thrust him before the camera just as he was, and somewhat mussed from moving merchandise. So at noon he went home, washed, shaved and changed his clothes. The shave could be obliterated with make-up...but it was necessary for store-owner Galloway to return home and don the togs in which he had been registered by the cameras during the morning!

Just as local blacks had not wanted to cooperate with Brown by willingly jailing themselves, so this local merchant, George Galloway, wanted to avoid being filmed in the trappings of the lower class, because of the separation of this class from the empowered classes that was occurring at the time.

Faulkner's novel is replete with middle-class success stories of the sort that would have appealed to Oxford's Chamber of Commerce. Most of these involve transplanted farmers who now own property in town, sometimes their own homes, and are prospering as office workers or in some profession. This is true of individual characters like Sheriff Hampton (105) and Jefferson's town marshall (133); but the phenomenon is also evinced in Faulkner's descriptions of neighborhoods, "where the prosperous young married couples lived with two children each and (as soon as they could afford it) an automobile each and the memberships in the country club/and the bridge clubs" (118). Following Faulkner's interest in Jefferson's changing class structure, the story of Brown's filming, as it is told in the pages of the *Oxford Eagle*, offers the city's mayor as a symbol of the "arrived" middle class in the South. R. X. Williams figures prominently, as a promoter of the city, as the owner of the local theater where the "world premiere" took place, and, as one *Eagle* photo caption reads, "practically the 'location manager' for the M-G-M film company."[36] He is also one of the city's residents chosen to play a character in the film, the role of Mr. Lilley, "a countryman," Faulkner's text reads, "who had moved to town a year ago and now owned a small shabby side street grocery" (46). The text dwells upon Lilley's house as a harbinger of middle-class suburbia: "a small neat shoebox of a house built last year between two other houses already close enough together to hear one another's toilets flush." And in the film Mayor Williams's suit, seemingly out of place for someone watering his grass, suggests the story of a transplanted yeoman pursuing a nobler class identity for himself. Williams—by extension, all the merchants and business owners who participated in the filming—thus performed roles both in Brown's film, and in the story of the New South that grew out of Hollywood's presence in Oxford.

In the process of producing Oxford as a white, middle-class success story, Brown's filming followed Faulkner's text in sacrificing lower-class whites in order to demonstrate equal racial treatment under segregation. Like the removal of black subjectivity that describes Reconstruction historiography, we should recognize that the removal of poor whites from the image of the New South fashioned in both Faulkner's text and Brown's film is predicated upon a certain revision of the middle and upper classes' role in the South's racial past. After all, it was a former U.S. Senator from Mississippi, W. V. Sullivan, who asserted with pride to a reporter for the Jackson *Daily Clarion-Ledger* that he had led the mob against Nelse Patton.[37] And as late as 1950, Faulkner had identified a prominent banker as the author of a hate letter in response to Faulkner's advocacy of integrated public schools.[38] Thus the dialectic of class identity-formation relies upon a process of dependency and disavowal similar to that with regard to race: the middle and upper classes depended upon their rural, agrarian past to demonstrate their own economic progress, but disavowed this dependency by explaining the South's remaining prejudices as a problem of the lower, unreconstructed classes.

As with any process founded upon artificial binary oppositions, Oxford's fashioning of a white, middle-class identity for itself is fraught with contradiction and irrationality. Perhaps the fantasy of a unified, white middle class is exposed most when it is confronted by the double-impossibility, according to its logic, of a black middle class. As the cotton farm included in the list of "authentic" film scenes suggests, the ownership of property—as Lucas owns the ten acres at the center of the antebellum McCaslin plantation—qualifies one for middle-class status in Jefferson as in Oxford. Lucas's final appearance in Faulkner's fiction, demanding a written record of the financial transaction he had conducted with the most visible white professional in Jefferson, thus confirms his own "arrival" in the face of efforts by the white community in general, and by Gavin Stevens in particular, to exclude him. As I have already suggested, Hernandez's Hollywood celebrity presented the people of Oxford an analogous refutation of the system of exclusions upon which their segregated society was based.

I would not want to reduce these various instances of subject-formation to a *single* formula of dependency and disavowal, however. Doing so would be to participate in the same longing for order and cohesion this dialectic served to support. Doing so would allow one to rationalize the white South's history of racial exclusion, for instance, as fundamentally the same as the wealthy white South's economic and political scapegoating of poor whites. Middle-class whites have depended upon blacks, poor whites, and politically active women, and have disavowed this dependence in similar ways. But the consequences of the dialectic are different in each case. When Chick says the people of Jefferson will "make a nigger" (31) out of Lucas, his phrase refers to the same process by which Nelse Patton became the figure of the Negro in the 1908 *Oxford Eagle*. The actual Lucas with a home, a family, and a history would be transformed into an ideological object of ridicule and mutilation, which could be used in subsequent retellings of his lynching to reinforce the white fantasy of uncorrupted racial boundaries. When Crawford Gowrie emerges as the real murderer, the nearest thing to an ideological figure for the people of Jefferson and Beat Four to transform him into is a fratricide, understood in terms of the Old Testament. But in the postwar context of Faulkner's story, this rhetorical transformation anticipates no communal violence against Crawford, as it does in the case of Lucas. Instead, Crawford conveniently is allowed to take his own life with comparative honor. A final, perhaps obvious difference between these cases is the speed with which the two objects of disavowal are inserted into the dominant class's dialectic of self-ratification. Lucas is immediately accepted as a suitable object of scorn and ritual erasure, whereas Crawford, still a visible reminder of the white middle class's own recent experiences, is only disavowed when the facts of Vinson's murder become irrepressible.

Previous schools of literary criticism tended to reduce narratives of social injustice to a single plot, without considering the differential spaces between them. One important goal of cultural criticism should therefore be to retrieve the details of cultural events that seem most impossible, most irreducible to a single narrative of symbolization. A final example from what happened to Faulkner's novel during Brown's filming will illustrate this point. Literally, we know the body of Jake Montgomery gets lost somewhere between Faulkner's novel and Clarence Brown's film. Like the details of the Nelse Patton affair which would have confused the formula of "white womanhood protected" for the readers of the *Oxford Eagle* in 1908, Jake Montgomery's connection to the Gowries, and the second corpse this subplot introduces to Faulkner's narrative, would have complicated Ben Maddow's screenplay beyond the coherence of a Hollywood film. But cultural events like the filming of *Intruder in the Dust* are best understood if we retrieve the incoherent details that others have determined to forget, and seek all the technologies of removal that have collaborated to disavow them.

Notes

1. "Negro Lynched by Mob," *Oxford Eagle*, 17 September, 1908, 1. The story gives "Lawson" as Patton's proper name. The spelling of the female victim's surname differs in the various discussions of this case, further evidence, to me, that the particulars were of less importance than the formula these events reproduced.
2. For answers to some, but not all, of these questions, see John B. Cullen, *Old Times in the Faulkner Country* (Chapel Hill: University of North Carolina Press, 1961), 89–98.
3. William Faulkner, *Intruder in the Dust* (1948; New York: Random House, Vintage Books, 1991), 134; subsequent page references are to this edition.
4. This is a reformulation of Slavoj Žižek's discussion of the ideological figure of the Jew in *The Sublime Object of Ideology* (New York: Verso, 1989), 48.
5. Ibid., 45.
6. Ibid., 43.
7. See Philip Weinstein, *Faulkner's Subject: A Cosmos No One Owns* (New York: Cambridge University Press, 1992); and Cheryl Lester, "Racial Awareness and Arrested Development: *The Sound and the Fury* and the Great Migration (1915–1928)," *The Cambridge Companion to William Faulkner*, ed. Philip Weinstein (New York: Cambridge University Press, 1994), 123–45.
8. For an analysis of film as fantasy-construction, see Timothy Murray, *Like A Film: Ideological Fantasy on Screen, Camera, and Canvas* (New York: Routledge, 1993). Žižek provides numerous readings of film, desire, and ideology in *Looking Awry: An Introduction to Jacques Lacan through Popular Culture* (Cambridge: Massachusetts, MIT Press, 1991).
9. Dudley Andrew, *Concepts in Film Theory* (New York: Oxford University Press, 1984), 23.
10. On the representation of slavery in American historiography, see John David Smith, *An Old Creed for the New South: Proslavery Ideology and Historiography, 1865–1928* (Westport: Greenwood Press, 1985). For Du Bois's revisionist historiography, see *Black Reconstruction in America, 1860–1880* (1935; New York: Atheneum, 1992).
11. The relation between minstrel stereotypes of the nineteenth century and the development of the American film industry is the subject of Donald Bogle, *Toms, Coons, Mulattoes, Mammies, and Bucks: An Interpretive History of Blacks in American Films* (1973; New York: Continuum, 1989); and Edward Campbell, *The Celluloid South: Hollywood and the Southern Myth* (Knoxville: University of Tennessee Press, 1981).

12. A Brandt's Mayfair advertisement in the *New York Times*, for example, proclaims the following: "*The Birth of a Nation* created a sensation in 1915; *Gone with the Wind* did the same in 1939; *Intruder in the Dust* gives the dramatic answer in 1949." *New York Times*, 21 November 1949, 29.
13. Other examples of taxable black labor in the novel occur on pages 94, 119, and 145.
14. "These Lafayette Scenes To Become Movie Sets," *Oxford Eagle*, 17 February 1949, 1.
15. See Cheryl Lester's essay in this collection. Emigration from Mississippi slowed during the 1930s, but by the 1940s it had regained its pre-Depression pace. The 1950 census recorded a black population in Mississippi of 986,494, down 8.2 percent compared to 1940, according to Donald B. Dodd, *Historical Statistics of the States of the United States: Two Centuries of the Census, 1790–1990* (Westport: Greenwood Press, 1993), 50.
16. Marc Ferro, for instance, writes that "Unlike a work of history, which necessarily changes with distance and analytical developments, a work of art becomes permanent, unchanging." *Cinema and History*, trans. Naomi Greene (Detroit: Wayne State University Press, 1988), 159.
17. This definition comes from Trevor Whittock, *Metaphor and Film* (New York: Cambridge University Press, 1990), 59.
18. Joseph Blotner, *Faulkner: A Biography*, 2 vols. (New York: Random House, 1974), 1284.
19. Quoted in Blotner, 1277.
20. "MGM Seeking More Local Actors As Movie Progresses," *Oxford Eagle*, 17 March 1949.
21. Žižek, *Sublime Object*, 43.
22. Felix S. Cohen, *Handbook of Federal Indian Law* (1941; Washington: U.S. Government Printing Office, 1945), 83.
23. "In Most Any Newspaper in the Country, May Appear Something About Oxford," *Oxford Eagle*, 6 October 1949, 10.
24. See James Snead, *Figures of Division: William Faulkner's Major Novels* (New York: Methuen, 1986), 197.
25. Much of this history of the 1948 Democratic Convention comes from Irwin Ross, *The Loneliest Campaign: The Truman Victory of 1948* (New York: New American Library, 1968).
26. Ibid., 121.
27. Ibid., 122.
28. Indeed, one reason Walter White of the NAACP worked the Democratic Convention as thoroughly as he did was the pressure Southern members of Congress exerted upon Senate and House committees earlier that spring to write weak antilynching legislation. See Robert L. Zangrando, *The NAACP Crusade Against Lynching, 1909–1950* (Philadelphia: Temple University Press, 1980), 192–94.
29. Ross, 132.
30. For the history of this and other antilynching organizations, see Jacquelyn Dowd Hall, *Revolt Against Chivalry: Jesse Daniel Ames and the Women's*

Campaign Against Lynching (New York: Columbia University Press, 1993).
31. Blotner, 1277.
32. "Negro Star Was Well Liked, Well Respected in Town," *Oxford Eagle*, 6 October 1949, 19.
33. "Movie Folk Enthused Over Oxford: Expect Film Start Early in March," *Oxford Eagle*, 10 February 1949, 1.
34. Ibid.
35. "In Most Any Newspaper in the Country, May Appear Something about Oxford," *Oxford Eagle*, 6 October 1949, 9.
36. "A New Star Is Born!" *Oxford Eagle*, 21 April 1949, 6.
37. See Cullen, 97.
38. See the "Weeping Willie" letters in James B. Meriwether, ed., *Essays, Speeches, and Public Letters by William Faulkner* (New York: Random House, 1965), 93–94.

NEGOTIATING THE NATIONAL VOICE IN FAULKNER'S LATE WORK

Joe Karaganis

Broke, all but out of print and trying to join the Air Force in the spring of 1942, Faulkner wrote "Shall Not Perish," a short story centered on one of his minor avatars of poor rural virtue, the Grier family. The story is set in the present and concerns the efforts of Mother and her nameless younger son (the narrator) to understand the death of the older son, Pete, in the war. It was rejected by no less than eight magazines and went through nearly as many versions before Faulkner managed to pawn it off to *Story* magazine for $25. Although he included it in his *Collected Stories*, "Shall Not Perish" has been consigned, for the most part, to critical oblivion. Nonetheless, it marked, I would argue, a watershed in Faulkner's literary trajectory, inaugurating his efforts to reintegrate Southern history into a redeemed and unified vision of national life. It also marked something of a professional watershed: once it became clear that at age forty-four the best he could expect from the military was a desk job in Washington, he returned to Hollywood as a scriptwriter under a penurious seven-year contract with Warner Bros.[1]

In retrospect, "Shall Not Perish" shows early signs of the ambition that would occupy Faulkner for the next decade: the extrication of social and political positions from what had become virtually a stock repertoire of themes, characters, and situations in his work. This moralizing turn has often perplexed and frustrated admirers of his novels of the thirties. As Michel Gresset has put it, expressing a near consensus on Faulkner's late work, "To put values on stage, as once he had put fantasies, may well have been the mad dream which guided Faulkner during and after the Second World War" (276).

Mad dream or not, "Shall Not Perish" records an interesting moment in this transition just after the complex triumph of *Go Down, Moses* (1942). It was a moment when Faulkner essentially broke with the historical and epistemological dilemmas that had previously underwritten his presentation of Southern and national life. "Shall Not Perish" illustrates how a solution to at least a partial set of those dilemmas was made possible by the reorientation of his art towards the political imperatives of the world war. Being too old to realize his dreams of aerial combat and with no indication that his novels would ever return to print (much less be celebrated as a major achievement), Faulkner reconceived the task of authorship in order that he might "leave [a] better mark on this our pointless chronicle than I seem to be about to leave" (*Selected Letters* 182).[2] He imagined this new role in generational terms: "We will have to make the liberty sure first, in the field....Then perhaps the time of the older men will come, the ones like me who are articulate in the national voice, who are too old to be soldiers...yet are not so old that we too have become another batch of decrepit old men looking stubbornly backward at a point 25 or 50 years in the past" (*Selected Letters* 166).

Faulkner's assumption of this "national voice" was given a boost by Malcolm Cowley, whose crusade on his behalf in the mid-forties led to the publication of *The Portable Faulkner* in 1946. Cowley's "rediscovery" of Faulkner was then massively confirmed by Faulkner's receipt of the Nobel Prize for Literature in 1950. *The Portable Faulkner* and the Nobel Prize were the two landmarks of Faulkner's rapid critical and popular sanctification after the war. As Lawrence Schwartz has argued, they were part of his appropriation by cold-war literary culture both in and outside the United States as a symbol of "American" rather than, more narrowly, "Southern" culture. It was increasingly from this position of, if not intellectual authority, then at least literary celebrity that Faulkner turned towards the subjects of global politics and species, survival after the war. On matters closer to home, however, he put his notoriety to somewhat different use, drawing on his position as a Southerner with considerable legitimacy in the Northern literary establishment to address the emerging civil rights crisis.

This essay is a consideration of that trajectory, reading the evolution of Faulkner's political ideas from the forties onward as the impetus for the evolution of his narrative technique. I begin with Faulkner's early attempt to find a form proper to his "national voice" in "Shall Not Perish" and end with a look at *Intruder in the Dust* (1948)—in many respects his most overtly politicized novel. By the time Faulkner published *Intruder*, his transition away from the core logic of his earlier work was essentially complete; the complex negotiation of form and content that epitomized Faulkner's modernism was subordinated to his programmatic exposition of the ethical and political dilemmas of the contemporary South.

It is perhaps not surprising that this shift coincided with what was widely perceived to be the decline of Faulkner's creative powers. By the early forties Faulkner had completed his canon. The usual roster, comprising *The Sound and the Fury, As I Lay Dying, Light in August, Absalom, Absalom!, The Hamlet*, and *Go Down, Moses* lay behind him and six years would pass before he published another novel (*Intruder in the Dust*). All of these earlier novels chart the social crisis of the South after the devastation of the Civil War—a subject which, by any measure, constituted his great theme of the thirties. The Southern crisis is figured in these novels through an elaborate network of symptoms and metaphors of decline, from the generational disintegration of great planter families and all they represented politically and socially to the vast panoply of resentments born out of the defeat. Sartre, one of Faulkner's earliest and best critics, drew the connection between these ubiquitous dooms and Faulkner's formal innovations, particularly in regard to the broken chronologies and streams of consciousness that emerged full blown in *The Sound and the Fury* (1929). What these techniques produce in the novel, Sartre argued, is an "obscene and obstructing presence" that we "discover…under each word." Instead of "unfolding," the whole story is simultaneously "condensed" into each part and dispersed into all of them. With so much collapsed upon the narrative present, the future itself is obstructed; any space in which action might be taken (and this is the fundamental vocation of the present in Sartre's existentialism) is always already determined by the terrible sovereignty of the past. Echoing Faulkner's own paradoxical formulations, Sartre described this sovereignty as a "frozen speed at the very heart of things" that admitted no change "except in the form of a cataclysm" (*Literary Essays* 79, 81, 87).

If cataclysm is the only way out, as Faulkner's subsequent novels tend to confirm, those novels also make clear that cataclysm was the way in. By rooting the collapse of the present in the disaster of the Civil War, as he began to do more emphatically after *The Sound and the Fury*, his formal repertoire acquires a historical rather than predominantly existential justification.[3] Throughout the thirties, Southern identity in Faulkner's work is defined through the misfortune of having survived its own apocalypse—of having outlasted the South's historical reason for being. The New South persists as an after-image of that event, caught in the trap of excessive retrospection and materially under siege, so to speak, from the pressures of its troubled modernization and by the cultural and political domination of the North.

Unlike the unapologetic fantasies of the Old South that guided much of the emerging Southern literary scene in the thirties, however, Faulkner's obsession with the past had little to do with sanitized visions of plantation life.[4] The powerful nostalgia in Faulkner's writing is not for plantation or slave culture per se, whose iniquities he well understood, but for the intensity of the moment of rebellion and defeat in which the South, "primed for fatality," fulfilled its distinct historical identity and brought upon itself a long accrued retribution for the collective "crime" that marked its origin as a society. This vague but foundational social transgression, associated at times with the inception of slavery (in *Absalom, Absalom!*) or with the original appropriation of the land from the Indians (in *Go Down, Moses*) persists in the double sins of miscegenation and incest that haunt Faulkner's family cycles as signs and ultimately as causes of their destruction. These are the local crises that make the transmission of family legacies and family property, the pillars of the genteel South, so disproportionately costly in his novels. Such is the doom of the McCaslin and Compson families in *Go Down, Moses* and *The Sound and the Fury*, respectively, and the destruction of Sutpen's dynastic "design" in *Absalom, Absalom!*

What "endures" the general cataclysm of the war is the residue of unappeased loss, manifest in the "baffled, angry ghosts" that echo in the heads of so many of the protagonists of these novels. What survivors have to look forward to is a series of more intimate cataclysms: suicide, familial disintegration, the renunciation of birthrights, murderous community action, and visions of racial degeneration. If at times such outcomes are tempered by grotesque comedy, as at the end of *As I Lay Dying* when Anse Bundren introduces wife number two or in *Absalom, Absalom!* where the Sutpen legacy devolves upon a howling fool who haunts the ashes of the mansion, such comic relief does less to mitigate the foreclosure of the future than to indicate the failure of these latter day disasters to achieve the tragic grandeur that might make them commensurate with 1865—that might mark them, even in failure, as the continuation of the Old South's chivalric dream.

"Shall Not Perish" differentiates itself from this major line, I would argue, by working towards a different historical vision of the Civil War, one that by refusing to posit it as a cataclysm refuses, in equal measure, the crushing sovereignty of the past. Instead, "Shall Not Perish" reimagines the Civil War as part of a continuous and progressing national history, and thus as a contribution to the present rather than a constraint on it. The context of World War II is crucial to this revision: the war furnishes a model of national crisis and patriotic response that bridges the mythical gap between the gigantic figures of the Civil War and the present day sons gone to fight in the name of a reunified nation. Through this association, the sacrificed sons figure not as pale afterimages of Confederate heroes (as was explicitly the case in Faulkner's treatment of World War I in his early novel *Sartoris*) but as men driven by the same mysterious, almost instinctual "call to war." This equality is nominally introduced in "Two Soldiers," Faulkner's earlier story about the Grier family which recounts Pete's gradual surrender to the "call." The importance of this equality, however, is underplayed in the story, which dwells instead on Pete's younger brother's comic attempt to follow him to Memphis. "Shall Not Perish," by opening with the very different problem of mourning Pete's death, recenters itself around the meaning of the call to war.

The task of deciphering this obscure impulse, however, falls to those who haven't heard it. Mother, its chief theorist, can only gesture towards a vague "it" or "something" denied to women and even to men like Major de Spain whose rank, the story notes, is purely honorific. Mother is cognizant of this limit: "Maybe women are not supposed to know why their sons must die in battle; maybe all they are supposed to do is just to grieve for them" (109). The most she is certain of is that "it came from a long way....So it must have been strong to have lasted through all of us. It must have been all right for him to be willing to die for it after that long time and coming that far" (110).

In its novelty, this strange blood-knowledge (for want of a more precise term) is one of the less plausible compulsions that so often underwrite Faulknerian psychology. It is part instinct (indeed "it" functions here as a sort of recessive gene), part atavistic code of honor, and part parcel of a culture devoted to fatalistic essences of character. This vagueness is reflected in Mother's resignation to her own incomplete knowledge and in her description of Pete, who, as the bearer of "it," inarticulately "knew why" he went to war. As Faulkner himself suggested in a letter from the same period in which he encouraged his stepson to enlist, it's "something in the meat and bone and blood from the old cave-time"—"the public proof of his [man's] masculinity" displayed through "his courage and endurance, his willingness to sacrifice himself for the land which shaped his ancestors" (*Selected Letters* 166). However casually advanced here, this archaic will to fight for one's country is a variation on a theme that would assume increasing importance in Faulkner's post-war writing: the "enduring" qualities of the human species that, however mortal their particular vessels (in this case, Pete) "shall not perish."

One could well add, "from the earth," to complete the last phrase of Lincoln's Gettysburg Address, with which "Shall Not Perish" shares not only a vocabulary and, to a considerable degree, a tone, but also the larger purpose of transforming mourning into an act of rededication to the national cause. Faulkner invites us to associate Lincoln's admission of his (and more generally, our) insufficiency before the spectacle of massive sacrifice with Mother's reflections on the death of her son. Standing before the "living and dead" who "have consecrated it [the battlefield], far above our poor power to add or detract," Lincoln, like Mother, invokes both the necessity of the effort to understand sacrifice and the inadequacy of explanations to compass loss.

If this lesson brings into relief a somewhat sententious modesty on Faulkner's part in which he connects Mother's simple wisdom to the most iconic figure of post-bellum national unity, it is also something of a digression—a supplement to the deeper functioning of blood-knowledge in the story. The real value of the concept becomes clear in relation to the conciliatory historiography that underlies the narrative structure of the story. In what might be called the manifest content of the story, the fact that Pete goes to war because of the demands of blood-knowledge constitutes a counterpoint to the various state-sponsored and relentlessly propagandized answers to the question of why we fight—as Faulkner put it another letter, "the shibboleths they glibly talk about freedom, liberty, human rights" (*Selected Letters* 176). Blood-knowledge thus reconstructs national unity and the bond between the nation and the individual at a level below political traditions, in something passed across generations and from man to boy.

This rejection of the official reasons, however, is only part of the story. As events demonstrate, the claims of blood-knowledge prove inadequate either to overcoming the acid remains of Southern sectionalism or to providing a utopian dimension to the national project. In the effort to solve this double problem, Faulkner arrived at something like a dramatized dialectical method; "Shall Not Perish" winds its way through a series of discretely articulated "positions" on national unity and national identity toward the construction of a nationalism not only worth dying for, but worth coming home to.

"Shall Not Perish" is composed of three vignettes. The first opens with the Grier family's receipt of the news of the Pete's death. It continues some months later when, after reading of the death of Major de Spain's son, Mother and her younger son pay the Major a visit of condolence. This generous impulse is, however, sidetracked by the Major's vituperations—products of a despondent cynicism about the national cause and, consequently, about the meaning of his son's death. The Major explains: "He had no country: this one I too repudiate. His country and mine both was ravaged and polluted and destroyed eighty years ago, before even I was born. His forefathers fought and died for it then, even though what they fought and lost for was a dream. He didn't even have a dream. He died for an illusion" (108). Mother answers the Major's venom with her explanation of the blood-knowledge, marking it, rather than the nation, as the agent that drew their sons into the war. Recognizing an unexpected, if somewhat cryptic wisdom, Major de Spain turns to her: "You have had three months...to find out why; mine happened yesterday. Tell me" (109).

The turn to blood-knowledge as a rationale for their sons' deaths effectively depoliticizes the war, moving its awful demand for bodies into the murky depths of the male psyche. It is significant, though, that this maneuver doesn't refute the Major's diatribe against the national war effort. In the Major's Civil War centered universe, World War II is a corrupt enterprise, orchestrated by "the interests of usury...the folly and rapacity of politicians...[and] for the glory and aggrandizement of organized labor" (108). If his protests are superseded by Mother's explanation, they are also substantially uncontradicted by it. Her response turns on a pregnant "Yes" (and in the drafts of the story, a clearer "Yes, but...") that grants the Major's arguments while preparing the way for her own completely different register of meaning. Faulkner glosses this double logic—the "Yes, but"—in his letter to Franklin: "I'm afraid that the same old stink is rising from this one as has risen from every war yet....But it is the biggest thing that will happen in your lifetime. All your contemporaries will be in it before it is over, and if you are not one of them, you will always regret it" (*Selected Letters* 166).

Mother's explanation of the blood-knowledge quiets Major de Spain before its mystery, but the failure of this logic to refute his indictment of the war has an interesting consequence; it prevents the ideological closure that the scene's nationalist pretext seems to anticipate and, indeed, require. It prevents what might be called the typical Hollywood ending (about which Faulkner knew a great deal) in which the shared sacrifice of the Griers and Major de Spain would "represent" the social equality so manifestly absent from their encounter in his luxurious parlor. It prevents, finally, their shared condition of grief from being further recycled as the utopian solidarity that makes the nation worth fighting for. That Faulkner leaves this scene effectively hanging suggests a refusal on his part to falsify the depth of that division through a funereal communion with the nation. The way is blocked, and, as if furnishing a symbol of this failure to achieve ideological closure, their interview ends with a puzzling incident in which the Major's negro butler magically ends the threat of violence (of Major de Spain's self-violence, one is left to suppose) that had hung vaguely over the scene. The narrator explains: "one flick of the black hand and the white sleeve and the pistol vanished without me even seeing him touch it" (110).

What has the makings of a consummate Faulknerian collision between race and class fails to materialize, however, because nothing further happens. The butler's slippery act is a kind of residue or anticipation of meaning that the scene fails, ultimately, to deliver. "Shall Not Perish" was revised several times in the course of its rejections by different magazines, and the manuscripts of the story give some indication of what it was the butler was there to do. In at least one of the earlier versions, the scene with the gun is fleshed out in less mysterious and less interesting fashion to emphasize Mother's consoling power; she disarms the suicidal de Spain and places the gun on the table for the butler to take away. Although the butler's role in this version doesn't change, his actions signify differently by referring to an earlier scene that finds the Griers at Major de Spain's door. That scene, which Faulkner cut entirely from the final version, turns on the Griers' encounter with the butler:

> And it never mattered whether our shoes was shined at all or not: the monkey nigger's face and the whites of his eyes for jest a second when he opened the door, the white of his coat for jest a second at the far end of the hall before it was gone too, his feet not making no more noise than a cat's, already running even before he opened the door, as niggers do from white folks' trouble in the house, leaving us to find the right room by ourselves. (*Short Stories* 429)

What the negro butler does, in short, is get out of the way, leaving "the rich and the pore" to their uncertain reconciliation over their dead. Stripping out this scene, Faulkner not only undermined that utopian solution, but prevented the story from, in effect, mapping the negro contribution to the national cause as self-effacement in the name of white solidarity. His revisions, in effect, removed race and class in the story from the framework of legibility that had dominated his earlier work—particularly *Absalom, Absalom!* in which another negro butler at the door serves to illuminate and enforce class distinctions between whites (187). One might conclude that, as Faulkner economized in the revisions, he decided that the war effort didn't require the mapping of race—that the problem of national unity was first one of region (of north vs. south, figured by Major de Spain), and, second, of class (of planter vs. poor farmer). At least one of his letters from the same period, however, suggests that in fact the opposite was closer to the truth:

> There is a squadron of negro pilots. They finally got Congress to allow them to learn how to risk their lives in the air. They...did well at Pantelleria, on the same day a mob of white men and white policemen killed 20 negroes in Detroit....A change will come out of this war. If it doesn't, if the politicians and the people who run this country are not forced to

> make good the shibboleth they glibly talk about freedom, liberty, human rights, then you young men who live through it will have wasted your precious time, and those who dont live through it will have died in vain. (*Selected Letters* 175)

For Faulkner, the war adumbrated the civil rights crisis, and indeed it would take the latter crisis to transform the scrambled racial signals of "Shall Not Perish"—of appropriate and inappropriate ways for negros to carry guns and of indefinable hereditary legacies—into a newly legible map of Southern and national society. Thus the foundation was laid for *Intruder in the Dust*, which engages the national problem in the context, some years later, of the incipient civil rights struggle. In *Intruder*, the question of guns, their origins, and their racially circumscribed uses returns, in effect, as the obscure object around which the narrative develops. In *Intruder*, blood-knowledge, no longer enlisted in the war effort, comes into its own as a theory of racial authenticity.

The vignette involving the Griers and Major de Spain ends with a departure rather than a reconciliation and on an ambiguous note of mystic inquiry, grief, and unappeased bitterness rather than healing. If the utopian national vision fails to materialize here, however, it's not long in coming. Immediately following this scene is the second vignette, barely a page long. The young narrator begins:

> There was an old lady born and raised in Jefferson who died rich somewhere in the North and left some money to the town to build a museum with. It was a house like a church, built for nothing else except to hold the pictures she picked out to put in it—pictures from all over the United States, painted by people who loved what they had seen or where they had been born or lived enough to want to paint pictures of it so that other people could see it too. (110)

The passage ends: "there was only the last sunset spoking out across the sky, stretching all the way across America from the Pacific ocean, touching all the places that the men and women in the museum whose names we didn't even know had loved enough to paint pictures of them, like a big soft fading wheel" (111). This series of images, of course, paints a nationalist pastoral. In the museum, looking tranquilly at the pictures, the spectator metaphorically occupies the place of the sun that bathes the diverse parts of the country in its light. This visual harmony stages, in effect, a successful version of the earlier failed encounter between the Griers and Major de Spain, finding a common measure between unequal social actors. The contemplative gaze echoes, this time in positive form, the earlier "look" of the child as he surveyed the disproportionate luxuries of Major de Spain's hall: the "gold-colored harp that would have blocked our barn door and the mirror that a man on a mule could have seen himself and the mule both in" (107). In this way, the gaze overcomes social and geographical distance, staging a soft focus performance of national unity starkly opposed to the nation of death, bureaucracy, and social struggle described by Major de Spain. It is, moreover, a vision sponsored by an old woman, a privileged type in Faulkner's universe, who furnishes by association both a gendered counterpart to the invisible solidarity of fighting men and an aged counterpart to their youth.

The last vignette involves Grandpap, whose periodic and vocal flashbacks to the Civil War (which like Major de Spain he was too young to know first hand) are a regular source of embarrassment to the Grier family. One Saturday they take Grandpap to town to see the weekly matinee, a serialized Western. He nods off until he is startled by the noise of galloping horses:

> Then Grandpap waked up. For about five seconds he sat perfectly still. I could even feel him sitting still, he sat still so hard. Then he said, "Cavalry!" Then he was on his feet. "Forrest!" he said. "Bedford Forrest! Get out of here! Get out of the way!" clawing and scrabbling from one seat to the next one whether there was anybody in them or

not...still hollering, "Forrest! Forrest! Here he comes! Get out of the way!" (113)

Grandpap's outburst refers us to the early history of the cinema—to the reported experiences of audiences confusing film with the real event, and more saliently, I would argue, to the images of cavalry charges and Klan rides from D. W. Griffith's landmark film *Birth of a Nation*. Grandpap's choice of Bedford Forrest, the notorious cavalry commander of the Confederate Army and later the first Grand Wizard of the Ku Klux Klan, lends weight to this allusion. Forrest is, in turn, the implied historical protagonist of *Birth of a Nation*, which loosely fictionalized the events that made him a hero to both the Old and the New South.

It was Griffith's film in 1914, perhaps more than any other single cultural event, that recuperated Southern sectionalism into a revised narrative of national destiny.[5] *Birth of a Nation* drew upon Thomas Dixon's romances of the Klan and on a growing body of scholarly historical revisionism to reimagine the Civil War as a product of abolitionist villainy, tragically responsible, in the national family allegory that constitutes the center of the film, for forcing white brother against white brother. The majority of the film, however, dwells not on the war itself but on the supposed tyranny of the Reconstruction government and the outrages of its black henchmen after the Southern surrender. The Ku Klux Klan is formed in this crucible, saving the day and giving birth, in no uncertain terms, to the new unified nation. In this fashion, the "rebirth" of the union is credited not to the war, but to the restoration of the racial order and the reassertion of Southern self-rule—the "Redemption" that followed Reconstruction.

From this perspective, Major de Spain's diatribe is something of an anachronism. The war that more or less reconciled the South to national unity was not the second but the first world war, built on the mythology of unity that *Birth of a Nation* brought to a mass audience. I would argue that the Grandpap vignette can be read through this allusion to *Birth of a Nation* as an implicit revision of Griffith's ideological tour de force. Faulkner scorned Griffith's brand of white supremacist mythology and its incarnation in the Klan. Nonetheless, his concern with Southern sectionalism was similar, and, by this point, he has given us the components of a new and different myth of Southern nationalism. It's Mother who recognizes the hidden wisdom of Grandpap's outburst: "'Fool's yourselves!' Mother cried at Father and Pete and me. 'He wasn't running from anybody! He was running in front of them, hollering at all clods to look out because better men than they were coming, even seventy-five years afterwards, still powerful, still dangerous, still coming!'" (114).

Mother's evocation of the return of those powerful spirits—Lincoln included—sets the stage for the synthesis of the two visions of the national character: the blood-knowledge that drives men to fight and the domestic aesthetic contemplation that provides coherence to "all the little places quiet enough to be lived in and loved" (115). Together, these visions form an image of conquest and settlement, of war and peace that subsumes the Civil War and even World War II into the greater, if mistier destiny of the American people. Faulkner pulls this off, moreover, with an apocalyptic resonance that, in retrospect and from beyond the massive horizon of world war, reads as much like a threat as a promise. He concludes:

> ...all the little places quiet enough to be lived in and loved and the names of them before they were quiet enough, and the names of the men and the women who did the deeds, who lasted and endured and fought the battles and lost them and fought again...and tamed the wilderness and overpassed the mountains and deserts and died and still went on as the shape of the United States grew and went on. I knew them too, the men and women still powerful seventy-five years and twice that and twice that again afterward, still powerful and still dangerous and still coming, North and South and East and West, until the name of what they did and what they died for became just one

single word, louder than any thunder. It was America, and it covered all the western earth. (115)

TEMPERAMENTAL EDUCATION—*INTRUDER IN THE DUST*

If the war, for Faulkner, presaged the Civil Rights crisis and if the elegant *e pluribus unum* structure of "Shall Not Perish" rested on fudging the question of race, it was perhaps inevitable that this "formal" solution to his desire for a national voice was unstable. Just how unstable became apparent when Faulkner addressed the problems of the postwar South in *Intruder in the Dust*.

The plot of *Intruder* turns on the arrest of Lucas Beauchamp, an iconic figure of tangled racial bloodlines from *Go Down, Moses*, for the murder of Vinson Gowrie, one of the clan of "brawlers and fox-hunters and whiskeymakers" (35) that inhabits the outer reaches of Yoknapatawpha County. The circumstantial evidence of Lucas' guilt, in due course, degenerates into the threat of lynch-mob justice. Most of the action of the novel occurs in the shadow of this threat, as Chick Mallison, the young protagonist, agrees to Lucas' enigmatic request to dig up the victim's body. Doing so, he discovers that Lucas could not have been responsible for the murder and, after further developments, that Lucas has been framed by Vinson's brother Crawford, the true culprit.

To most critics, however, these "events" have seemed somewhat peripheral in the novel, or worse, a perfunctory and awkward scaffold used to stage a series of lectures on social questions. Gavin Stevens' manic discourses on race, region, and nationalism in the second half of the novel have been a consistent problem for critics, both for the way that they clumsily derail the narrative and for the idiosyncratic position on race that they outline. The question that the novel insistently baits in regard to this didactic turn is whether or not Stevens expresses Faulkner's views. This debate is fueled by an apparent conflict within the narrative between the manifest authority of Stevens' expositions and what appears to be, on occasion, the parodic undercutting of his position. Thus, if Stevens almost always has the last word, his moral triumph comes only late in the novel, after Chick's discovery of Lucas' innocence has shocked him out of his complacency and, indeed, his complicity with white prejudice. The most damning sign that pedantry wins out over authority, however, is Stevens' obscurantist project, à la Pierre Menard, of translating the Bible back into ancient Greek.[6]

Regardless of how one reads Faulkner's undermining gestures, I think it's clear that Stevens' discourses are essentially of a piece in tone and content with the erratic but always highly opinioned course that Faulkner charted on race and nationalism after the war. This course is well documented in the many newspaper editorials, speeches, and essays that he wrote as he tried to parlay his literary celebrity into a mediating role in the civil rights crisis. I would argue, though, that this is not the only question to be asked about Stevens' discourse. In particular, I question the tendency to treat Stevens' monologues as isolated, incongruous, and momentum-killing digressions. For better or for worse, these speeches are the centerpieces of, if not a narrative logic, then at least an argument that structures, albeit somewhat loosely, the whole novel. Although *Intruder* is nominally a detective story, Stevens' set speeches testify to a different and sometimes competing ambition on Faulkner's part to write a novel of education, in which the "lessons" learned by the young protagonist, Chick Mallison, culminate in a lesson for the novel's readers. What most critics have reacted to negatively in *Intruder* is precisely this didactic ambition, which Faulkner exacerbated by transparently mining his "high" art for resources in his effort to disseminate a new social contract for the South and, in grander terms, a new model of national unity.

Intruder in the Dust begins by modifying Faulkner's obsession with innocence lost, both as a metaphor of personal maturation and as an allegory of the white South's imprisonment in its nostalgia for antebellum glories. Recall that Sutpen, at the outset of *Absalom, Absalom!*, is a blank slate whose encounter with a negro butler at a planter's door initiates him into knowledge of the class and racial hierarchies that organize Southern life. His innocence of these matters is an ambiguous signifier which, if not quite a condemnation of the Southern social order is at least testimony to its mystified and brutal character. Chick, who at the end of *Intruder* can look back on his days as a "tenderfoot," nonetheless undergoes a very different kind of initiation into social knowledge. Inverting Sutpen's complete alienation by origin and then, as it were, by choice, from Southern society, Chick is at home in the racially divided South. Faulkner's complex metaphor for this state of comfort emphasizes not the division between the races, but rather Chick's lifelong proximity to negroes, to the point where race barely registers as a social artifact. For Chick, knowledge of race resides chiefly in the "smell which he had accepted without question all his life as being the smell always of the places where people with any trace of Negro blood live" (10).

This unreflective association of a particular smell with "Negro blood" is what stands in for innocence in the novel, soon to be fundamentally shaken by the life-shaping traumatic encounter that underlies so much of Faulknerian psychology:

> …if it were not for something that was going to happen to him…he would have gone to his grave never once pondering speculating if perhaps that smell were really not the odor of a race nor even actually of poverty but perhaps of a condition: an idea: a belief: an acceptance…by them of the idea that being Negroes they were not supposed to have facilities to wash properly or often…that in fact it was a little to be preferred that they did not (11).

In large part, Chick's education involves his developing awareness of this knot of elements that make up a "race." More importantly, it involves his recognition of the ignorance and indignity imposed on him by his submission to the racial norms of the community. This submission is the substance of Chick's crucial "mistake" at the beginning of the novel: his attempt to pay for a simple kindness that Lucas had done him. Lucas' refusal of payment constitutes a rebuke to Chick's clumsy obedience to racial codes. This rebuke returns to Chick as a form of unpayable debt—a source of "shame" at having to acknowledge not Lucas' equality, a term that has little meaning in Faulkner's universe, but rather a superior quality of character marked by his refusal of Chick's naïve condescension (14). Lucas' quality resides in what constitutes a virtual refrain in Faulkner's late work, in his capacity for being "not arrogant at all and not even scornful, just intolerant inflexible and composed..." (13). He is thus a bearer of Faulkner's increasingly categorical fantasy of individual autonomy: a definition of character marked less by positive qualities than by a refusal to participate in the ubiquitous injustice of society. No longer a quality reserved for those who withdraw from life (like Ike McCaslin in *Go Down, Moses*, Mr. Coldfield in *Absalom, Absalom!*, or Quentin in *The Sound and the Fury*) or for the paradigmatic mulattoes whose lack of identity drives them to self-destruction (Joe Christmas in *Light in August*, Charles Bon and Bon Jr. in *Absalom, Absalom!*), Lucas recasts refusal as a manifestation of essential identity—of permanence of character. He becomes master over himself, and ultimately, over the white community, by refusing to "act like...[a] nigger" (48).

This is the nature of his rebuke to Chick and his posture of defiance of the white community more generally. It places him, not surprisingly, in constant danger of the normalizing violence of that community. As Chick puts it, "We got to make him be a nigger first. He's got to admit he's a nigger. Then maybe we will accept him as he seems to intend to be accepted" (18). Such an occasion is, in effect, what the town has been waiting for—whence the general relief when Lucas is arrested for a crime whose meaning is clear to everyone. Stevens explains the theatrical performance of the racial order that awaits Lucas: Lucas "blew his top and murdered a white man...and now the white people will take him out and burn him, all regular and in order and themselves acting exactly as he is convinced Lucas would wish them to act: like white folks; both of them observing implicitly the rules...and no real hard feelings on either side..." (48). If Stevens is cynically resigned to this outcome, Chick is less insulated from the social ritual, tied to Lucas by his shame and, as Lucas insists, by a certain openness towards the improbable that all marginal people—blacks, children, and old women—share. With Lucas facing certain death, these ties force Chick to face the full meaning of his place in the racial order of the New South: the demand that he approve the violent enforcement of the community's racial norms.

At least initially, Lucas' arrest comes as a secret balm to Chick's shame. Chick reads the inevitable reflex of the racial order as a form of absolution of his debt—a verdict on its original perversity. His lynching, Chick understands, will succeed in making "a nigger out of him once in his life anyway" (31). Lucas denies him this relief, however, by calling in his obligation. Although he asks Chick to set a price on his help, Chick understands that Lucas' request refers only to that source of debt ("So this is what that plate of meat and greens is going to cost me" [67]) and that the defense of Lucas' freedom not to "act like…[a] nigger" constitutes, in the end, the only meaningful form of currency between them.

Thus begins the complicated course of Chick's adventure: the enlisting of his allies Miss Habersham and Aleck Sander, the digging up of bodies and the scares in the woods that situate *Intruder* in the tradition of another novel ostensibly about a boy's racial enlightenment, *The Adventures of Huckleberry Finn*. As Cleanth Brooks and other critics have noted, the machinery of this adventure doesn't make much sense, in large part because there isn't, strictly speaking, a mystery to be solved. The plot hinges on the implausible and somewhat grotesque proposition that, believing he would never be believed, Lucas would refuse to finger a white murderer in order to save his own life. Thus it isn't Lucas' innocence but, perversely, his silence that sets in motion the long deferral of information about the crime and its circumstances that constitutes, such as it is, the narrative arc of the novel.

Chick's deepening involvement with Lucas leads him to a series of reflections on his place in the New South: "now he seemed to see his whole native land, his home—the dirt, the earth which had bred his bones and those of his fathers for six generations and was still shaping him into not just a man but a specific man…a specific kind and even race: and even more: even among a kind and race specific and unique"

(148). If the first part of this passage signifies Chick's reassertion of an organic Southern identity, the final phrase marks the transformation that has taken place in the course of his adventure. Overcoming both his shame and his identification with the racial order, Chick's sense of identity resolves itself into a notion of belonging to an enlightened minority, of being a "specific man" "even among a kind and race" that distinguishes itself, as Stevens explains later, chiefly by "refusing to bear...injustice and outrage and dishonor and shame" (201). This notion of being, in effect, a minority within a race is one side of the novel's argument about racial authenticity. Reflecting Faulkner's own situation as the civil rights crisis grew, it is rooted less in a search for racial essences than in a concern for the internal dynamics of individual adherence to a racial community. Authenticity, in this context, lies in the principle of autonomy or "refusal" that permits an individual to separate him or herself from the indignities of a shared racial "condition," whether those of the oppressor, as in Chick's refusal to accept mob justice, or the oppressed, as in Lucas' refusal to act the nigger. Race thus emerges as an object of ethical contention in the novel, split between the individualistic values that Chick and Lucas defend and the logic of race as a mass identity that crushes the space for moral autonomy. Chick's refusal of the expiatory violence of the community, like Sutpen's refusal to ride with the white vigilantes after the war, documents the persistence of Faulkner's fear of the latter version of racial community: the "invasion of the self" suffered through incorporation into the "monstrous unraveling omnivorous" "Face" of the white mob (190).

The pre-rational solidarity of the mob is the closest thing to a conception of evil in Faulkner's writing and a particularly important subject in *Intruder*. It signifies the dilution of personal responsibility into an anonymous mass, such that "the individual red hand which actually snapped the thread [that is, that kills] may vanish forever into one inviolable confraternity of namelessness" (198). In broader terms, the mob is the "complete relinquishment of individual identity into one We" (135) that Faulkner associates not only with white supremacist violence, but with political authoritarianism in general and, perhaps most importantly in the context of the emerging civil rights crisis, with the principle of majority rule embodied in federal authority. Chick's hard-won autonomy lies in this tenuous space between the threat of the lynch mob on one side and the threat of federal authority on the other—the latter, like the former made up of "massed uncountable faces looking down at him and his" (150).

In this way, Chick revisits Major de Spain's anti-national position in moderated and modernized form. Jettisoning the anachronistic defense of Southern independence, he situates the Civil War within a larger metaphor of organic national unity: "the great River itself flowing not merely from the north but out of the North circumscribing and outland—the umbilicus of America joining the soil which was his home to the parent which three generations ago it had failed in blood to repudiate" (148). This convoluted imagery of oedipal rebellion and the legitimacy of "natural" bonds expresses a political contradiction: how to maintain the "natural" union of America (coded as a family) without the threat of paternal authority (the North or the federal government) over the children (the South or, stretching the point as Faulkner does, the various regional identities of the United States). From this perspective, the encroaching power of the federal government is a divisive, rather than unifying force, responsible for the "curving semicircular wall" that "circumscribes" the South in Chick's imagination. This immaterial wall marks the growing barrier of miscomprehension that separates North and South, "between whom and him and his there was no longer any real kinship and soon there would not even be any contact since the very mutual words they used would no longer have the same significance" (149–50).

Chick's reflections reach their limit in this double movement from national unity to the growing divide between North and South and from Southern unity in resistance to federal authority to the increasingly problematic division between enlightened and unenlightened whites. It is left to Stevens to take the next step. Stevens revises and synthesizes Chick's insights, providing, in no vague terms, the lessons of the novel. Chick himself authorizes these conclusions in a manner that echoes

Quentin's and Shreve's collaborative narrative in *Absalom, Absalom!*, while effacing the differences in priorities that kept the two of them distinctly "two" through to the end. As Chick characterizes it, his uncle simply takes over his thoughts: "once more his uncle spoke at complete one with him...he saw his thinking not be interrupted but merely swap one saddle for another" (150).

Where Chick had begun to understand the uniqueness of his scruples in Southern society, Stevens elaborates on the responsibilities of that enlightened minority. Where Chick had seen North and South at an ever worsening impasse, Stevens articulates a means of retrieving national unity through the defense of local and regional autonomy. Perhaps most significantly, where Chick had recognized the "emotional idea" (149) of Southern defiance of the North, Stevens extends the ethical argument of personal responsibility into a kind of Southern existential mission, such that freeing "Sambo" would free the white South from the authoritarian consequences of its collective guilt. All of these issues come into play in Stevens' densest and most problematic monologue:

> We are defending not actually our politics or beliefs or even our way of life, but simply our homogeneity from a federal government to which in simple desperation the rest of this country has had to surrender voluntarily more and more of its personal and private liberty in order to continue to afford the United States....Only a few of us know that only from homogeneity comes anything of a people...and perhaps most valuable of all a national character worth anything in a crisis....That's why we must resist the North: not just to preserve ourselves nor even the two of us as one to remain one nation because that will be the inescapable byproduct of what we will preserve: which is the very thing that three generations ago we lost a bloody war in our own back yards so that it remain intact: the postulate that Sambo is a

> human being living in a free country and hence must be free. That's what we are really defending: the privilege of setting him free ourselves. (150–51)

Having for all intents and purposes set Lucas free, Chick accomplishes something very much like this existential liberation at an individual level. If, within the logic of the narrative, Lucas' freedom constitutes payment of Chick's personal debt, however, this balancing of accounts vastly multiplies the corresponding social debt owed Lucas by the rest of the community, which has simply reaffirmed its guilty conscience through the affair. The town is shamed, Stevens explains, not by its eagerness for violence, but by having its root prejudice contradicted by the facts. "What sets a man writhing sleepless in bed at night," Stevens notes, "is not having injured his fellow so much as having been wrong" (194). In this way Lucas becomes "the tyrant over the whole county's white conscience" (195), and the dilemma that occasions Chick's ethical liberation is laid before the community.

This passage also presents what is perhaps Stevens' broadest revision of Chick's thinking—his assertion of the respective *homogeneity* of different peoples. Homogeneity, here, intersects the usual signifiers of race, but by way of the complexities of Chick's earlier reflections on race as a "condition," rather than through the crude biologism of white supremacist discourse, which Faulkner had disowned in the course of years of convoluted miscegenation plots. Given the weight the concept is expected to carry, Stevens makes a vague and contradictory case for homogeneity, even to the point of exempting it from rational understanding:

> We dont know why it [homogeneity] is valuable. We dont need to know. Only a few of us know that only from homogeneity comes anything of a people or for a people of durable and lasting value—the literature, the art, the science, that minimum of government and police which is the meaning of freedom and liberty, and perhaps most

valuable of all a national character worth anything in a crisis—that crisis we shall face someday. (151)

At this intersection of biology and culture, in this "condition" that persists from generation to generation binding a "people" together as a "homogeneous" body, one can see the resurrection of the logic of blood-knowledge, restored to its signifying, if deliberately ambiguous register of race. Here is a model of collectivity that privileges neither the mindless action of the community, nor, as Stevens makes clear, the leveling forces of political enfranchisement and commercial culture, but rather the power of individual and collective endurance in the face of adversity. In this latter quality, Stevens argues, the negro race is superior—not only in terms of its ability to survive oppression and injustice, but because of its relative exclusion from the political and cultural cheapening of American life:

> And as for Lucas Beauchamp, Sambo, he's a homogeneous man too, except that part of him which is trying to escape not even into the best of the white race but into the second best—the cheap shoddy dishonest music, the cheap flash baseless overvalued money...all the noisy muddle of political activity which used to be our minor national industry and is now our national amateur pastime....I dont mean that Sambo. I mean the rest of him who has a better homogeneity than we have. (152)

Stevens presents modernization and commercialism as the cultural counterparts of federal encroachment into Southern life. They are agents of dissolution of the different conditions that underlie racial identity and symbols of the larger tradeoff of personal autonomy for comfort that, he argues, constitutes the central proposition of modern nationalism. These nominally distinct tendencies are combined in what Stevens calls the "national religion of the entrails" in which man "has been absolved of soul to owe duty to and instead is static heir at birth to an inevitable quit-claim on a wife a car a radio and an old-age pension" (197). Stevens' thumbnail account of the growth of the modern state and the emergence of the commercial South completes the picture of the forces allied against his double ethic of racial solidarity and individual autonomy. Authentic racial identity, as an ethical as well as material condition, is threatened with erasure from all sides by white authoritarianism, by the inauthentic culture of the commodity, and by the misguided ideal of social equality promoted by the federal government.

The "better" racial homogeneity borne by Lucas and the vision of enlightened "white" homogeneity exemplified by Chick thus set the stage for Stevens' proposition of a *confederation* between the races. This appropriation of the political vocabulary of the Old South marks the novel's unstable revision of the Southern dream of independence. Stevens' new utopian space is demarcated by the novel's broad concept of autonomy, by its notion of racial authenticity, by an implicitly rural anti-modernism, and, finally, by the political horizon of the nation. The key, Stevens concludes, is that "We—he and us—should confederate: swap him the rest of the economic and political and cultural privileges which are his right, for the reversion of his capacity to wait and endure and survive. Then we would prevail; together we would dominate the United States" (153).

The logic underlying Stevens' idea of national dominance is clarified in a later monologue in which he scales his case for homogeneity beyond the limits of the Southern racial crisis. Citing the virtues of the New Englander's isolation "from the coastal spews of Europe" (150), Stevens recasts the preservation of homogeneity as a ubiquitous dilemma facing the other peoples of the United States. *Confederation*, in this respect, is not just a regional solution to the race question, but a model of national redemption in which the white South stands, unexpectedly, in the vanguard.

Letting the white South set Sambo free, in Stevens' lexicon, is the only way to defend both racial homogeneity and moral autonomy.[7] Analogously, it is the only way to free the negro race not to a vulgar imitation of vulgar white materialism, but to the deeper idea of racial identity that Stevens reads in Lucas' power for resistance. Thus, just as this act would, in a sense, realize the white race, so it would realize the negro race—freeing it from that "part" of itself tied to the false idols of commercial and political life. Those "rights" could then be granted easily because they would be understood in their proper place; the homogeneity of authentic peoples and the solidarity between them would be the stronger bond, guaranteeing the national community below the level of civil, political and, commercial society.

To say that this argument is politically and even logically problematic is, of course, something of an understatement. Stevens assigns primary responsibility for the South's culture of racial repression and violence to the North and tries to limit the racial crisis to the problem of white *bad conscience*. Consequently, he writes out any space for social struggle in favor of a valorization of negro reserves of "patience" and "endurance." As marginal as this line of thinking turned out to be, however, it raises two issues that merit consideration. The first is the obvious resonance of Faulkner's defense of difference with contemporary multicultural rhetoric—a fact that testifies not to Faulkner's prescience, but, as Walter Benn Michaels has pointed out, to the problem common to both: the desire to retain the essentialist contours of racial identity while losing the biological determinism associated with American racism. Second, one should credit Faulkner with an attempt to work through a dimension of the racial dilemma that remains fundamentally incomplete: the transformation of the racist consciousness, which *Intruder* situates at the heart of the crisis of the post-bellum South. As the economy of debt and repression in the novel illustrates, no one was free, in Faulkner's view, until everyone was free— until collective white guilt was expunged not *in specie* (the trap of dependence that Faulkner, an increasingly vocal economic liberal, railed against in the name of personal autonomy), but in defense of that freedom that the white South alone, he believed, could confer.

Inevitably, this complex evacuation of the racial regime for the purpose of redeeming racial difference involved Faulkner in a series of contradictions. If the negro race had to be set free in order to preserve the white race, then continued repression of the negroes must have been a threat to it. Such indeed was the case; for nearly two decades Faulkner had been nothing if not insistent on how the structural inequalities of the racial order produced miscegenation, yielding a modern South in which racial difference frequently cut through the center of families and in which racial identity was often obscure. The problem for Faulkner was that the modern solutions to that repression—the expanding social mobility of the commercial South or the enforced social equality of federal intervention—promised still further destruction and/or erasure of the public signifiers of race. They would destroy the different "conditions" through which racial difference was intelligible, and in so doing, destroy the circumstances through which particular forms of racial authenticity—Lucas' or Chick's, for instance—could be recovered and defended.

This vexed logic comes to a head in Stevens' well-known statement from *Intruder*: "we are in the position of the German after 1933 who had no other alternative between being either a Nazi or a Jew" (211). To be sure, this imperative to choose resonates with Chick's decision to defend Lucas at the risk of his own safety. Such an interpretation feeds into the ethical version of Faulkner's racial politics outlined by Stevens and subscribed to by, among others, Gilles Deleuze and Felix Guattari in their frequent references to this passage (292). On the other hand, one might also read in it a return to Stevens' obsessions with white authenticity—with a *becoming-negro* that signifies not a political or social alliance with blacks but rather the achievement by Southern whites of that "homogeneity" that negroes possess in greater measure. If, finally, both of these interpretations refer to the problem of white bad conscience in the South—to the problem of freeing the oppressor from himself—there is still another possibility rooted in the priority that Stevens accords the external conflict between North and South. According to this logic, Northern imperialism not only prevented the South from doing the right thing, but had actually worsened the condition of blacks in the region. On this basis he could claim that "the victory of 1861–1865...probably did more than even John Brown to stalemate Lucas' freedom" (211).

Under such circumstances, the choice between becoming a Nazi or a Jew might well fall to the former. As Faulkner notoriously remarked some years later in the wake of *Brown vs. Board of Education* (probably, as an extenuating circumstance, while "tight" and in reference not to the Nazis but to Robert E. Lee's famous choice of loyalties): "As long as there's a middle road, all right, I'll be on it. But if it came to fighting I'd fight for Mississippi against the United States even if it meant going into the street and shooting Negroes" (*Lion* 262).

This is not, in any sense, the "final" attitude of *Intruder in the Dust*, nor did it sum up Faulkner's social peregrinations of the 1950s, which on balance sought to calm tempers and reduce the risk of white violence. His remarks, however, reflected the contradictions of a position years in the making. As he well understood, they totally destroyed his legitimacy on the subject and wisely proved to be the last of his public interventions. As for *Intruder in the Dust*, it is, I would argue, too fundamentally at cross-purposes on the question of political and social freedoms and too cognizant of the difficulty of fleshing out a viable "middle road" in an increasingly polarized political climate to do more than hint that the choice between Nazi and Jew represented a real quandary. If an ambivalent identification with the culture of slavery was, in some respects, the bread and butter of Faulkner's art, Nazism, circa 1948, was a different matter altogether.

By posing the existential problem of the white South as a problem of racial authenticity, *Intruder in the Dust* proposes a model of national unity that, like that in "Shall Not Perish," consists of separate and unique components—in this case, "peoples" instead of "places." Though this vision remains vague in *Intruder* and nowhere constitutes, exactly, a principle of political unity, it may be that Chick's defense of Lucas should be read as more than just an allegory or prefiguration of that redeemed future. If the redeemed nation consists of authentic "peoples," and if national unity is justified through the mutual defense of the right of those "peoples" to be, however differently, themselves, then the commitment to their defense is necessarily an individual commitment—a refusal of the totalitarian "Face" and its communal bond of guilt. In these terms, the defense of the other is, paradoxically, the means by which one achieves one's own autonomy and authenticity. If this is the case, then national redemption isn't really a collective movement at all (which for Faulkner almost always signified mob), but rather a liberation in a series of individuals such as Chick, who thus both represents the process *and begins it*. The political sequence outlined in *Intruder*, from the individual to the minority within a race, to the confederation of such minorities, to, finally, their dominance of the nation is the defense of individual conscience in increasingly large *combinations*. After *Intruder in the Dust*, this is the idea that Faulkner increasingly brought to bear against the cold war logics of authoritarianism and militarism, both at home and abroad. It is the territory, in particular, of *A Fable*, which recounts the almost viral spread of the idea of peace among troops on the Western Front, enabling each soldier to lay down his weapon as if in perfect association with soldiers up and down the line and across the battlefield.

Even if Faulkner had found a more palatable ideological line to toe in the civil rights struggle, his efforts to legitimize his "national voice" faced an uphill battle. Ultimately, this ambition spoke to and, in a sense, closed the book on a paradigm of literary nationalism that had dominated the American literary imagination during the twenties. Faulkner was in a unique position to register this disintegration because, in many respects, the racial impasse of the New South was the last entrenched obstacle to the formal consolidation of a liberal political culture in the United States. Its official resolution in the early sixties emptied political identity of its last group privileges and prioritized the nation as, in effect, the set of all sets of social, political, and private identity. One of the major axes of cultural critique in the twenties had been, precisely, a romantic contestation of that real and symbolic hegemony, championing the local or its equivalents as a beleaguered principle of difference whose recovery might, in the end, redeem national identity from the homogenizing tendencies of modernization.[8] Operating within this horizon, cultural critics and literary modernists from across the political spectrum had had little trouble conceiving a ubiquitous division in American life between the local and the national. Faulkner, in the forties, had to extrapolate this distinction rather uncertainly from his sense of Southern exceptionalism, extending it to other threatened and largely imaginary "peoples" of the United States. Ultimately, this is where his proposition confronted not just its contradictions, but its cultural obsolescence.

In short, the pox that Faulkner cast on both North and South proved to be a quixotic and untenable position. The stridency of his efforts to articulate and defend that position suggested, moreover, that the conditions that legitimated this sort of redemptive criticism were coming to an end. Perhaps the most significant change was that there was now little broader anxiety about the legitimacy of the nation in which Faulkner's redemptive critique could lose its regionalist trappings. In an era not only of emerging racial struggle but also deep ideological consensus, Southern intransigence failed to find much resonance as an instance (as Faulkner would have it and as the rhetoric of states' rights had traditionally maintained) of a more general crisis of the union.

In other ways, too, the nationalist literary paradigm of the twenties was breaking up. The self-evidence of post-war American hegemony largely obviated the fears of cultural inferiority that had always lurked behind the efforts to produce an "American literature" worthy of comparison to Europe. That project had by and large dropped off the list of cultural obsessions by the forties and, with it, the fundamental ambition of literary nationalism to imaginatively connect writing to the national body. The imperative to constant cultural reinvention that characterized such efforts had itself become an object of institutionalized scholarship—the subject of far more debates about the past than about the future.[9] Without these active concerns, Faulkner's careful finessing of the question of racial and national identity fell between the cracks of the reconsolidating territories of literature and politics.

NOTES

1. Most of the biographical information on Faulkner used here can be found in Blotner's exhaustive biography.
2. *Sanctuary* (1931), which contained a lurid rape scene that had briefly made Faulkner infamous if not famous, was his only work that remained in print.
3. Sartre's relative blindness to this dimension of Faulkner's work is particularly clear in his own foray into American Gothicism, *The Respectful Prostitute*. Lizzie, the protagonist, stands in for the universal subject of existentialism, an "outsider" (in this case, a Northerner) faced with the choice of becoming a "bastard" (in this case, a party to racist violence). Faulkner's characters never have this privilege of being outside. The historical crisis constitutes them and binds them.
4. Like those of *I'll Take My Stand* (1930), a collection of nostalgic defenses of Southern cultural autonomy that constituted the *cri de coeur* of the "Agrarian" movement.
5. Rogin examines this reconciliation of Southern resentment through the rewriting of the Civil War, and particularly the role of Woodrow Wilson in this revisionism.
6. Even this apparent mockery, however, is placed on dubious footing by Faulkner's own attempt to produce a modernized Gospel in *A Fable*. Howe, Snead, Sundquist, and Gresset belong to the majority that holds Stevens to exemplify or express the worst of Faulkner's ideological wandering and stylistic excess of the late novels. Brooks and Urgo make cases for Stevens' relative marginality to the more important trajectory of Chick's rebellion and education.
7. Since this is a piece about how the meaning of race was constructed in a particular context—Faulkner's, in the forties—I have elected to preserve Stevens'/Faulkner's diction. To do otherwise introduces anachronisms and suggests a faith in the coherence of racial categories. I don't want to imply that black or African American are simply present-day equivalent terms for the same, preexisting racial identity.
8. See, for instance, Dewey or Lawrence's meditations on the spirit of "place" (7-15), and Williams' defense of "locality" (216-31).
9. Reising provides a useful account of the institutionalization of American literature in the thirties, forties, and fifties around questions of inclusion/exclusion from the national canon. By that time, the existence of that usable past—still a postulate and a project for Van Wyck Brooks and Williams in the twenties—is no longer in question. What matters are the criteria of inclusion and exclusion, and these undergo a shift in the course of those decades, very roughly, from a canon that privileged the "representation" of "American" materials, groups, or events as a kind of democratic practice (associated with V. L. Parrington and Granville Hicks) to the general rejection of those criteria in favor of more discreetly aesthetic concerns (whence the repertoire of New Critical values: ambiguity, irony, style—although these too could be articulated in nationalist terms). The values underlying this shift find

perhaps their most telling illustration in the inverse relationship of the fortunes of Theodore Dreiser and Henry James in the period—the former the champion of the literary left of the thirties, the latter the epitome of writerly craft and textual isolation from mundane realism that the New Critics took to be the measure of literary greatness.

WORKS CITED

Blotner, Joseph. *Faulkner: A Biography. One-Volume Edition.* New York: Random House, 1984.
Brooks, Cleanth. *Faulkner: The Yoknapatawpha Country.* New Haven: Yale University Press, 1963.
Deleuze, Gilles, and Felix Guattari. *A Thousand Plateaus: Capitalism and Schizophrenia.* Minneapolis: University of Minnesota Press, 1991.
Dewey, John. "Americanism and Localism." *Dial* 68 (1920): 684–88.
Faulkner, William. *Absalom, Absalom!.* New York: Vintage, 1986.
-----. *Collected Stories.* New York: Vintage, 1977.
-----. *A Fable.* New York: Random House, 1954.
-----. *Intruder in the Dust.* New York: Vintage, 1991.
-----. *Lion in the Garden: Interviews with William Faulkner, 1926–1956.* Eds. James B. Meriwether and Michael Millgate. New York: Random House, 1968.
-----. *Sanctuary.* New York: Vintage, 1987.
-----. *Selected Letters of William Faulkner.* Ed. Joseph Blotner. New York: Random House, 1977.
-----. "Shall Not Perish." *Collected Stories.* New York: Vintage, 1977. 101–15.
-----. *Short Stories: Holograph Manuscripts and Transcripts.* Ed. Joseph Blotner. New York: Garland, 1987.
Gresset, Michel. *Fascination: Faulkner's Fiction, 1919–1936.* Trans. Thomas West. Durham, NC: Duke University Press, 1989.
Griffith, D. W., dir. *Birth of a Nation.* Mutual/Reliance-Majestic, 1914.
Howe, Irving. *William Faulkner: A Critical Study.* Chicago: University of Chicago Press, 1951.
Lawrence, D. H. *Studies in Classic American Literature.* New York: Penguin, 1977.
Michaels, Walter Benn. *Our America: Nativism, Modernism and Pluralism.* Durham, NC: Duke University Press, 1995.
Rogin, Michael. *Ronald Reagan, the Movie and Other Episodes in Political Demonology.* Berkeley: University of California Press, 1988.
Reising, Richard. *The Unusable Past: Theory and Study of American Literature.* New York: Methuen, 1986.
Sartre, Jean Paul. *Literary Essays.* Trans. Annette Michelson. New York: Philosophical Library, 1957.
-----. *The Respectful Prostitute. No Exit and Three Other Plays.* Trans. Lionel Abel. New York: Vintage, 1989. 243–75.
Schwartz, Lawrence. *Creating Faulkner's Literary Reputation: The Politics of Modern Literary Criticism.* Knoxville: University of Tennessee Press, 1988.
Snead, James A. *Figures of Division: William Faulkner's Major Novels.* New York: Methuen, 1986.
Sundquist, Eric. *Faulkner: The House Divided.* Baltimore, MD: The Johns Hopkins University Press, 1981.

Twelve Southerners, *I'll Take My Stand: The South and the Agrarian Tradition*. Baton Rouge: Louisiana State University Press, 1977.

Urgo, Joseph. *Faulkner's Apocrypha: A Fable, Snopes and the Spirit of Human Rebellion*. Jackson: University Press of Mississippi, 1989.

Williams, William Carlos. *In the American Grain*. New York: New Directions, 1956.

Faulkner's Comic Narrative of Community

Donald M. Kartiganer

"These characters and incidents are fictional, imaginative, and—some will say—impossible."
William Faulkner[1]

Intruder in the Dust is a novel about a lynching that does not take place. "Nobody lynched anybody" (199), Gavin Stevens reminds his nephew Chick Mallison during one of their debates on the behavior of the people of Yoknapatawpha County toward Lucas Beauchamp, the black man virtually everyone assumes, from the first sentence, has "killed a white man" (3). Not only does the lynching not take place, but as the novel gradually makes clear to us, it never could. At every stage of the action, Lucas Beauchamp's life is presumably in great danger, yet no harm comes to him nor to any of his unlikely allies. Although the novel compels us to acknowledge that danger—necessary both for the purpose of suspense and to point up the great significance of the fact that the lynching does not, after all, occur—it also consistently assures us that Lucas is never really at risk. In contrast to such earlier Faulkner texts as "Dry September" or *Light in August*, in which public outrage at an accused black man moves inevitably towards its violent climax, *Intruder in the Dust* unfolds within a particular social setting and narrative convention that combine to render such violence improbable and fictionally inconceivable.

Although he has clearly picked the wrong place—Beat Four—to be found standing, with a recently fired pistol in his pocket, over the body of a dead white man, and despite the overwhelming evidence of his guilt as well as ample precedent for quick and brutal communal vengeance, Lucas Beauchamp remains alive, without a single hand being lifted against him. During the two days following his arrest, he is vulnerable to attack should the assembled crowd of townspeople and countrymen choose to mount one. Nevertheless, whether chained to a bedpost in the constable's home in Beat Four, imprisoned in the jail in Jefferson, eating breakfast in Sheriff Hampton's kitchen, or in the back seat of the Sheriff's car as "bait" to flush out the real murderer, Lucas Beauchamp is perfectly safe.

He is safe because Faulkner has chosen to embed the story in a thoroughly idealized fictional representation of what the novel terms a homogeneous society, one that, for all its persistent, habitual racism and its apparent penchant for violence, is finally capable of behaving with exemplary justness and fairness. Moreover, in depicting that society in action, Faulkner has aptly resorted to the narrative mode of social comedy, specifically that version which enacts and celebrates the reintegration and triumph of community. Our sense that *Intruder in the Dust* will not conform to the historically proven possibility of the lynch mob is in part owing to the pressure of its comic form, the structural embodiment of that homogeneity which, in this novel, becomes the best guarantee of social justice.

The claim that the South in general and Yoknapatawpha County in particular are homogeneous societies is made explicitly by Gavin Stevens. The tendency to interpret Stevens as a mouthpiece for Faulkner in this novel is one that has recently been challenged by critics, most comprehensively by Noel Polk (220–24). Given his unceasing loquaciousness, his inclination to talk when he should be listening, his maddening inability to absorb new information that contradicts his working assumptions, Stevens is clearly a foil for his flexible and quick-acting nephew, Chick Mallison—who clearly has much to learn, but does in fact learn it. Nevertheless, Stevens's central point about the homogeneity of the South as its distinctive and most valuable quality, and the necessary instrument of social justice, is one that the novel consistently and concretely represents, if at times in ways that Stevens is himself too blind to recognize.

By a homogeneous society, Stevens implies what Cleanth Brooks refers to as not "a mere collection of people who happen to live in a place called Jefferson...[but] an organic society that shares basic assumptions...[and whose] members can, without thinking or prior consultation, suddenly move together in a concordant action" (291); "they have a community of values that is rooted in some kind of lived experience" (421). The authority of such a society, as M. E. Bradford has noted, is historical and family and clan based (478), a condition that leads Stevens to the pronouncement that fratricide is the crime that society finds most threatening: the ultimate violation of its conception of communal life, the repudiation of which becomes the value that will save Lucas Beauchamp's life.[2]

Pervading *Intruder in the Dust* is an imagery of interrelation, of Yoknapatawpha as a web of commonalities ranging from shared blood to shared attitudes, a world of collective participation (sometimes unconscious) in traditions that are potentially destructive, but that—in this idealized fictional account—are finally the foundation that holds that world intact, fulfilling the promise of harmony. The concept of social homogeneity, so often employed as a code term for exclusion, becomes in this novel a celebration of inclusion, of a culture constituted by the blurring of racial, social, and economic boundaries.

Lucas Beauchamp is himself the core of a series of links tying together not only the black and white communities but aristocrat and peasant classes. The grandson of Old Carothers McCaslin, blood descendant of black slaves and their white owner, Lucas joins the divided races of his society even as he boasts of his separation from both. Deriving from "the old lot," the McCaslins, rather than "the new folks" (19), the Edmondses, Lucas insists on his aristocratic origins, yet his ties to the Gowries—"a connection of brawlers and farmers and foxhunters and stock-and timber-traders" (35)—are also manifest.

Chick Mallison is the astonished witness to the fact that Lucas and

Nub Gowrie are equally capable of grieving for their dead: Chick "thinking how he had seen grief twice now in two years where he had not expected it or anyway anticipated it, where in a sense a heart capable of breaking had no business being: once in an old nigger who had just happened to outlive his old nigger wife and now in a violent foulmouthed godless old man who had happened to lose one of the six lazy idle violent more or less lawless a good deal more than just more or less worthless sons" (158). This common expression of grief over wife and son allows Chick to see a bond between Lucas and Gowrie that destroys at least some of his preconceptions regarding both men. He discovers not only a capacity for grief in men he has regarded as his racial and social inferiors, but also a bond between two men he has regarded as natural enemies.

Less dramatic but equally significant is the quality of unapologetic independence and stubbornness that Lucas and Gowrie alike assume and indeed brandish before the world. Lucas cultivates an expression, a manner, "not black nor white either, not arrogant at all and not even scornful: just intolerant inflexible and composed" (13). He is a man the very placement of whose property holdings testifies to his autonomy: a ten-acre "oblong of earth set forever in the middle of the two-thousand-acre [Edmonds] plantation like a postage stamp in the center of an envelope"(8). Gowrie is the representative of a family, an entire subculture of the county, "a synonym for independence and violence: an idea with physical boundaries like a quarantine for plague so that solitary and unique and alone out of all the county it was known to the rest of the county by the number of its survey coordinate—Beat Four" (35).

The stark singularity of both men extends to the structures they live in and the churches they use for worship. Lucas's house sits on a hill "with an air solitary independent and intractable too" (8), the house itself "gray and weathered and not so much paintless as independent of and intractable to paint" (9). The church in which the Gowries worship is "solitary but not forlorn, intractable and independent, asking nothing of any, making compromise with none" (154).[3]

While Lucas Beauchamp asserts his link to Old Carothers McCaslin,

Nub Gowrie (Nub stands for the initials N.B.) is named after Nathan Bedford Forrest and in turn has named his first son after him as well—both Lucas and Nub recognizing the need to buttress independence with past authority, however remote from their particular social situations that authority may appear to be.[4] In sum, in this diverse yet oddly coherent community, the suspected murderer and the murdered and bereaved share common traits, claim comparable inheritances, command similar stances toward the world—a range of commonalities consistent with the fact, discovered only towards the end of the novel, that the Gowries apparently have always realized that Lucas did not kill Vinson and have never planned to take vengeance on him (214).

Particularly significant is the novel's developing realization that Lucas and the Gowries, in many ways self-willed outcasts, indifferent to common opinion, prepared to offend, actually stand at the center of value in their community. They represent a combination of independence and tradition that is not only the foundation of the community but even validates it: the tiny postage stamp in the center of the envelope, without which it cannot reach its destination.

The shared traits of Lucas Beauchamp and Nub Gowrie exemplify a cohesion that obtains throughout the society. Lucas wears a sheep-lined coat and felt hat, "such as [Chick's] grandfather had used to wear" (6), a gold toothpick "such as his own grandfather had used" (12). Miss Habersham is joined to Lucas through her relationship with his late wife Molly, "both suckled at Molly's mother's breast and grown up together almost inextricably like sisters, like twins" (86), as well as to the Gowries, with whom she shares a willful spirit, "independent solitary and forlorn" (183). To touch this organically structured society anywhere is to set off echoes throughout the whole, crossing class and racial lines, linking individuals and groups remote from, and often antagonistic to, each other, composing a community that, as Brooks claims, "shares basic assumptions."[5]

The foundation of this society is the anonymous "crowd," the townspeople who hang about the barbershops and poolhalls, the country people who pour into town to join them in the square and outside the jail: to wait, to watch, to be on hand to register the violent events that have become, if not inevitable, then clearly possible. Unable or unwilling to assume individual identity or individual opinion, too large, too leaderless to act, they are the chorus of the drama. They are there not to initiate but to witness, to give voice to what have become conventional attitudes. But they are also there to represent—as Brooks writes, "without thinking or prior consultation"—a revision in communal thinking that more active forces in the society have persuaded them to accept.

They rely on their past experience to predict the future, not realizing that events are already in motion that will bring about an entirely different outcome than they can possibly imagine. For example, concerned primarily with when and where Lucas Beauchamp will be lynched, the crowd speculates that he is safe at the constable's house in Beat Four because it will soon be Sunday, and the Ingrums and Gowries and Workitts would not "want to have to hurry, bolt through the business in order to finish it by midnight and not violate the Sabbath" (33). Then they decide the lynching will take place when Skipworth hands his prisoner over to Hampton, who "might be sheriff in Yoknapatawpha County but he's just another man in Beat Four" (39). But then, when the sheriff arrives with Lucas Sunday morning, apparently having received his prisoner from Skipworth without incident, the crowd—like resourceful prophets of an ever-retreating apocalypse—revises still again its expectations regarding Lucas's fate: "Lawyer hell. He wont even need an undertaker when them Gowries get through with him tonight" (44).

The callousness and lack of empathy are clear enough, but so is the absence of anything resembling an inclination to take action. The crowd is no danger to Lucas or to anyone else. They are easily kept at bay by token defenders of lawful procedure: the single sharpshooter, Will Legate, propped conspicuously in the open doorway of the jail, and his eventual replacements, the two women, Miss Habersham and Chick's mother, Maggie Mallison. Neither Legate nor the women, as everyone realizes, would be able to prevent an attempted lynching; they merely symbolize the traditional authorities of law and womanhood that the crowd is expected to—and does—honor.

The crowd momentarily resists the sheriff's and marshall's attempts to disperse it, yet "not at all defiant, not really daring anyone: just tolerant, goodhumored, debonair almost," and eventually it moves, if "still without haste" (138). What is evident here is that, even as they assemble to witness, possibly to participate in, illegal violence, the people are in fact adhering to communal standards of order, expressing their impatience with the law (the impatience also part of their tradition) even as they admit its legitimacy.

The crowd is not the creator of the culture but the product. At the end of the novel they withdraw from the scene of the nonlynching—perhaps in flight, as Chick Mallison claims, from the shame of their false accusation of Lucas Beauchamp, or perhaps, as Gavin Stevens claims, from their repudiation of the true murderer, the fratricide Crawford Gowrie. Still passive, never wholly aware, they are yet the bearers, the embodiment of the communal culture, responsive to the surprising shift in events, representing the renewal of the culture and the possibility of its fulfillment.

The great threat to community in *Intruder in the Dust*, that will prevent it from fulfilling its promise of complete homogeneity by indelibly dividing it, is racism: the belief of whites in the inherent inferiority of blacks. This belief is the offense of the novel, the stain that sets the plot in motion, as if the murder of Vinson Gowrie would be of little moment were Lucas Beauchamp not discovered standing by the corpse. Just another killing among the violent inhabitants of Beat Four, it arouses all of Yoknapatawpha County because a black man murdering a white man is a crime that requires instant vengeance, regarded by whites as a violation of the fundamental order of society.

What is clear in *Intruder in the Dust*, constituting Faulkner's major insight into Southern society, is that this racism is not the foundation of homogeneity, but the tragic contradiction to it. Racism is the name and essence of division, a division so deeply cut that it assumes the validity of natural fact rather than human construction. Within the context of the elaborate network of affiliations that the novel weaves, racism is the great aberration, the deviation that *undermines* society, since, as Chick Mallison has learned from the voluminous speeches of Gavin Stevens, division is *"the anteroom to dissolution"* (212).

The novel takes great pains to establish as unjust and indefensible the conviction of black inferiority, although there remains a residue of racist thinking that continues to praise with faint contempt: the familiar notion, for example, that black strengths reside primarily in endurance and patience or in abilities, such as seeing in the dark, that are found primarily in animals. For the most part, the novel quietly depicts the racist conventions that contradict both common sense and the common bonds tying black and white together. For example, in the novel's opening chapter, Aleck Sander and Edmonds's "boy" hunt rabbits with tapsticks while Chick Mallison carries a shotgun; in the scene at Sheriff Hampton's house, Aleck Sander, after participating fully with Chick and Miss Habersham in the discovery of Jake Montgomery's corpse in Vinson Gowrie's grave, eats breakfast alone in the kitchen while the others adjourn to the dining room. These arbitrary and irrational distinctions become elsewhere the differences in behavior that Faulkner explains as the results of cultural habit and attitude: Chick's unquestioning assumption, matched by the assumptions of blacks themselves, "that being Negroes they were not supposed to have facilities to wash properly or often" (11); that the food they ate "was what Negroes ate, obviously because it was what they liked, what they chose; not...that out of their long chronicle this was all they had had a chance to learn to like" (13).[6]

The most vivid image of the offense of racism is the initial encounter between Chick and Lucas. Faulkner prepares the scene by having Chick, quite unexpectedly, "who had walked the top rail of a fence many a time twice that far," fall off a log into a creek: "all of a sudden the known familiar sunny winter earth was upside down" (5). The complete reversal of things is precisely what Chick is going to have deal with when, at Lucas's house, he attempts to financially compensate hospitality he would not think of offering money for were the Beauchamps white. This condescension to Lucas, the refusal to acknowledge in a black man the privilege of providing a meal without payment, becomes Chick's particular initiation into what in *Go Down, Moses* is referred to as "the old curse of his fathers" (107). Instantly rejecting the payment, Lucas turns Chick's world "upside down," collapsing his preconceptions, condemning his racism, leaving him "forever now too late" (15) in his hope of withdrawing the offense.[7]

Chick's subsequent attempts to relieve himself of the humiliation of his rejected payment only repeat the original insult, the need to remind Lucas of his inferior status: "*We got to make him be a nigger first. He's got to admit he's a nigger*" (18). Lucas easily parries Chick's offerings with gifts of his own, making it clear that there can be no additional "payment" in the form of goods or service that can cancel the first one. All that Chick can do is to embrace consistently the ideal of the homogeneous society itself, to accept Lucas Beauchamp for what he undoubtedly is, a member—through blood, through convention, through loyalties and habits the novel documents throughout—of the community that is Chick's own.

Acceptance manifests itself not in compensation (there can be none that is adequate) but in a form of faith. This faith is the ground of the idealized homogeneous society: a trust both in one's own intuitions and the fundamental worth of another, a trust in human relationship, in a true integrity within which one can know and accept the value of another human being. The depth of trust is measured by what Miss Habersham claims is a willingness to recognize the superiority of truth to fact, to probability and evidence (88).

As Gavin Stevens summarizes it, although he has been incapable of putting it into practice, Chick's triumph is his ability "to believe truth for no other reason than that it was truth, told by an old man in a fix deserving pity and belief, to someone capable of the pity even when none of them really believed him" (124). Going out to Vinson Gowrie's grave to dig up the body with Miss Habersham and Aleck Sander, without really believing Lucas's story, probably without being sure of just what he believes, Chick Mallison is fulfilling, even as he is learning, the existential meaning of the organic society. His is an action of faith, without hope of success—"they had never had time, they had known that before they ever left Jefferson" (100)—and unsure of just what it is he is trying to accomplish.[8]

A faith of this sort, the novel argues, is at once the ground and the triumph of the organic community. In order, however, to confirm and demonstrate that fact, to correct the community's most prominent aberration—the disenfranchisement of its black members—Chick must engage, paradoxically, in an act of rebellion. A striking quality of that rebellion is that it is built into the fabric of the community itself. It rests on a tradition of its own, one seldom invoked but apparently appropriate in times of crisis. That tradition is first stated in the novel by Ephraim: "In fact, you mought bear this in yo mind; someday you mought need it. If you ever needs to get anything done outside the common run, dont waste yo time on the menfolks; get the womens and children to working at it" (70).

The tradition involves both a particular object—accomplishing something "outside the common run"—and a particular means—women and children—because they are the ones most likely to possess that faith that distinguishes the homogeneous from the heterogeneous society. Corroborating Ephraim's charge, although there is no indication she has ever heard him give it, and confirming his advice as conceivable within the scope of communal practice, is Miss Habersham: "Lucas knew it would take a child—or an old woman like me: someone not concerned with probability, with evidence. Men like your uncle and Mr Hampton have had to be men too long, busy too long" (88).

Chick's willingness to act against the apparent will of his community, in other words, does not blind him to the source of his rebellion in the community itself, "since it had also integrated into him whatever it was that had compelled him to stop and listen to a damned highnosed impudent Negro" (148). Regardless of his anger at the townspeople for failing to make some kind of restitution for their false assumption of Lucas's guilt, Chick proclaims his oneness with them: "his people his blood his own with whom it had been his joy and pride and hope to be found worthy to present one united unbreakable front to the dark abyss the night" (190).

Moreover, he knows that his value to the community will be his willingness to continue that rebellion; as his uncle Gavin says, "Just dont stop" (205). He imagines himself as always being among the marginal people who foment revolution: "*Because they always have me and Aleck Sander and Miss Habersham, not to mention Uncle Gavin and a sworn badgewearing sheriff.*" If he will "defend them from anyone anywhere," it will be only "so that he might excoriate them himself without mercy since they were his own and he wanted no more save to stand with them unalterable and impregnable" (205).

Having described the Southern community as a uniquely homogeneous one—the full implications of which Chick Mallison has been left to resolve and implement for himself—Gavin Stevens also provides an anthropological account of the value system underlying such a community. As Wesley and Barbara Alverson Morris have pointed out, Stevens's resort to fratricide as the unpardonable social sin calls up Freud's *Totem and Taboo* and its attempt to identify fratricide as "the foundation law of civilization" (232). It replaces the murder of the father with the murder of the brother as the primal crime determining future social behavior. None of the brothers, Freud argues, who have banded together to overthrow the father, is capable of replacing him. Their only recourse is to unite, agreeing to "institute the law against incest by which they all alike renounced the women whom they desired and who had been their chief motive for dispatching their father. In this way they rescued the organization which had made them strong" (Freud 179).

Stevens's extrapolation from Freud's theory of social origins is to establish brotherhood as the basis of the homogeneous community, emphasizing its organic nature by stressing the blood dimension. As Freud explicitly asserts, the law against fratricide precedes the law against murder itself: "It was not until long afterward that the prohibition ceased to be limited to members of the clan and assumed the simple form: 'Thou shalt do no murder'" (181). Stevens borrows this notion in his explanation to Chick Mallison: "*Thou shalt not kill* you see—no accusative, heatless: a simple moral precept"; even when violated it still stands as law, "and maybe next time we even wont"

(195). "But t*hou shall not kill thy mother's child*" holds in its horror a greater power: "no maybe about it, no next time to maybe not Gowrie kill Gowrie because there must be no first time. And not just for Gowrie but for all" (195–6).[9]

This brotherhood and the compulsion to protect it is the brotherhood that includes Lucas Beauchamp, and therefore best insures his safety. Without the law against the murder of the brother, "'how hope ever to reach that one where *Thou shalt not kill at all*, where Lucas Beauchamp's life will be secure not despite the fact that he is Lucas Beauchamp but because he is?'" (196).

The crowd at the jail, according to Stevens, runs not from shame at the false accusation of Lucas but in total rejection of the fratricide: "They didn't want to destroy Crawford Gowrie. They repudiated him. If they had lynched him they would have taken only his life. What they really did was worse: they deprived him to the full extent of their capacity of his citizenship in man" (198). For Crawford Gowrie there is no help within the community, no tradition of rebellion that has authorized Chick and Miss Habersham and Aleck Sander to violate one social convention in the service of a larger one. Crawford has violated the very foundations of the society; no one in the community, no one in his family will come to his aid. "Who would he get?" asks Gavin Stevens (213).

In the opening paragraphs of this essay I refer both to a particular social setting and a narrative convention that combine to insure that *Intruder in the Dust* will avoid its tragic potential, that it will be a novel in which "[n]obody lynched anybody" (199). The social setting is Faulkner's idealized portrait of a homogeneous Southern community fulfilling its genuine communal character: freeing the innocent man, who is in every important respect an integral part of that community, and "repudiating" the true violator, the fratricide. The narrative convention is a version of what Northrop Frye calls New Comedy, a mode Faulkner seldom used in his Jefferson fiction prior to this novel, and that he employs here in order to provide structural support for, and deepen thematically, his idealized social vision.[10]

While New Comedy has multiple variations, its basic plot, originating in Greek drama with Menander, involves a hero in conflict with his society, usually over his desire for a woman forbidden to him by her father or guardian. The society is temporarily controlled by unjust and irrational minds who support the prohibition. The normal thrust of the comedy is to resolve the conflict and reform the society, an action Frye summarizes as "the integration of society, which usually takes the form of incorporating a central character into it" (43).

In *Intruder in the Dust* that central character is dual, comprised of Lucas Beauchamp and Chick Mallison, both of whom find themselves threatened with expulsion from the community—Lucas by virtue of being a black man suspected of murdering a white man, Chick by virtue of his violation of communal custom for the sake of protecting that black man. The object of their quest is not a woman but rather a form of social relationship, also forbidden, based on the fundamental principle of racial equality. Although the comic plot occasionally swerves into dangerous territory—part of its distinctive power being just that willingness to risk disaster, like the comic hero on the verge of being sent to the gallows—it generally returns to its major goal, which is to achieve that fortunate outcome fundamental to comedy that Frye calls "a redeemed society" (185).[11]

In his discussion of comedy as "the mythos of spring," Frye describes the general conversion of a corrupt society to a redeemed one. Although the movement is corrective, making it clear that certain characters have been misguided, the tendency is always toward inclusion rather than exclusion, "the blocking characters...more often reconciled or converted than simply repudiated" (165). It is not so much individuals at fault as it is their submission to "some absurd, cruel, or irrational law: the law of killing Syracusans in the *Comedy of Errors*, the law of compulsory marriage in *A Midsummer Night's Dream*" (166)—or, in *Intruder in the Dust*, the Jim Crow laws of segregation and their irrational, racist underpinning.

The turning point in the action of comedy, the recognition leading to the reversal that makes resolution possible, is often gimmicky—a highly implausible episode within a mode whose happy conclusion is inevitable, but whose means of reaching it are not. The collective action of Chick Mallison, Miss Habersham, and Aleck Sander, bent on digging up one corpse only to find another, is a perfect example. What Ephraim advises in times of crisis—"dont waste yo time on the menfolks; get the women and children to working on it" (70)—becomes the novel's version of the comic turn, leading directly to the exoneration of Lucas, the identification of the true murderer, and the restoration of Chick Mallison and Lucas to their places within the community.

Ultimately included within that community, evidence of comedy's tendency to incorporate rather than expel, are almost all the "blocking characters": the Gowries, the crowd outside the jail, Gavin Stevens—a version of the *senex iratus* (angry old man) of New Comedy, who has been engaged in his own form of antagonism with the dual hero. The only character left outside is Crawford Gowrie: "Who would he get?" He is granted a certain pathos in the description of his frantic need to dig up two corpses: Chick "thought of that too: the anguish, the desperation, the urgency in the black dark and the briers and the dizzy irrevocable fleeing on seconds, carrying a burden man was not intended to carry" (169). And yet by no means does he acquire the depth or the sympathy of a Shylock, whose punishment in *The Merchant of Venice* threatens to shift the comic emphasis from the restored community to the tragic fate of the scapegoat. Crawford is the fratricide whose outcast state clarifies by contrast Lucas Beauchamp's authentic membership in the community.

The comic action, Frye writes, moves "from law to liberty" (181), "from a society controlled by habit, ritual bondage, arbitrary law and the older characters to a society controlled by youth and pragmatic freedom…a movement from illusion to reality" (169). The effect of this comic mode, almost formulaically implemented in *Intruder in the Dust*, is to assure us—despite even the dual hero's occasional hopelessness—that the outcome will be fortunate, that there will be no lynching, that within this seemingly divided society lie all the necessary ingredients of its redemption.

In the real United States of 1948 the idealized comic world of *Intruder in the Dust* was a world powerless to be born. In his *New Yorker* review, Edmund Wilson suggested that the novel is "too positive, too optimistic," that it gives in to "the temptations of the novelist's power to summon for innocence in difficulties the equivalents of the United States Marines" (333). Such, of course, is the charge we can direct at most comedy; it makes us more hopeful than reality entitles us to be. Nevertheless, given the increasingly explosive climate within which Faulkner was working, it is necessary to situate this fiction in relation to its historical moment, to determine its merit as a comment on the events taking place as it was written.

In general, *Intruder in the Dust* seems to me a book of great moral courage and clarity. In emphasizing homogeneity as a priceless, uniquely Southern social value and convicting Southern racism of the crime of violating it, Faulkner is making an original and crucial social statement. Especially significant is the novel's refusal to rationalize a "go slow" approach to civil rights by claiming that black people must first "earn" their right to equality.

We find that rationalization in Faulkner's remarks outside his fiction, most notably in a letter he wrote in 1960 to Paul Pollard, who had asked Faulkner to become a lifetime member of the NAACP. In declining, Faulkner wrote: "As I see it, your people must earn by being individually responsible to bear it, the freedom and equality they want and should have. As Dr. Carver said, 'We must make the white people need us, want us to be in equality with them.' I think that your organization is not doing that." That blacks must earn what any white citizen is born with—even Crawford Gowrie—is clearly specious. Faulkner's defense of that stipulation depends on an exhortation that barely conceals its twisted logic: "Since they are a minority, they must behave better than white people. They must be more responsible, more honest, more moral, more industrious, more literate and educated. They, not the law, have got to compel the white people to say, Please come and be equal with us" (*Selected Letters* 444).

But the demand that blacks must earn their rights is not made in

Intruder in the Dust.[12] Lucas Beauchamp does nothing to deserve equality before the law, nothing to deserve justice and his eventual freedom other than to *not* be the murderer of Vinson Gowrie. Clearly, in his explicitly described individualistic stance to the community, white and black, he has not sought to ingratiate himself. Philip Weinstein has noted the passivity of Lucas, who "emerges less as an imagined subjectivity than as an object." He is a character literally fixed and static: "The motion denied him is transferred to Chick Mallison" (76-77), a shift that Weinstein regards as in its own way demeaning, a violation of autonomy that reduces Lucas to a fetishized object of white discourse and action.

My own reading is that Lucas's passivity has a more positive dimension, that it is an implicit rejection of the notion of "earned" equality. As Faulkner frequently said in his public comments, it is the responsibility of the South to grant the blacks equality, not under Northern pressure, but under the pressure of social justice itself. What becomes clear in *Intruder in the Dust* is the additional insistence that whites must grant this equality not as a reward for anything that blacks may do to deserve or demand it, but because that equality is their unquestionable right by virtue of their membership within the homogeneous community.

Just as blacks did not "lose" their equality out of some failure of character or courage, so there is nothing they need or can do to regain it. Lucas Beauchamp's role is to remain in custody until "the womens and children" carry out the task of setting him free. He cannot actively take hold of his equality, but can only accept it from those who have deprived him of it; he cannot assume his rightful place in the homogeneous community until he is recognized as always having belonged there.

As a result, Lucas's only significant action is to identify the one person who, having attempted once to confirm Lucas's inequality by offering money for customary hospitality, has recognized the moral debt that he must now pay. The rest is up to Chick Mallison and the community that he gradually summons to his side.

If *Intruder in the Dust* avoids the quid pro quo rationalization for continued legalized racism, it nevertheless, at least once in the text, falls back on the need to postpone indefinitely its abolition. Even in this idealized comic universe, Gavin Stevens is permitted to say, with no objection from Chick Mallison, that "it wont be next Tuesday" (152). And yet perhaps the novel provides a counter to Stevens's familiar qualification. At the end of the third chapter, Chick Mallison visits Lucas in jail, where Lucas tells him to go and look at the buried corpse of Vinson Gowrie. Chick agrees to do so, but not without expressing his complete skepticism as to the usefulness of the project:

> He looked at Lucas, at the old man holding gently to the bars inside the cell and not even looking at him anymore. He drew a long breath again. "But the main thing is to get him up out of the ground where somebody can look at him before the....." ... He looked at Lucas. "I'll have to get out there and dig him up and get back to town before midnight or one oclock and maybe even midnight will be too late. I dont see how I can do it. I cant do it'."
> "I'll try to wait," Lucas said. (71–2)

Lucas's laconic reply refers both to his awareness that he is in jail and therefore going nowhere himself, and that he is also obviously vulnerable to the lynch mob that may take him from that jail before Chick can complete his task. But perhaps at some level Lucas is also answering Gavin Stevens's complacent assurance that although injustice endures, it will not prevail. "Soon this sort of thing wont even threaten anymore" he tells Chick, "It shouldn't now. It should never have" (151). But apparently it will, at least for a little longer. " I'll try to wait" implies that the time of waiting indeed was running out.

Notes

1. From a rejected prefatory note to the novel (Blotner, *A Biography*, Vol. 2, Notes, 165).
2. Richard Gray points out that for pro-slavery theorists the concept of an organic community was essentially Aristotelian: "one which defines the social group as an organism, complex and inegalitarian, a harmony of different

interests and castes" (140). In *Intruder*, neither Stevens nor the novel as a whole proposes that inegalitarian dimension. The linkages among the very different social levels in Yoknapatawpha, as we shall see, suggest not so much a "harmony of castes," but a harmony of peers.

3. Faulkner's respect for the people of Beat Four as admirably self-sufficient, if violent, and self-protective against government is evident in the similarity between his description in *Intruder* and the one of Frenchman's Bend in *The Hamlet*. See, for example, *Intruder* (35) and *The Hamlet* (5).

4. Both Brooks (465) and Kirk and Klotz (126) err in identifying N. B. Forrest Gowrie, named as Amanda Workitt's husband on her tombstone (*Intruder* 100), as Nub's oldest son. If we assume that the novel takes place around the time of its writing, Amanda, whose dates are 1878–1926, must be Nub's deceased wife. Forrest Gowrie has married (160), but not to a woman born in 1878.

5. At one point Gavin Stevens seems to imply that black homogeneity is separate and different from white, in that the Negro "has a better homogeneity than we have," (152). Presumably the white community can combine with the black and "dominate the United States" (143). Whether this is an example of what Towner calls "deeply misguided babble on racial matters" (33), or simply of Stevens's penchant for talking faster than he can think, the fact remains that commonalities shared by Lucas and Gowrie and Miss Habersham suggest that a single, shared homogeneity already exists and needs only to be acknowledged by both black and white communities. See, for example, the early review by Walter Allen, "The truth, as Mr. Faulkner sees it, is that the South, white and coloured alike, is inextricably one family...it is a family relation as well as an opposition between colours" (105–6).

6. See for example the discussion by Schmitz (251–55).

7. The scene repeats the fall into racism of Roth Edmonds in *Go Down, Moses*, who also sees that his regret and subsequent shame over his show of superiority is "forever and forever too late" (109).

8. Towner's version of this faith is "Chick's recognition of Lucas as Subject" (32). It is interesting to note that, although the community apparently comes to complete agreement as to the identity of the murderer, no real "proof" is ever supplied. Sheriff Hampton tells Nub Gowrie that Vinson was shot with a German Luger, known to belong to Crawford Gowrie (161, 175), but there is no medical examination of Vinson's body before the Gowries (re)bury him. "Shared assumptions" remains the only evidence.

9. A translation of *Totem and Taboo* by A. A. Brill was published in 1918, and was reissued by Random House in 1938.

10. Prior to *Intruder in the Dust*, *The Hamlet* (1940), focusing on Frenchman's Bend, is the Faulkner novel that comes closest to the depiction of the homogeneous community at work.

11. One such disaster, according to Frye, occurs at the more ironic levels of comedy, "in which comedy consists of inflicting pain on a hopeless victim, and tragedy in enduring it," as for example, with "the black man of a lynching" (45).

12. M. E. Bradford's reading of the novel as "a parable about the relation of the

sections within the context of the United States and about the worthlessness of racial reforms that are merely 'given' to the Negro before he has earned them" (47) seems to me wholly erroneous.

Works Cited

Allen, Walter. "Mr. Faulkner's Humanity. In Claridge, vol. 4, 104–107.
Bassett, John. *William Faulkner: The Critical Heritage*. London: Routledge & Kegan Paul, 1975.
Blotner, Joseph. *Faulkner: A Biography*. 2 vols. New York: Random House, 1974.
Bradford, M. E. "Faulkner, James Baldwin, and the South." In Claridge, vol. 4, 477–86.
-----. "Text and Context: Reading Faulkner's *Intruder in the Dust*." *The Intercollegiate Review*. 27 (1992): 45–50.
Brooks, Cleanth. *William Faulkner: The Yoknapatawpha Country*. New Haven: Yale University Press, 1963.
Claridge, Henry, ed. *William Faulkner: Critical Assessments*. 4 vols. The Banks, Mountfield: Helm Information, 1999.
Faulkner, William. *Go Down, Moses*. [1942] New York: Vintage International, 1990.
-----. *The Hamlet*. [1940] New York: Vintage International, 1991.
-----. *Intruder in the Dust*. [1948] New York: Vintage International, 1991.
-----. *Selected Letters of William Faulkner*. Ed Joseph Blotner. New York: Random House, 1977.
Freud, Sigmund. *Totem and Taboo*. Trans. and Ed. James Strachey. New York: W. W. Norton & Co., 1950.
Frye, Northrop. *Anatomy of Criticism: Four Essays*. Princeton: Princeton University Press, 1957.
Gray, Richard. *Writing the South: Ideas of an American Region*. Cambridge: Cambridge University Press, 1986.
Kartiganer, Donald M. and Abadie, Ann J., eds. *Faulkner in Cultural Context: Faulkner and Yoknapatawpha, 1995*. Jackson: University Press of Mississippi, 1997.
Kirk, Robert W. with Klotz, Marvin. *Faulkner's People: A Complete Guide and Index to the Characters in the Fiction of William Faulkner*. Berkeley: University of California Press, 1963.
Morris, Wesley with Morris, Barbara. *Reading Faulkner*. Madison: University of Wisconsin Press, 1989.
Polk, Noel. *Children of the Dark House: Text and Context in Faulkner*. Jackson: University Press of Mississippi. 1996.
Schmitz, Neil. "Faulkner and the Post-Confederate." Kartiganer and Abadie, 241–62.
Towner, Theresa M. *Faulkner on the Color Line: The Later Novels*. Jackson: University Press of Mississippi, 2000.
Weinstein, Philip. *Faulkner's Subject: A Cosmos No One Owns*. Cambridge: Cambridge University Press, 1992.
Wilson, Edmund. "William Faulkner's Reply to the Civil-Rights Program." Bassett, 332–39.

CONTEXTUALIZING FAULKNER'S INTRUDER IN THE DUST: SHERLOCK HOLMES, CHICK MALLISON, DECOLONIZATION, AND CHANGE

Richard C. Moreland

To contextualize a Faulkner novel is difficult even on the generalized level of literary epochs like realism, modernism, and postmodernism. Not impossible or futile, but difficult. This is not just because some of his readers have attempted to elevate his fiction above most history, politics, and institutions (for reasons partly historical, political, and institutional). It is also because Faulkner wrote and has been read in times and circumstances that have themselves become difficult to contextualize in the manner of most humanist, Hegelian attempts to explain a society in terms of one "expressive totality" or one "primary and fundamental principle of power which dominates society down to the smallest detail," tendencies criticized by Louis Althusser (17) and Michel Foucault (224) respectively,[1] and in cultural criticism more generally. Without minimizing the effects of such domination, Faulkner's novels suggest the complexity of its sources, its effects, and its intersections with forces and forms of resistance and social change. In a memorial lecture for James Snead, whose work many Faulkner readers know, Cornel West has attempted to historicize, pluralize, and contextualize recent debates about postmodernism in terms of the current vocation of intellectuals, arguing especially for a role for intellectuals that "fundamentally links the life of the mind, the best of the life of the mind, to the best of organized forces for social change, even in this conservative moment in which we find ourselves" (3, 19). West's lecture may also help to contextualize a novel like Faulkner's *Intruder in the Dust* (1948), a book which articulates and offers to its readers a series of intellectual vocations, roles, or subject-positions significantly different from those offered to readers of, say, Arthur Conan Doyle's popular stories in turn-of-the-century England about the detective-intellectual Sherlock Holmes.

West recalls the intellectual vocations proposed by a series of four cultural critics—Matthew Arnold, T. S. Eliot, Lionel Trilling, and Frantz Fanon—in the context of three overlapping historical changes. The first of these three changes, marked especially by "World" Wars I and II, was the end of the age of Europe as the center of world power (also the end of a certain cultural confidence in realism and humanism). The second change was the U.S. ascent to a similar position of almost uncontested world power from about 1945 to 1973, with the important difference that its colonized Third World existed more obviously both without and within its home borders. This meant that this high tide of U.S. world power was accompanied by persistent questions of hybridity and heterogeneity both abroad and at home, in the canonization, for example, of a modernist aesthetic of contradiction, tension, and paradox. The third change, running alongside or beneath these changes of dominant world powers, was the Third World's decolonization throughout this century, a change characterized especially by increased cultural attention to questions of violence and identity. All of these cultural changes impinge on a novel like *Intruder in the Dust* (1948) and intersect there as dominant, residual, emergent, and otherwise marginalized forces and forms in a variety of discursive and social fields, including several in which "the intellectual" as writer, reader, and activist is significantly involved.

West summarizes Matthew Arnold's influential acknowledgment that religion, "the glue that fragilely held together the old aristocratic-led regimes in the sixteenth, seventeenth and eighteenth centuries, could not do so in the nineteenth century," so that Arnold proposed instead a "new secular culture of critical discourse…that would contain and incorporate the frightening threats of an arrogant aristocracy and especially an anarchic 'working majority'" (West 6–7). When these and other threats could not be contained either as individuals or cultures under the influence of cultural "sweetness and light," the new critical-intellectual discourse of secular culture would be able to justify the state's repressing them on the model of imperial Rome's casting convicted murderers off the Tarpeian Rock (7–8). Already important here, obviously, are questions of hybridity and heterogeneity, more characteristic of modernist culture, as well as questions of violence and identity, more characteristic of postcolonial and postmodernist culture, but the emphasis is on humanist European culture's imperial power—rather, its obvious cultural obligation—to define and confirm the human and the real.

In several ways this is the function of one of the most well-known intellectual figures in English-language literature, Sherlock Holmes. As read by Franco Moretti, Doyle's fiction has continued to articulate and offer to its realist readers a subject-position that provides them with an imaginary social coherence and personal identity in the conformity and empirical common sense of nineteenth-century imperial Britain's emergent middle class. This reassuring subject-position for the middle-class reader is produced especially by means of Holmes's ability to detect and demonstrate for Watson (the reader's most accessible stand-in) the potentially confusing but eventually plain signs of difference and anomaly that distinguish crime from its antithesis in the uneventful and innocent everyday workings of middle-class capitalist society. Such telltale signs of (class) difference and anomaly characterize not only crime's perpetrators (usually aristocratic hoarders or defiant proletarian thieves), but also its detectors (the refined Holmes, not to mention Poe's Dupin) and even its victims (whose own anomalies somehow "ask for" criminal victimization). The familiarity of these formulations suggest how persistent and powerful such realist discourses of crime and detection remain even today.

Faulkner's *Intruder* can hardly avoid comparison with Doyle's stories insofar as this novel evokes the detective genre as an important precedent for its own signifying practice, less pointedly than the stories of *Knight's Gambit* do, but more pointedly than *Absalom, Absalom!* and *Go Down, Moses* do.[2] Chick Mallison, from whose, or rather for whose, point of view the novel is narrated in free indirect discourse, admires his European-educated and cultured uncle and moral and intellectual mentor Gavin Stevens (much as Watson does Holmes), but Chick does not entirely trust, understand, or communicate with Stevens, and Chick eventually grows impatient and acts without him, acts instead with his black friend Aleck Sander and an old, odd woman named Miss Habersham. In other words, the innocent, middle-class conformist subject-position prepared by Holmes for Watson and for the readers led to occupy Watson's place in the story is recapitulated here between Stevens and Chick, but it is a subject-position shown in this novel not to work according to the expected (perhaps unconsciously expected) genre script. It becomes a false lead, an almost untenable imaginary identity for the reader. But Stevens's moral and intellectual authority (by virtue of genre, gender, class, race, profession, and historical moment) does not therefore simply disappear, any more than "classic realism" is superseded by modernism or postmodernism except in particular currents in particular texts—particular discursive and social practices. His authority is, however, historicized and contextualized in Faulkner's novel.

Like Arnold or Holmes, Stevens is inclined to pronounce Lucas Beauchamp guilty by anomaly, guilty by virtue of his highly ambiguous, unstable (and potentially destabilizing) association with the classes both above and below the white middle class, though that white "middle" needs to be translated and redefined from the nineteenth-century British context to that of the early twentieth-century American South. The class tensions focused on by Moretti between the British aristocracy and working classes are here mediated by a racially defined white "middle" that still contains significant tensions, for example, between what Numan Bartley calls the "plantation-oriented county-seat governing class," such as Stevens, and the "white common folk" and "poor whites" of Beat Four (1154). That is, on the one hand, Beauchamp looks suspicious because of his dignified manner and outspoken pride in his aristocratic, patriarchal descent, both of which dangerously evoke a residual plantation discourse that irks both the "common folk" and "poor white" elements within the unstable "white" ideological coalition. On the other hand, Beauchamp also looks suspicious because of his unspoken but unmistakable defiance of the low social station to which he is assigned by social and legal definition, thereby also evoking another dangerous discourse in the potentially emergent resentment and resistance of the working classes (see Michael Goldfield). These ambiguous differences from the white "middle" (and the differences within that middle to which they call disturbing attention) have earned Beauchamp the longstanding suspicion, the unstable but thus also intensely defensive suspicion, of those Stevens calls the "homogeneous people" of the white South (400). In this Arnoldian voice with a Southern accent, Stevens suggests both a knowing assurance of homogeneity and a sense that this assurance may be a defensive shield against an impending or even an already present crisis:

> Only a few of us know that only from homogeneity comes anything of a people or for a people of durable and lasting value—the literature, the art, the science, that minimum of government and police which is the meaning of freedom and liberty, and perhaps most valuable of all a national character worth anything in a crisis.... (400)

Nor is Chick himself immune to the seductive identity offered him in the image of "one unalterable durable impregnable one: one people one heart one land" (442). But while *Intruder* registers the continuing force of this (adapted) humanist legacy even in a small Mississippi town after the end of World War II, the novel soon denies Chick and the novel's readers and even Stevens himself any such reassuring identification with a homogeneous European or even European-American middle class, in ways that parallel changes West describes in intellectual vocations since the times when Doyle and Arnold wrote. The image of this homogeneous people, heart, and land gathered under the watchful eye of the critical intellectual will turn out here to be rather a defensive back-formation by an intellectual speaking on behalf of a people, heart, and land that is already much more hybrid and heterogeneous than this intellectual and this model of the intellectual recognizes, not just recently but throughout its various histories. It is a people, heart, and land that has always defined itself in its relationship to this hybridity and heterogeneity.

Arnold's confidence in secular European culture was not shared by his successor in West's genealogy of critics, T. S. Eliot, due perhaps in part to intervening events that removed Europe from the world's center-stage, notably the devastation, division, and disillusionment left behind by Europe's two World Wars. World War I "brought to the surface," West writes, not merely the violence of outsiders against the middle class but also the violence of "the very institutions that Arnold valued, the violence of the state itself" (9). As an expatriate American, Eliot may also have been more sensitive than Arnold to signs of the hybridity and heterogeneity that would become increasingly obvious, according to West, during the coming period of relatively undisputed world power for the United States (1945–73). This would be a hybridity and heterogeneity not just to be kept at bay by means of sweetness and light or to be detected and occasionally expelled by force, but to be found almost everywhere already well *within* the pale of "civilization," even within the predominantly middle-class society of the mid-twentieth-century United States. While Eliot's poetry may in some ways and moments gather the courage now apparently necessary to "force the moment to its crisis," his cultural criticism tends more clearly to turn back in reaction against the specter of a chaotic modern waste land toward a European religious tradition older and supposedly more stable and profound than Arnold's secular traditions. Comparable to this attempted retreat from impending crisis to Eliot's higher Tradition are a number of other religious, ideological, and nationalist revivals throughout this century in the Second and Third Worlds, as the centrality first of Europe and then of the United States is challenged and displaced and the Third World is gradually decolonized. This decolonization is the third historical moment in West's chronology, overlapping or running under the other two, and many of its implications are partly recognized as well in Eliot's poetry, even if they are also more clearly fended off in his cultural criticism. Eliot's modernism represents the second of these three historical moments, a kind of precarious stopping point, both recognizing the emergence of and warding off decolonization as the third of these historical moments.

Faulkner's novel also registers something of this influential religious, apocalyptic, modernist reaction to the end of the age of Europe and the rapid rise of the United States "from a stage of perceived innocence to corruption [and violence] without a mediating moment of maturity" (F. O. Matthiessen; cited without references by West 10). This modernist sense of unpreparedness is evident, for example, in Chick's adolescent consciousness in moments of helpless horror before the potential violence of the white citizenry toward Lucas Beauchamp:

> ...it seemed to him now that he was responsible for having brought into the light and glare of day something shocking and shameful out of the whole white foundation of the county which he himself must partake of too since he too was bred of it, which otherwise might have flared and blazed merely out of Beat Four and then vanished back into its darkness or at least invisibility with the fading embers of Lucas' crucifixion. (388)

He may have brought this quasi-state violence to light and exposed its connection to "the whole white foundation of the country," but his own initial reaction to this discovery is flight, and he does not expect this shock and shame to prevent, but rather to exacerbate, the rest of the white coalition's scapegoating violence toward Beauchamp. That is, Chick doubts here the historical effectiveness of this modernist recognition either against the patterned response of the town's white coalition or in his own response, since the tendency of such a modernism of shock and shame is to cast doubt on all moral and political action that is in any way derived from this "white foundation of the country." It suggests instead an individualized retreat, a moralistic, characteristically American retreat from the corruption of action and politics, which effectively leaves an open field to the social operations of American capitalism's "invisible hand." It is thus all too easy to see in this 1948 novel "the degree to which modernism became part of the ideological arsenal used in the cold war against the Soviets" (West 5). Thomas Schaub has shown how such modernist suspicions of all "political" action were read in the Cold War context of U.S. politics as a criticism of actively oppositional, that is, left-leaning politics as opposed to the business-as-usual of an apparently non-political American version of democracy and capitalism. And Lawrence Schwartz has shown how Faulkner and Trilling (West's third cultural critic) figured more specifically in this Cold War politics.

But at least this modernist recognition about the corrupt "foundation" of the white coalition is forceful enough in this novel to make the realist Arnold-Holmes position (usually articulated by Stevens) almost untenable for Faulkner's readers, even if no easily recognized or unsuspicious alternative readily presents itself. Stevens is shown clearly not to be the character who would normally masterfully *detect* who the criminal is and thus empirically *solve* the crime for his innocent listening and reading audiences, according to the genre's script of expectations. Even those members of the white coalition within the novel who were most ready to lynch Lucas Beauchamp come to recognize that the *criminal* has in this case turned out not to be Beauchamp as the anomalous outsider, as they had thought and as Stevens thought, but one of their own. Likewise, the *crime* has turned out not to be the expected danger from outside (a black-on-white murder), nor only the murder of one white brother by another white brother out in the less civilized, lower-class corner of the county known as Beat Four. The crime has come to include also the white coalition's own method of detection and their own near murder of another of their racially hybrid and heterogeneous "brothers" in Lucas Beauchamp, another brother whose family relation and racial likeness-in-difference the white coalition has tried unsuccessfully to expel and deny. Even

Chick has hoped at one point that "he was no longer Lucas' keeper" (315). Their readiness to deny and murder another supposedly threatening outsider has exposed their capacity to murder each other more generally within and throughout the hybrid, heterogeneous history of the United States. But this long history of lynchings is represented here as coming close to an end. Why? How?

If this modernist knowledge has made Chick feel, and has invited readers to feel, alternately, both an observer's self-righteous horror and an implicated guilt and shame, neither position leads anywhere practically or historically in this novel, and somehow Chick knows better than Stevens not to attempt to stop there on the modernist (especially American modernist) watershed between innocence and its apparently inevitable, contradictory, paralyzing alternative in violence and corruption. As Stevens articulates what he has learned not from his own or from Chick's realist or modernist knowledge but from Chick's actions with Aleck Sander and Miss Habersham during the course of this novel, "Tenderfoot is, Dont accept. Eagle Scout is, Dont stop. You see? No, that's wrong. Dont even bother to see. Dont even bother to not forget it. Just dont stop." As Chick replies, "We dont need to worry about stopping now. It seems to me what we have to worry about is where we're going and how" (442). Whatever the temptation to stop or to turn back may be for Arnold, Doyle, Eliot, Trilling, and Stevens, at least Stevens might also be learning here from Chick that stopping is not only not to be recommended, but is not an option, at least not for long, if history and politics are allowed to enter into this novelistic account.

To this novel's credit, I think, Stevens's topical remarks do allow such history and politics to enter openly into this novelistic account. While Stevens stopped, as Chick was also tempted to stop, Chick himself recognized that the community and others would continue to act in one way or another, whether or not he participated in determining "where we're going and how." As an intellectual figure, Stevens functions here less as state power's Arnoldian guide, explainer, or justifier (something like what Althusser would call an ideological state apparatus) than as an ineffectual, perhaps co-opted figure on the sidelines of power—though one who might learn something important from that very ineffectiveness.

I have argued elsewhere that the South's history of slavery, defeat in the Civil War, Reconstruction, and a kind of colonization of its economy for decades afterward forced Matthiessen's logic of innocence and corruption into at least some quarters of the South's consciousness earlier and to a greater extent than in other parts of the United States. This makes the twentieth-century South ripe not only for what C. Vann Woodward has called the largely modernist "Irony of Southern History," but also for a local version of the generally later American turn away from modernisms whose transgressive power would come to seem circumscribed, diluted, and co-opted (as in the cases of Chick and especially Stevens, discussed above), toward postmodern problematics "of difference, of marginality, of otherness, of alterity and subalternity, of being subjugated and subordinated" (West 5-6). More than the rest of the United States, the South has also shared many of the decolonizing Third World's experiences of the "long-festering underside of modernity...not only within European colonies but also within the United States itself":

> The first thing to note here is the centrality of violence, the degree to which a person begins to recognize just how ugly and brutal the world really is. Not simply, of course, the mushroom clouds of Hiroshima and Nagasaki, not simply the concentration camps—the Holocaust—but also the everyday violence...the European [or European-American] violence and brutal subjugation of colonized persons. Also it has to do with issues of identity...in which persons no longer view themselves as objects of history, but rather as subjects of history. (13)

Frantz Fanon, the cultural critic in West's genealogy most concerned with such histories of decolonization, stresses especially the "long-festering scent of denial and deep degradation" and "the impetuous ferocity of moral outrage" whose articulation is characterized especially by a sense of unbuffered violence, intense polemics, and polarized identities (whether of ideology, nation, gender, race, or class). According to West, the organized social movements and cultural critiques associated with postmodernism and decolonization may indeed "focus principally on the silences and the blindnesses and the exclusions of the male WASP cultural homogeneity and its concomitant notions of the canon." And this unavoidable engagement with dominant traditions may often appear manichean and apocalyptic, as if to suggest that the empire is not just striking back but exploding into inexplicable chaos. But these same social movements and cultural critiques have drawn on the radical scepticism of "travelling theories" from Europe in ways that have helped not only to create opportunities for attacks against the metaphysics of presence, but also to create openings for ongoing social and cultural change, including the revision of American historiography in the light of those it has tended to exclude, as well as a new attention to the impact of these and other groups and individuals on both popular and "highbrow literate culture" (West 14–16). Decolonization and postmodernism together bring into focus a set of forces and questions that both realism and modernism have tended to blur.

Chick's question about where we're going and how, after the shock of modernism (unlike Yeats's more rhetorical, apocalyptic question, "After such knowledge, what forgiveness?"), is directed beyond or aside from that sometimes stalling or fixating moment of horror and reaction, toward the changing and multiple social and personal histories within which it also has its place. Stevens's "go-slow" argument against the imposition of civil rights legislation on Southern states by Northern states is in part the argument of an apologist for the status quo, and in part the argument of a white Southerner understandably suspicious of Northern attempts to project and reduce the pervasive, structural problems of race in the United States onto a simple moral problem for the white South (on the humanist, Hegelian model of an expressive or spiritual totality). But he is also concerned with the problem of how

Southern white society can move beyond the logic of violent, repeated denial and repression of the (therefore) violent, repeated return of the repressed—much as Freud came to recognize that the psychoanalytic cure depends not simply on a recovery of and confrontation with the repressed, but on a changed representation of and relationship to such knowledge, developed by means of the imaginative and social work of transference and analysis. Stevens is fully aware of the characteristically modernist risk of denial and reaction if this knowledge is simply thrust in the face of the white South, but he is less aware of how such denial and reaction might be avoided through some such imaginative and social transference and analysis.

In the course of Faulkner's novel, however, Lucas Beauchamp (like Old Ephraim and Miss Habersham) knows better than Stevens does, and can even help Chick (along with the reader) to discover that Chick already knows better himself than Stevens does, that the knowledge that Stevens thinks of as so completely and dangerously repressed by the white population and familiar only to the black population (as the supposedly passive objects of a tragic history) is a knowledge already accessible and familiar to many whose identities are less unified and less polarized according to race and historical moment than Stevens tends to think, many who are not confronting the everyday violence of the state's repressive apparatuses for the first dramatic time. As Chick wonders about his own relationship to the knowledge uncovered in the Gowrie grave, wondering why Lucas would appeal to him and his black friend Aleck Sander and the old Miss Habersham (who was "born in the same week" as Lucas's late wife Molly and had "suckled at Molly's mother's breast and grown up together [with Molly] almost inextricably like sisters, like twins" 349)—as Chick wonders why an old woman and two boys are left to "solve the crime" instead of someone like Stevens or the sheriff, Chick remembers and reconsiders at least three times in the novel something he already half-knew, something another old black man named Ephraim once explained to him about finding something that was lost:

Young folks and womens, they aint cluttered. They can listen. But a middle-year man like your paw and your uncle, they cant listen. They aint got time. They're too busy with facks. In fact, you mought bear this in yo mind; someday you mought need it. If you ever needs to get anything done outside the common run, dont waste yo time on the menfolks get the womens and children to working at it. (*Go Down, Moses* 337)³

Too busy with the empirical facts most readily defined by and therefore fitted and counted within the dominant capitalist economy, too busy with the unified subjects that same economy attempts to define and sort by race, gender, class, or age, and too busy defining the historical moment in terms of the fate of dominant powers, the (white) "menfolk" are all too liable to think themselves and others incapable of dealing with anything "outside the common run": other definitions of knowledge, other less unified and autonomous definitions of subjectivity, and other more complexly historicized definitions of events.

This may be why Lucas Beauchamp at the end of the novel insists on a written receipt from Stevens, who has charged him two dollars not for his legal services but for the fountain pen point Stevens says he broke in frustration "trying to write down all the different things you finally told me in such a way that Mr Hampton could get enough sense out of it to discharge you from the jail" (468). Beauchamp tells Stevens, "whether you know your business or not I reckon it aint none of my red wagon as the music box says to try to learn you different"; nevertheless, Beauchamp does insist on challenging and encouraging Stevens's capacity for a suppler (more subtly contextualized) humor, courage, and intelligence (and intellectual role) by waiting for Stevens to write him a receipt. Beauchamp effectively urges Stevens, that is, that he can listen to the different things Beauchamp (along with the popular blues lyrics from the music box) is telling him and can try writing it down again in a different form of his own language, however factual and inflexible that language of business receipts may seem to be. Stevens can listen and learn from Chick and Beauchamp, and Chick can listen and learn from Old Ephraim, Beauchamp, Aleck Sander, and Miss Habersham, because they have all always already heard it before in this less moralistic, more specifically historicized, pluralized, and contextualized sense of cultural reality. It is a matter of learning how to listen and learn from what they have already heard.

Beauchamp has urged this same kind of analytic, transferential learning on Chick, and the novel urges a similar learning on its readers. The novel is organized around a few dramatic, isolating, and polarizing events, but they are repeated under a number of different lights that suggest ways in which powerful cultural myths, or "narratemes," such as those of lynching or detection figured here, might not change, but also might change, might be changing. The novel's readers, like its characters, then and now, are defined by their histories and contexts, but in a complex variety of ways, such that apparently isolated events and actions can have unexpectedly far-reaching implications and effects.[4] The novel's readers and characters are already variously involved not only in the shift of world power from Europe to the United States, but also in the Third World's decolonization both abroad and at home in a number of different discursive fields. They are already affected in different ways by traveling theories of radical skepticism, by organized social movements of more or less marginalized groups, by changing historical accounts of our past and present, and by variously revisionist currents of popular culture. All these complexities make stopping or turning back from crisis on a single historical line difficult to imagine. Such complexities thus make it difficult to contextualize such a novel as this one, not because the novel is above or outside history, but because the interaction between the novel and its readers takes place in so many different times and histories at once. Difficult to contextualize: not impossible or futile, but difficult. But the nature of this difficulty in turn makes learning and change possible. Not simple or certain, but possible.

Notes

1. See Easthope (216 and *passim*) for a useful discussion of these criticisms.
2. Patrick McHugh has suggested to me in a letter other intriguing connections between Faulkner's work and the detective genre as it continues to change after Sherlock Holmes. McHugh asks whether "the Gavin Stevens of *Knight's Gambit*, a sort of hard-boiled Prufrock, is Faulkner's answer to the Sam Spades and Philip Marlowes so popular in the Thirties, while the Stevens of *Intruder* might be some kind of critical comment on the (modernist) approach to justice? Similarly, the postmodern detective story might be connected to your reading of the direction Beauchamp points out to Chick Mallison and Stevens." I regret that these suggestions, which sound right to me in general, are beyond the scope of this essay.
3. See also *Intruder in the Dust* (351, 368).
4. Compare Ilya Prigogine and Isabelle Stengers on the idea of bifurcations in physical systems: "From the physicist's point of view this involves a distinction between states of the system in which all individual initiative is doomed to insignificance on one hand, and on the other, bifurcation regions in which an individual, an idea, or a new behavior can upset the global state. Even in those regions, amplification obviously does not occur with just any individual, idea, or behaviors, but only with those that are 'dangerous'—that is, those that can exploit to their advantage the nonlinear relations guaranteeing the stability of the preceding regime" (206).

Works Cited

Althusser, Louis and Etienne Balibar. *Reading Capital*. Trans. Ben Brewster. London: New Left, 1975.

Bartley, Numan. "Politics and Ideology." *Encyclopedia of Southern Culture*. Eds. Charles Reagan Wilson and William Ferris. Chapel Hill: U of North Carolina P, 1989. 1151–58.

Easthope, Antony. *British Post-Structuralism Since 1968*. New York: Routledge, 1988.

Faulkner, William. *Intruder in the Dust*. New York: Random House, 1948.

-----. *William Faulkner: Novels 1942–1954*. New York: Library of America, 1994.

Foucault, Michel. "Afterword: The Subject and Power." *Michel Foucault: Beyond Structuralism and Hermeneutics*. Eds. Hubert L. Dreyfus and Paul Rabinow. Brighton: Harvester, 1982. 208–26,

Goldfield, Michael. "The Color of Politics in the United States: White Supremacy as the Main Explanation for the Peculiarities of American Politics from Colonial Times to the Present." *The Bounds of Race: Perspectives on Hegemony and Resistance*. Ed. Dominick LaCapra. Ithaca: Cornell UP, 1991. 104–33.

Moreland, Richard C. *Faulkner and Modernism: Rereading and Rewriting*. Madison: U of Wisconsin P, 1990.

Moretti, Franco. "Clues." *Signs Taken for Wonders: Essays in the Sociology of Literary Forms*. Rev. ed. Trans. Susan Fischer, David Forgacs, and David Miller. London:

Verso, 1988. 130–56.
Prigogine, Ilya and Isabelle Stengers. *Order Out of Chaos.* New York: Bantam, 1984.
Schaub, Thomas Hill. *American Fiction in the Cold War.* Madison: U of Wisconsin P, 1991.
Schwartz, Lawrence H. *Creating Faulkner's Reputation: The Politics of Modern Literary Criticism.* Knoxville: U of Tennessee P, 1988.
West, Cornel. "Decentering Europe: A Memorial Lecture for James Snead, Introduced by Colin McCabe." *Critical Quarterly* 33.1 (1991): 1–19.
Woodward, C. Vann, ed. "The Irony of Southern History." *The Burden of Southern History.* 3rd. ed. Baton Rouge: Louisiana State UP, 1993. 187–212.

MAN IN THE MIDDLE: FAULKNER AND THE SOUTHERN WHITE MODERATE

Noel Polk

For Evans Harrington

William Faulkner wrote *Intruder in the Dust* in the winter and early spring of 1948, seasons during which the Mississippi Democratic party geared itself for a vital confrontation with the national Democratic party at the summer convention in Philadelphia, over the report of President Truman's Commission on Civil Rights. Truman was urging Congress "to adopt his civil rights program embodying voting rights, employment opportunities, and other provisions destined to draw fire from Southern Democrats."[1] Governor Fielding Wright called a meeting of Mississippi Democrats for February 12, Lincoln's birthday, in Jackson. All members of the legislature attended, hoping to find some way to counter in advance the proposed civil rights planks in the national party's platform. On February 22, Washington's birthday, Mississippi Democrats met with representatives from the Democratic parties of nine other Southern states to plan strategies to force upon the Democratic platform planks favoring states', rather than civil, rights. Failing to sway the national body at the August convention, the entire Mississippi delegation and part of Alabama's walked out. In a subsequent convention in Birmingham Southern delegates founded the so-called Dixiecrat party, which nominated the fiery states' righter Governor Strom Thurmond of South Carolina for president and Mississippi's own Governor Wright for vice-president. Mississippi voted 87 percent for the Dixiecrat ticket, and was joined in the colossal losing battle by South Carolina, Louisiana, and Alabama.[2] The political and emotional issues at stake in this Dixiecrat year—states' rights, anti-lynching laws, mongrelization, the future of the white race, and other associated issues—were surely not lost on William Faulkner as he wrote *Intruder* in the spring and then saw it through the press during the summer.

Intruder was published on September 27. On October 23 Edmund Wilson wrote in the *New Yorker* that *Intruder* seemed to have been, at least "partly...stimulated by the crisis at the time of the war in the relations between Negroes and whites and by the recently proposed legislation for guaranteeing Negro rights. The book contains," Wilson went on, "a kind of counterblast to the anti-lynching bill and to the civil-rights plank in the Democratic platform." This was a line that many reviewers would take, and most commentators since have agreed with Wilson's assessment that "the author's ideas on this subject are apparently conveyed, in their explicit form, by the intellectual uncle, who, more and more as the story goes on, gives vent to long disquisitions that seem to become so 'editorial' in character that...the series may be pieced together as something in the nature of a public message delivered by the author himself."[3] About the time Wilson's review appeared, Faulkner paid his first visit to the New England home of Malcolm Cowley, a friend since their collaboration on *The Portable Faulkner* of 1946. Cowley had reviewed *Intruder* for *The New Republic* along the same lines as Wilson, although he had been a bit more generous than Wilson about the novel. In writing about Faulkner's visit, Cowley reports that Faulkner discussed *Intruder* in terms that might have been an "indirect answer" to his review: "[Gavin] Stevens, he [Faulkner] explained, was not speaking for the author, but for the best type of liberal Southerners; that is how they feel about the Negroes."[4]

In this comment to Cowley, Faulkner seems to be distancing himself from Stevens and his views on the South's racial problems in a way that should make the average New Critic very proud, although to be sure, it is not a distance many new or old critics either have been successful at finding. Yet barely three months later, in January 1949, he sent to Robert Haas, at Random House, a two-page addition to *Intruder* that he wanted inserted if there were ever a second printing: it was something, he wrote, that he had "remembered…last year only after the book was in press."[5] What he sent Haas, on February 7, was a two-page addition to Stevens's long speech on Southern blacks and whites as the only homogeneous groups left in the United States. In the addition Faulkner has Stevens conclude this speech with the prediction that social and political assimilation of whites and blacks will eventually result in the extinction of the black race. In the closing lines of the speech, Faulkner makes Stevens actually refer to and quote from *Absalom, Absalom!*, a book, Stevens says, by "a mild retiring little man over yonder at Oxford"; he quotes what he calls the book's "tag line," from a conversation, he says, between a "Canadian [and a] self-lacerated Southerner in a dormitory room in a not too authentic Harvard." He identifies the "tag line" as Shreve's parting shot to Quentin on the subject of the amalgamation of the races—"I who regard you will have also sprung from the loins of African kings."[6]

In identifying Stevens as "the best type of liberal Southerner," Faulkner was placing him in pretty good company—the company of such people as Hodding Carter, P. D. East, James Silver, Frank Smith, Duncan Gray, and many others, all of whom risked lives and fortunes in numerous ways in the fight for racial justice in the South. If Faulkner, in responding to Cowley, was distancing himself from Stevens, was he simultaneously taking himself out of the company of what he called "the best type of liberal Southerners"? If so, why did he go out of his way to inject himself, by way of Stevens's reference, into what Stevens has to say? If he were trying to distance himself, did he have in mind another category for such Southerners as himself? Was he trying to make some sort of statement about the "best type of liberal Southerner"? Was he, in speaking to Cowley, being serious, then, or was he simply putting on his novelist's mask of anonymity? Did he have a different opinion of this "type" of "liberal Southerner" in 1948 than he was to develop during his association and public identification with them during the fifties?

Granted, it is difficult to escape a considerable sense of urgency, of "message" in Stevens's diatribe against the North, and equally difficult to resist assuming that Stevens is mouthing Faulkner's own sentiments, especially given the similarity of Faulkner's rhetoric to Stevens's as his own public involvement in civil rights issues grew over the next few years. Nevertheless, we need to take seriously Faulkner's effort to distance himself from Stevens. The novel itself insists that we be careful about Stevens's opinions about race. Stevens is, in *Intruder*, as in the other works in which he appears, more interested in talking than doing. The essence of Stevens in *Intruder* is not the political relevance to 1948 of his diatribe against the North, but rather, I would argue, his inability to see past the persiflage of his own words. Three times in the closing pages Faulkner describes Stevens as talking while he smokes his cob pipe:

> his uncle even struck the match to the cob pipe still talking not just through the smoke but into it with it;

> his uncle struck the match again and puffed the pipe still talking, talking through the pipe stem with the smoke as though you were watching the words themselves;

> again his uncle was striking the match, holding it to the pipe and speaking through with into the smoke.[7]

It could hardly be clearer that in *Intruder* Gavin Stevens is largely blowing smoke—not altogether because of what he says, however, but because of the relationship between what he says and what he actually does. Stevens says to the North: let the South free the black man; we owe it to him and we will pay him and we don't need anybody to interfere. Yet *Intruder* is precisely about the wrongful imprisonment of an innocent black man; given the opportunity to defend Lucas in court, or even to listen to his side of the story, Stevens—the "type" of the best of liberal Southerners—hastens to an assumption of Lucas's guilt that is worthy of even the reddest of Beat Four necks. Proven wrong by his nephew's impetuous trust of Lucas, Stevens takes some pains to elbow, and mouth, his way into Lucas's salvation. Much of what he has to say, then, should be taken as a vain attempt to fill up the gap between what Chick has done and what he has failed, with all the best intentions, to do: to act.

Stevens talks about everything but his own failure: he is defensive about the hypocritical North, fearful of government interference, worried about amalgamation of the races; he is concerned whether blacks are ready for full equality; he is bothered that they imitate the ways of the lowest class of whites (instead of, apparently, the more acceptable manners of the Gavin Stevenses of the world); he condescendingly concedes that the reason rednecks fear blacks is that blacks can work harder and do more with less than whites can. What he has to say is in fact very much in line with what other moderates of the forties and fifties in Mississippi had to say and not at all unlike the sorts of things Faulkner himself said publicly during the same period; but as they come from Stevens in the dramatic context of the novel, all of these topics are merely his devices to avoid having to confront his own particular guilt in regard to a very particular Lucas, his failure to operate according to the rhetoric, at least, of his own highest moral and social standards. He is, as I say, blowing smoke to hide behind: he throws up Sambo, the condescending abstraction, to avoid Lucas, the concrete human being. This is the same Stevens, we should remember, who in *Light in August* pontificates so superfluously on Joe Christmas's ambiguous blood, and the same Stevens whose good intentions in the concluding chapter of *Go Down, Moses* are seriously undercut by his consternation upon confronting Molly Beauchamp's real, impenetrable grief and by the reader's simultaneous discovery of how arrogantly Stevens has presumed to know what Molly—The Negro—wanted, and of how terribly little he understood of her life: how much he talked, how little he said: how much less he did. Among the other important things Chick comes to recognize is the "significantless speciosity of his uncle's voice" (80), and his "uncle's abnegant and rhetorical self-lacerating, *which was...phony*" (133, my emphasis).

What is novelistically at stake in *Intruder*, then, is Chick Mallison and his efforts to find his own way through the tangle of Southern race relations. In this, Lucas and Aleck Sander and even the Gowries themselves represent the quality of his concrete experience of that tangle; Stevens represents its abstraction, the looming and ponderous weight of history, of the tradition of black-white relations as seen from the secure financial and social position of the educated aristocrat who can afford their easy platitudes, can afford to be "concerned" about Sambo precisely because, unlike the rednecks in Beat Four, they do not have to compete with Sambo for what living they can muster with their own sweat.

Faulkner's attitude toward Stevens in *Intruder*, then, seems reasonably clear from the context that the novel creates: that is, the novel provides sufficient evidence of Stevens's shortcomings to make us wary of accepting his words at their face value. The extent to which Faulkner endorsed Stevens's opinions, if not Stevens himself, may be discerned in the series of speeches, public letters, and more formal essays of the next few years, which got him more and more embroiled publicly in the problem and more and more formally associated with the moderate point of view. As with other moderates in the South, Faulkner's moderation earned him the contumely and spite of both sides—whites, including family and friends, who were outraged at his break with traditions; and blacks, who felt that such moderates were more a part of the problem than of the solution. The middle was not an easy position to hold. Faulkner gave his white neighbors and friends plenty to scream at him about and, on one occasion, at least, gave black accusers a real reason to question his racial sensibilities.

In February of 1956 Faulkner submitted to an interview by Russell Howe. Among numerous thoughtful responses to questions in which he articulated both his abhorrence of the injustices of racial segregation and his fear that the current crisis would precipitate bloodshed, he also, according to the interviewer, said this amazing thing:

> If I have to choose between the United States government and Mississippi, then I'll choose Mississippi. What I'm trying to do now is not have to make that decision. As long as there's a middle road, all right, I'll be on it. But if it came to fighting I'd fight for Mississippi against the United States even if it meant going out into the street and shooting Negroes....I will go on saying that the Southerners are wrong and that their position is untenable, but if I have to make the same choice Robert E. Lee made then I'll make it.[8]

When published, the remark created such controversy that Faulkner wrote a public letter in which he contended that the statement, as reported, was "more a misconstruction than a misquotation." Without explaining how the statement could have been misconstrued and still be accurately quoted, he went on to say that such statements were both "foolish and dangerous"; they were "statements which no sober man would make and, it seems to me, no sane man believe."[9]

There seems to be no question that Faulkner was accurately quoted in the interview, that he actually said he would shoot Negroes in the street to defend Mississippi. He himself did not directly deny having said it and his editor, Saxe Commins, who was present at the interview, never denied it—and one has to assume that he would have been quick to defend his author from the effects of such an admission if he could have.[10] Faulkner apologists in the matter take some comfort in his implicit admission that he was drinking during the interview, and indeed, according to Blotner's account, he had been drinking heavily during the period of the interview, responding to pressures of the mounting racial crisis in his native state and particularly to that developing at the University of Alabama. His critics suspect that, liquor or not, the statement reveals William Faulkner for what he *really* was, at heart: a white Mississippian, with all the moral and cultural and even intellectual limitations that soubriquet implies.

The episode is a significant one in Faulkner studies because in it are crystallized and intertwined all of the biographical and historical and political considerations and, radiating outward from it are a number of artistic and aesthetic considerations, which make "Faulkner and Race" a hellishly complex topic. One can hardly call "moderate" his purely outrageous confession that he would shoot Negroes in the street to defend Mississippi—a statement that seems to be such a dramatic departure from the very straightforward moderate positions he had been taking during the decade of the fifties, a far cry, indeed, from a more personal, intimate, view he had offered to Else Jonsson not quite a year earlier, in a letter of 12 June 1955:

> We have much tragic trouble in Mississippi now about Negroes. The Supreme Court has said that there shall be no segregation, difference in schools, voting, etc. between the two races, and there are many people in Mississippi who will go to any length, even violence, to prevent that, I am afraid. I am doing what I can. I can see the possible time when I shall have to leave my native state, something as the Jew had to flee from Germany during Hitler. I hope that wont happen of course. But at times I think that nothing but a disaster, a military defeat even perhaps, will wake America up and enable us to save ourselves, or what is left. This is a depressing letter, I know. But human beings are terrible. One must believe well in man to endure him, wait out his folly and savagery and inhumanity.[11]

There is a very long distance between on the one hand abandoning in despair a homeland one loves and, on the other, being willing to go to armed battle against overwhelming odds in defense of the very land, people, who have caused the despair that makes him consider leaving. He made his comment to Russell Howe in the context of a discussion of Autherine Lucy's attempts to enroll at the University of Alabama; he expressed a fear that she would be killed, and worried over the consequences of that eventuality. Just three months after Faulkner died, James Meredith enrolled at the University of Mississippi. I doubt very much that Faulkner, had he lived, would have taken up arms, along with other Mississippians, against the Federal Marshals who were posted here to keep the peace and to insure Meredith's right to an education.

I said that Faulkner's statement to Howe that he would shoot Negroes in the street *seemed* to be a departure from his more moderate statements; for if the part of his statement about shooting Negroes is an appalling contradiction of his previous positions on racial justice, his willingness to "defend Mississippi against the United States" is at the same time perfectly consistent with his often reiterated desire to hold at bay any sort of outside intervention into Mississippi's affairs. While racial matters clearly dominate Faulkner's nonfictional pronouncements of the fifties, they are not his only concerns; there are others whose relationship to the Negro question, in Faulkner's mind, or at least in his rhetoric, has not, I think, been sufficiently noted.

Part of his anxiety about the modern world was caused by the degree to which social, economic, and political phenomena seemed to be conspiring to rob individual man of his capacity to act and even think as an individual. The very idea of collective man, which he found abhorrent, expressed itself politically in the post–World War II world as a product of Communism and of the American government's various welfare and support programs that, in Faulkner's view, were depriving individual man of his capacity and of his right to depend upon himself; socially and economically it expressed itself in Madison Avenue's enforcement of a consumer conformity through the brand new power of television advertising; psychologically, it expressed itself as an increasing dependence upon technological gadgetry to do not just our work but our thinking for us. All of these forces were causing, in Faulkner's view, a standardization of life all across the world and, particularly in America, an intolerable conformism that threatened to swallow up the individual, to render the individual human being invalid.

To be sure, many of the views on the modern world that Faulkner expresses in his nonfiction emerge from a deeply rooted political and personal conservatism. At one level, for example, he never seemed quite able to reconcile himself to many of the New Deal's welfare and assistance programs, especially those programs of farm subsidies designed to bring some sort of order and stability to farm produce markets that were increasingly involved in very complicated national and international economies that made his own implicit ideal, the Jeffersonian self-consumer, not only obsolete, but virtually impossible even to imagine, except as a historical oddity. His world vision also seems to be marked by a kind of xenophobia, which can be seen in a variety of his reactions both to the international problems connected with the Cold War and, especially, to the local and national problems connected with the racial antagonisms in his home state and region. That is, while he supported unequivocally equality of opportunity for all races as the morally right thing to do, he made his arguments along the very pragmatic lines that for the South not to solve its own problems would be to invite the federal government to intervene in its affairs. Southern whites and blacks, he argued, had more in common with each other than any Southerner had with any Northerner; therefore, Southerners, black and white, had better stick together to stave off any outsider's challenge to their way of life. By the same token, he felt, all Americans, black, white, Southern, Northern, needed to stick together in order to present a united front to combat the menace of Communism.[12]

It was therefore in the best interests of the white majority to abolish the system that kept Negroes in economic and educational slavery; not to solve our own problems was to invite the federal government to solve them for us, probably in ways not to our liking. It was also in the best interests of Negroes, who had made enormous gains and who now had the political and economic power to continue the initiative, to "go slow," not to precipitate crises which would weld the white majority, including moderates like himself, into a unit in backlash resistance, precipitate violence and bloodshed, and so create the conditions for yet another kind of federal involvement. Indeed, the violence and federal intervention he feared did occur. But it may also be true—how will we ever know?—that the positions Faulkner was advocating would have delayed those necessary social and political changes for many years, perhaps generations; certainly we look back now on the words and good wishes made by such moderates as Faulkner with an overwhelming sense of how empty the words advocating caution, patience, and good will must have seemed to blacks, who had practiced these virtues for generations. The violence that Faulkner feared had a bloody but immediate impact, and we seem now, on the other side of the chaos and misery of those awful years, to be at least some the better for it, though I, a male Mississippi WASP, may not be qualified to say how much better. It seems clear, in retrospect, that Faulkner simply underestimated the impatience of Negroes and their willingness to suffer and die for their rights as American citizens. He also may have overestimated the capacity of Southern whites to act in their own best interests. This, of course, is a mistake he never made in his fiction.

We should be very careful, however, not to read backwards from the public statements into the fiction, as the Faulkner field has done so readily, for his attitude toward the modern world, as writer and citizen, was neither simplistic nor simple, and he was not, as he has sometimes been thought, simply a reactionary retrenched against the modern world and longing sentimentally for the lost innocence of the Big Woods that he described so gorgeously and movingly in *Go Down, Moses*. Quite simply put, Faulkner was no mid-century Miniver Cheevy, born out of his time and resenting it. In fact no writer I know of places more value than he on the ability to cope with change—change of environment, of relationship, of historical and social circumstance. This was, from one way of looking at it, the point of his entire argument— certainly it was the point of the rhetoric he employed in all of his pronouncements on the race issue. That is, he did not waste his or anybody else's time trying to change the hearts of Southern whites, but only their behavior: he did not hope to bring about brotherly love and understanding overnight or any time in the future. What he did was argue very pragmatically that change was inevitable and that it was in everybody's best interest, blacks and whites, North and South, for Southern whites themselves both to effect that change and to learn to live with new social and political conditions. A large part of Gavin Stevens's problem in *Intruder* is that, unlike Faulkner, he is so completely wedded, even if he does not know it, to the status quo.

An even larger part of Stevens's problem is that he, like other Faulkner heroes, is so completely wedded to the abstraction of justice that he does not see the concrete; he is so completely concerned with what he would call the larger and very complex picture that he cannot see the details which make up that larger picture. We may indeed see many similarities between Stevens's and Faulkner's rhetoric; but Stevens's abstractions, his preference for talking instead of doing, his overriding interest in Sambo rather than in Lucas, point directly to the differences between Stevens and the public Faulkner. So far as there is any record, Faulkner's concern was consistently with the *individual* Negro. Even while making public and private generalizations about race that could be construed as racist, he never lost sight of the needs of the individual, black or white, or of the need to make concrete contributions to the solution of the problem, rather than just blow smoke. His chief concern during the crisis at the University of Alabama was for the life of Autherine Lucy, whom he feared would be killed if she tried to enroll there.[13] Rather than simply declare that blacks needed more education to be worthy of equality, he took a good part of his Nobel Prize money to establish a scholarship fund for needy and worthy black students who otherwise would not have a chance at an education.[14] Malcolm Cowley reported that Faulkner's farm was run by "three Negro tenant families....He lets them have the profits, if any, because—he said, speaking very softly—'The Negroes don't always get a square deal in Mississippi.' He figures that his beef costs him $5 a pound."[15] His actions in these and doubtless other cases did not, of course, speak louder than his words, but they certainly did help alleviate racial misery in these individual cases.

Faulkner, too, was a complex combination of historical, economic, psychological, and social forces; he was, like the rest of us, a product of his own time and place, and it would be surprising indeed if this were not reflected in his work. It would be astonishing if, writing fifty years ago and more, he had been able to please an audience of the 1980s, who are much more sensitized to the subtleties of racial prejudice than any white person in 1920s Mississippi, or in the entire United States either, for that matter, could possibly have been. Can we argue that Caspey and Simon Strother never existed? Can we argue that individual Negroes have never been irresponsible, have never looked like the stereotype even if they were deliberately puttin' on ol' massa? Have no Negroes ever played to their white bosses' prejudices either to save their skins or to keep their jobs? If we can allow Faulkner to describe the dark and violent and unsavory underside of the average Mississippi redneck as he saw and tried to understand him, why can we not also allow him the same privilege to describe the dark and violent and unsavory underside of the blacks he saw? Is there no coin for verisimilitude, much less historical accuracy? Should we then revise Faulkner to make him more up-to-date? Can we impose a 1970s and '80s social mentality upon folks of a bygone era who were simply trying to cope, the best of them, in the best way they knew how? I believe that we have tried too hard to discover the number and kinds of things that Faulkner *did not* or *could not* write about, and not nearly hard enough to find the profound and perplexing human drama that within his lights—illuminating ones they were indeed—he did draw so convincingly.

The closing scene of *Intruder* is significant in a number of ways. A proud, independent man, Lucas comes to Stevens's office to pay Stevens his lawyer's fee. Early in the novel, Lucas had had the dignity to refuse Chick's attempts to pay him for his hospitality after pulling him from the creek: he knows that there are some things you can't buy, some things you can't pay for. Stevens doesn't have that kind of knowledge, or that kind of dignity, and he takes Lucas's proffered coins, even though he in fact has done nothing to save Lucas's skin. It's a trivial, symbolic amount ($2), of course, and he does refuse to let Lucas pay him a "fee"; but Stevens, having by now effectively taken the initiative away from Chick, now safely on the other side of his guilt, does allow Lucas to pay his "expenses." This is a patently paternalistic ruse that can hardly be interpreted otherwise than as his allowing Lucas Beauchamp, an innocent black man, to pay him for something he, Stevens, did not do, allowing Lucas to pay for the very freedom that Stevens has throughout the novel said the South, if left alone, would eventually give him. In this way, Stevens, the "best type of liberal Southerner"—and with what irony that phrase now rings in our ears—tries to keep Lucas obliged to him, to keep him, in effect, in the bondage of gratitude. The shrewd Lucas understands what Stevens is doing, however, and in the novel's final line demands a receipt. Michael Millgate perceptively reads this scene as "Lucas's insistence on...keeping affairs between himself and his white 'benefactors' on a strictly business footing, makes it clear that he does not intend his recent experience to affect his behaviour in the slightest degree and that he will not even release Charles from that indebtedness, that sense of being always at a disadvantage, which prompted the boy to his original intervention on Lucas's behalf."[16] Lucas's demand for a receipt here is also a very direct way of saying that he does not trust Stevens, a symbolic way of protecting himself from any future demand Gavin Stevens and the best type of liberal Southerner might make on him. He wants proof that he is fully paid up.

Thus there is plenty of distance between Gavin Stevens and William Faulkner. I do not know certainly why Faulkner wrote that curious addition to *Intruder* four months after its publication, why he would want to associate himself with what Stevens was saying. I can only propose a partial answer that may be more ingenious than useful: even as other critics and reviewers like Edmund Wilson and Malcolm Cowley had quoted *Intruder* and others of Faulkner's novels to their own social and political purposes, making of *Intruder*, for example, a polemic where no polemic was intended, so does Faulkner have Stevens quote Faulkner out of context and for his own self-justifying purposes. Like others who have quoted Faulkner on the race issue, Stevens condescends to the author—Stevens's Faulkner is "a mild retiring little man over yonder at Oxford"—and to *Absalom, Absalom!* itself—Stevens, an old Harvard man, notes, just a little too archly, that Quentin and Shreve live in "a dormitory room in a not too authentic Harvard"—and he calls Shreve's flip and callous parting shot—"I who regard you will have also sprung from the loins of African kings"—the novel's "tag line,"[17] thereby glibly reducing the entire novel to that one line, a line that is hardly representative of the complexities or myriad meanings of *Absalom, Absalom!* And we cannot forget that Stevens quotes not the tortured and ambiguous testament—*"I dont hate it. I dont. I dont hate it."*—of Quentin Compson, but rather Shreve McCannon's nonsense. Shreve is, of course, a Canadian, an outsider who has no experience of the South but what he has learned from Quentin, but who nevertheless can reduce the South's problems to a clever rhetorical flourish. Faulkner, then, here makes Stevens a Faulkner critic. Like other critics, Stevens takes the words of one character more or less as Faulkner's own and, like many critics, he homes straight in on the easy, the simple, the clever, and avoids the hard and even dangerous complexities of a tragic situation. More critics than Stevens have done this: more critics than Stevens have misunderstood *Absalom, Absalom!*, and more critics than should have have taken Stevens in *Intruder* as Faulkner's voice.

Faulkner apparently did not pursue the insertion of the new material into new printings of *Intruder in the Dust,* and I suspect that he simply forgot about it, having written it on an impulse, perhaps even a whimsy, in response to being subjected yet again, by Wilson and even his friend Cowley, to the sort of manipulation and misunderstanding he had already had to put up with, and would increasingly have to endure during the coming decade.

Was Faulkner a racist? If by "racism" one means a hatred or fear of Negroes, one can say, I think, clearly No: Faulkner seems never to have been any more intolerant of blacks than of whites, or any more fearful of their capacity for mischief; he seems, in fact, to have been equally intolerant of just about everybody. If, however, by "racism" one means a belief in the inferiority of Negroes, one could probably answer that question with a Yes, but only by citing his numerous invocations of historical, rather than biological and genetic, circumstances as being responsible for the Negro's social and economic and cultural disadvantages. In this, too, he was fairly consonant with other moderate Southerners of his day. Even Hodding Carter did not generally argue for immediate social equality, perhaps not believing blacks capable of immediate social amalgamation; what he, and Faulkner, *did* confront was the issue of political and economic justice.[18]

But suppose it could be proven that in his very heart of hearts Faulkner was in fact a raging racist, that like his Southern and Mississippi brothers and sisters of the stereotype he imbibed from his mother's milk an absolute hatred of all people with black skins. Even if this were the case, shouldn't we still give him credit for the love and compassion and understanding with which he treated his black characters, his white ones too, and for the courage with which he spoke out, publicly, to try to correct a situation which his intellect, even if not his passions, found intolerable? One of his Negro characters opines that "Quality aint *is*, it's *does*." The same is true, I submit, of racism, since by certain psychological and social definitions we are all racists of one sort or another: however ingrained they are, whatever their sources, whatever their objects, our prejudices and their capacity to do mischief can only be measured by what they force us to *do*.

The fact is that even though a grandchild of slaveholders and a very defensive Southerner, Faulkner acted quite responsibly toward the Negro, both in his fiction and in the public forum. So even if in his early work some of his generalizations about Negro intelligence and physical characteristics offend, can't we still see in the works, from beginning to end, a powerful sympathy with both the individual and the race? And doesn't his concern with the problem of Negro humanity express itself more eloquently and more profoundly in *Light in August*, *Absalom, Absalom!*, and *Go Down, Moses* than in any other book by any other author, written any where, at any time, ever? What more could be expected of an artist?

If in his public declarations during the fifties he expressed moderation, we must remember that he hardly seemed "moderate" to white Southerners of the day. Even if black leaders were right in perceiving the white moderates of the day as part of the problem rather than as part of the solution, we must also remember that Faulkner made his public statements at a time when it was very dangerous to do so, and did so even though it cost him the contumely of his family and of his community and of the entire state. What more could be expected of a citizen?

As a novelist, Faulkner knew that nearly all significant problems are too large and complex to be contained by any single opinion or point of view; as a novelist, he could and regularly did dramatize those problems without being obliged to solve them. As a citizen he undertook the perhaps quixotic task of solving those problems precisely by talking about how complex they were. Thus he was man in the middle indeed, a sitting duck for the extremist activists on both sides.

In his life, then, as in his fiction, Faulkner focused on the individual human being, and we do his Negro characters an injustice if we do not at least try to see them as human first, and black only second. Part of the power of his depiction of black characters comes directly from his refusal to sentimentalize or simplify the humanity out of them. What makes "That Evening Sun" remarkable is not just its depiction of Mr. Compson's abandonment of his responsibility to Nancy, or of the children's inability to understand what is happening. What strikes one is rather the intensity and the complexity of the relationship between Jesus and Nancy. They do, in fact, seem to love one another very much; but their relationship is thwarted by a variety of forces, some of which they have no control over, others which perhaps they do. How victimized are Nancy and Jesus? Nancy is pregnant—by a white man? Apparently so, though there is no proof; Jesus certainly appears to think so. Has Nancy been raped, forced? Apparently not, since she has at least one "customer," a Mr. Stovall. One critic tells us bluntly that Stovall had "made her his whore and got her pregnant,"[19] though there is no direct evidence in the story to support such a conclusion. Is Nancy perhaps here, as in *Requiem for a Nun*, a "casual prostitute"? Does she entertain Mr. Stovall, and others, for enough money just to stay alive? for her own sexual pleasure? to get back at a husband who is apparently something of a philanderer? When Mr. Compson patronizingly thinks to comfort her by telling her that Jesus won't hurt her because he has probably gone away and "got another wife by now and forgot all about you,"

Nancy is outraged: "If he has," she says, venomously, "I better not find out about it....I'd stand right there over them, and every time he whopped her, I'd cut that arm off. I'd cut his head off and I'd slit her belly and I'd shove—."[20] Jesus' love and sexual fidelity are clearly important to Nancy. Her response indicates that neither she nor her creator subscribe, as Mr. Compson obviously does, to the myths of sexual casualness among all Negroes.

Is Jesus, by the same token, more outraged at a social structure that allows a white man to come into his house, for sexual and other purposes, but refuses him the opposite privilege, or only at Nancy, for cuckolding him in the first place and then for compounding the cuckolding by publicly humiliating him when she attacked Mr. Stovall in front of the bank? Clearly his outrage and his frustration spring from very complex combinations of both these things, and clearly there are significant ways in which he and Nancy are helpless victims of circumstance. Jesus is injured, yet impotent to strike back at the white world he blames, rightly or wrongly, for his troubles. Yet why should he take all of his frustrations out on Nancy if he blames the white man, particularly since Nancy is no less a victim of those same forces? The answers are, I'd suggest, more psychological than sociological; he strikes out at the only thing he feels he possibly can strike out at, the woman he loves—but is that his only recourse? Nancy, for her part, strikes rather at herself—out of what combination of guilt or self-reproach or simple despair it is impossible to say—when she attempts suicide in the jail, and when she confronts Mr. Stovall in front of the bank, asking for her money: one can only assume that she gets exactly what she expected, perhaps wanted, from him. Surely she knew that under the circumstances he was more likely to beat her than pay her. Perhaps she thought her own pain, even her death, was a small price to pay for a public humiliation of Stovall. Or was she simply so high on drugs she didn't know what she was doing? There are very many ways in which she deserves our deepest sympathy.

But the chemistry of our sympathy with her is seriously altered when we realize how dangerous it is for her to take the Compson children to her cabin with her to protect her. If Jesus decides to kill her, as she believes he will, does she think he will spare the little ones? Even if she does think he will spare them, if she has thought about it at all, it seems to me by no means responsible for her to try to hide behind them. Does she realize the danger, at any level? If Mr. Compson is the father of her child and so the author of her miseries, does Nancy deliberately, consciously or unconsciously, put them in harm's way to avenge herself on a white world which has wronged her?

I do not know the answers to these questions, and I do not believe that the story itself provides answers. But I insist that the story asks these and other questions, and that much of its power is directly related to the complexity of Nancy's characterization and to the complexities of the relationship between Jesus and Nancy. Faulkner's treatment of these two black characters is in very many ways a direct, frontal assault upon racial stereotypes that forces us to the astonishing knowledge that Jesus' and Nancy's feelings are, well, *white*: what we are really astonished at, even if we do not know it, is that those feelings are *human*. Criticism of this story, and of Faulkner's general treatment of blacks, seem stuck at considering them simply tragic victims of white oppresssion, and so symbols, rather than human beings.

His white characters are also too often read as stereotypes. "Pantaloon in Black" is, for many reasons, generally considered one of Faulkner's greatest stories. Most critics have, in my judgment, misunderstood "Pantaloon" not because of Faulkner's treatment of Rider, but because of their inability to see the deputy of the second part of that story as anything but a stereotypical Southern law man. He is, of course, a redneck deputy, a Southerner with all the prejudices associated with that type. Faulkner deliberately draws him that way. But if that is *all* he is, then "Pantaloon" seems to me an unsuccessful story that rather clumsily juxtaposes the moving story of Rider's love for Manny, his grief, his suicidal murder of the white man, and then his lynching, with the story of the redneck deputy and his crass, unloving wife.

Beyond those ironies, however, lies another story. Why does the deputy continue to tell his wife the story of Rider's lynching, in complete detail, long after she has made it clear that she doesn't care about Rider or about the deputy either? The answer, I think, is that he isn't talking to her at all, but rather to himself. He has just experienced something, Rider's griefstricken and doomed humanness, which nothing in his background has prepared him for, and he is clumsily trying to talk it out, trying to explain to his own mind, using a completely inadequate redneck vocabulary and conceptual system, something it cannot quite grasp. Most have accepted that Faulkner wrote "Pantaloon" to force white readers to go behind the stereotype of the black man. I would argue that he is also asking us to look behind the stereotype of the Southern lawman, even as Nub Gowrie's heartbreak forces Chick Mallision behind the stereotype of Beat Four rednecks: we who have eagerly seen Rider as a misunderstood human being have been unwilling to see the white man as equally human. The deputy is trying to make sense of his actual experience of Rider, which has made that magnificent black man something devastatingly different from the stereotype he has always presumed to think he knows: perhaps this deputy is also somebody devastatingly different from the redneck we have all presumed to know.

Thus that deputy seems to me far more educable than the more highly educated and sophisticated lawyer, Gavin Stevens, whose presence at the end of *Go Down, Moses* has for four decades muddied the racial waters of that novel. For with all the best intentions to be helpful, to demonstrate that he, at any rate, knows something of the civilized world, Stevens is completely blind to Molly's real humanity. Most critics have, of course, noticed this, and many have thought Stevens's paternalism a weakness in the novel. But I would suggest that Stevens is here set in sharp opposition to the deputy of "Pantaloon." Both become privy to grief, to human passion, where they had least expected it, in a Negro. The deputy tries to understand it; Stevens is arrogantly sure that he understands "The Negro" completely. It is thus much more likely to be that redneck deputy who will, one of these days, be able to meet black men and women as individual human beings. I suspect Faulkner would hold that the surer, the long-range solution to racial problems, if there is a solution, lies in the direction the deputy is facing, even if he hasn't yet begun to move forward; and I suspect that, at least as regards the question of race in his real South and in his fictionalized one, that deputy is nearer to Faulkner's position than any other character: he doesn't have any answers, but at least he is beginning to ask the right questions.

Notes

Portions of this essay appeared in slightly different form in "Faulkner and Race," *Review*, vol. 6, eds. James O. Hoge and James L. W. West III (Charlottesville: University Press of Virginia, 1984), 1–19.

1. William F. Winter, "New Directions in Politics, 1948–1956," in Richard Aubrey McLemore, ed., *A History of Mississippi* (Jackson: University & College Press of Mississippi, 1973), 2:141.
2. Ibid., 2:144.
3. Edmund Wilson, "William Faulkner's Reply to the Civil-Rights Program," in John Bassett, ed., *William Faulkner: The Critical Heritage* (London: Routledge & Kegan Paul, 1975), 335–36.
4. Malcolm Cowley, *The Faulkner–Cowley File: Letters and Memories, 1944–1962* (New York: Viking, 1966), 110–11.
5. Joseph Blotner, ed., *Selected Letters of William Faulkner* (New York: Random House, 1977), 285.
6. Patrick Samway, S.J., "New Material for Faulkner's *Intruder in the Dust*," in James B. Meriwether, ed., *A Faulkner Miscellany* (Jackson: University Press of Mississippi, 1974), 111.
7. William Faulkner, *Intruder in the Dust* (New York: Random House, 1948), 222, 226, 242. Hereafter cited parenthetically in the text.
8. James B. Meriwether and Michael Miligate, eds., *Lion in the Garden: Interviews* (New York: Random House, 1968), 260-62.
9. Joseph Blotner, *Faulkner: A Biography*, 2 vols. (New York: Random House, 1974), 2:1599. See also James B. Meriwether, ed., *Essays, Speeches, and Public Letters* (New York: Random House, 1966), 226, and *Lion in the Garden*, 265. Meriwether's and Millgate's introduction to the Howe interview (257) usefully argues the reasons that one must approach the interview with caution.
10. Blotner, *Faulkner: A Biography*, 2:1590. In the 1984 one-volume revision (*Faulkner: A Biography*, 1-vol. ed. [New York: Random House, 1984], 617–18) Blotner omits to mention Commins's presence at the interview.
11. *Selected Letters*, 381–82.
12. See, for example, "On Fear: Deep South in Labor: Mississippi" and the "Address to the Southern Historical Association" in *Essays, Speeches, and Public Letters*.
13. *Essays, Speeches, and Public Letters*, 108, and Blotner, 2:1591.

14. Blotner, *Faulkner: A Biography*, 1-vol. ed., 535.
15. *Faulkner–Cowley File*, 111.
16. Michael Millgate, *The Achievement of William Faulkner* (New York: Random House, 1966), 220.
17. Samway, 111.
18. See, for example, Hodding Carter's *Where Main Street Meets the River* (New York: Rinehart, 1953) and *Southern Legacy* (Baton Rouge: Louisiana State University, 1950), and David Cohn's *Where I Was Born and Raised* (Boston: Houghton Mifflin, 1948).
19. Walter Taylor, *Faulkner's Search for a South* (Urbana: University of Illinois Press, 1983), 55.
20. "That Evening Sun," in *Collected Stories* (New York: Random House, 1950), 295.

INTRUDER IN THE DUST:
A RE-EVALUATION

Patrick Samway, S.J.

In 1955, in Japan, William Faulkner said that a writer is not really writing about his social and cultural environment, but that he is telling a story about human beings in terms of that environment and thus any work must reflect the background out of which it emerges.[1] If a writer tells a story to explore the sociological background, then he is writing propaganda. The novelist, according to Faulkner, is concerned with people, with man in conflict with himself, and in this way with his environment. In the same year in Manila, Faulkner enlarged on his conception of the task of the writer, using some of the ideas he had previously expressed in his Nobel Prize speech:

> The writer must believe always in people, in freedom; he must believe that man must be free in order to create the art; and art is in my opinion one of the most important factors in human life because it has...been the record of man's rise from his beginnings. It is the writer's duty to show that man has an immortal soul.[2]

Thus Faulkner took his art seriously and did not use the novel form, as Dos Passos often did, as a channel for political thought, though that does not mean his fiction remained indifferent to the South's political environment. When he wanted to express himself in a strictly political way, he tended to write letters, short treatises, or essays which would deal specifically with civil rights problems.

Faulkner's overall approach to civil rights was moderate, too moderate for James Baldwin, who maintained "it is easy enough to state flatly that Faulkner's middle of the road does not—cannot—exist and that he is guilty of great emotional and intellectual dishonesty in pretending that it does."[3] Faulkner repeatedly said that the race problem was basically an economic problem and that children of both races normally feel free to intermingle: "It's only when the child becomes a middle-aged man and becomes a part of the economy that latent quality [of prejudice] appears."[4] He said that he opposed any evils in the South that would perpetuate segregation and, at the same time, he opposed forces from outside the South which would use legal or police compulsion to eradicate political and social evils overnight. He was against compulsory segregation in much the same way he was against compulsory integration. The Northerners, according to Faulkner, really know little about the South; they have a popular image of decadent people who through inbreeding and illiteracy are a kind of juvenile delinquent with a folklore of blood and violence.[5] He believed that the races should mix (or confederate) in order to preserve their freedom:

> And if we who are still free want to continue so, all of us who are still free had better confederate and confederate fast with all others who still have a choice to be free—confederate not as black people nor white people nor blue or pink or green people, but as people who are still free, with all other people who are still free; confederate together too, if we want a world or even a part of a world in which individual man can be free, to continue to endure.[6]

Writing for *Ebony*, Faulkner said that if he were a Negro he would want his fellow blacks to be "inflexibly flexible" and build on the decency and patience that have been part of their heritage for over three hundred years.[7] Patience, in this context, is not a passive quality, but an active weapon which can bring about peaceful unity.

Faulkner's novel *Intruder in the Dust* concerns race relations in the South and it is often thought that one of the main characters, Gavin Stevens, a white lawyer, represents Faulkner's views at face value. In an oblique way, Faulkner addressed himself to the problem of whether or not one should regard Gavin as his spokesman on one of the typescript pages of the original draft:

> These characters and incidents are fictional, imaginative, and—some will say—impossible. In which case let them be accepted not as the puppet-play of a whodunit but as the protagonist pattern of a belief that not government first but the white man of the South owes a responsibility to the Negro, not because of his past since a man or a race if it be any good can survive his past without having to escape from it (and the fact that the Negro has survived him in the way he has is his proof) but because of his present condition, whether the Negro wishes it or not.

Thus Faulkner saw *Intruder* as involving fiction and morality; the focus is on the white man's obligation to the Negro because of the Negro's present condition. If the work were solely a racial tract, however, then there might be some justification for the identity of Gavin and Faulkner. But, why would Faulkner want such a bewildering spokesman when he proved that he could be quite effective by himself? If Gavin were Faulkner's spokesman, then one would also expect that he dramatize Faulkner's views as well as articulate them. Yet, little or nothing in Joseph Blotner's biography of Faulkner even suggests that Gavin's experiences parallel any of Faulkner's. In fact, Faulkner was critical of Gavin and believed as an amateur Sherlock Holmes he was out of his depth.

In a review of Erich Maria Remarque's book, *The Road Back*, Faulkner wrote something about character study that might well apply to Gavin:

> It is a writer's privilege to put into the mouths of his characters better speech than they would have

> been capable of, but only for the purpose of permitting and helping the character to justify himself or what he believes himself to be, taking down his spiritual pants. But when the character must express moral ideas applicable to a race, a situation, he is better kept in that untimed and unsexed background of the choruses of Greek senators.[8]

As Faulkner hinted to Malcolm Cowley, Gavin assumes center stage in the last third of the novel and becomes the South's, *not* Faulkner's, liberal spokesman.[9] Though 16-year-old Chick Mallison listens to his Uncle Gavin's words, he does not, as Olga Vickery maintains, "accept all Gavin's ideas as he occasions their transmutation into an acceptable form which can encompass both their angles of vision, the idealist and the realist."[10] While it cannot be denied that some of Gavin's views approximate those articulated by Faulkner, Gavin never strays from being a fictional, dramatic character. If anything, however, Faulkner satirizes Gavin as the Southern spokesman.

Gavin firmly believes, as does the larger Jefferson community, that Lucas Beauchamp is guilty of killing Vinson Gowrie; he is perplexed as to why Lucas had to shoot a Gowrie of all people. When Gavin and Chick Mallison walk into town the evening after the murder, Gavin discusses the simple ways of the seemingly nameless, faceless country people. He notes they move into town to be close to human activity and rarely question life's deeper realities; in his opinion, a vocabulary of clichés often sustains them. When they meet Mr. Lilley, the representative *par excellence* of the town, Gavin interprets Mr. Lilley's philosophical stance to Chick: "He has nothing against what he calls niggers. If you ask him, he will probably tell you he likes them even better than some white folks he knows and he will believe it."[11] As a store owner, Mr. Lilley knows that Negroes steal small items occasionally and all he requires is that they continue to act like niggers, a position which paraphrases an earlier comment by Chick regarding Lucas, who lives neither in the white world nor the black one: "They're going to make a nigger out of him once in his life anyway" (p. 32). Like Gavin, Mr. Lilley has no doubts about Lucas' guilt; yet he harbors no ill feelings towards Lucas and would probably contribute money to help pay his funeral expenses. Gavin seems to understand Mr. Lilley's position so well that he accepts it and makes no overt criticism about it.

Gavin is presented not as a man with shrewd insight or a penetrating philosophy and he brings no real sense of history to the racial problems he discusses, and as such he represents a Southern intellectual who will not be an appropriate catalyst for change. When confronting Lucas in the jail cell, he intimidates Lucas by constantly proclaiming Lucas' guilt. He reflects, too, Mr. Tubbs' position when Tubbs says he has a wife and two children, and though he is the jailer, he does not want to get into a middle position between Lucas and the redneck Gowrie clan. Mr. Tubbs believes a quick lynching might have solved the problem. As a lawyer, Gavin is clear about his position: "I dont defend murderers who shoot people in the back…" (p. 60). On the other hand he admits, just by going to the cell, that he has taken the case, one that will be quickly expedited. Gavin wavers a little at the beginning, a sign, perhaps, that his words do not convey all that he thinks about Lucas.

When Gavin finally allows Lucas to talk about the murder, he interrupts him on a point of protocol, chastising him for not referring to a white man by a proper title. With laconic wit, Lucas responds by questioning whether he is to call each Gowrie "Mister" as they drag him out of the jail. Gavin does not really accept Lucas' version about Vinson Gowrie and another man storing lumber in order to later haul it away; he prefers to believe that Lucas called Vinson into the woods, told Vinson about the stealing, was called a liar, and then shot Vinson in the back. Lucas pleads that he has no friends; he wants to hire Gavin as a lawyer and not accept his services for free. In his haste, Gavin would even like to forget about buying tobacco for Lucas, something that Chick is more hesitant to do. Faulkner has clearly demonstrated the positions of the opposing forces and just as he dealt with triadic forces in *A Fable*, so too, he is beginning to show three views here in the jail cell.

Later in Gavin's office, Gavin remains unyielding and even suggests, in an off-handed way, that Lucas was actually shooting a tin can or a mark on a tree. He does not realize how close to the truth he is. Gavin cannot take the risk of going out and digging up Gowrie's grave; he feels secure in knowing that Lucas is locked up in jail, in preserving the accepted *mores* of the community. Chick tries to argue with Gavin, as Lucas did previously, and gradually fathoms the meaning of words and vocabulary—and of the limits of Vocabulary—as he confronts Gavin on Gavin's level; Chick knows his uncle's voice is filled with "significantless speciosity." This knowledge is a turning point for Chick and he does not really consult with Gavin again until after Gowrie's grave has been dug up. Only after the exhumation, not before as in the case of Chick, does Gavin change his stance; he admits that truth often comes out "of the mouths of babes and sucklings and old ladies—" (p. 106). Still, it should be noted that Gavin exerts some leadership by suggesting that the strategy they use should include driving to Harrisburg and consulting with the District Attorney. And he encourages Miss Habersham, here reduced to the town's comic guardian, to sit by the entrance to the jail so she can be seen by the townsfolk and help ward off any trouble.

It is only after Gavin has dropped Miss Habersham off at the jail that he begins to get closer to Chick, although Chick is aware of his "naive and childlike rationalising" (p. 122). Chick hopes that Gavin will not side with his mother, and when Chick finally utters at the hopelessness of the situation, "You're just my uncle," Gavin replies he is worse than that, "I'm just a man" (p. 122). Gavin knows after Montgomery's body is discovered, it "took an old woman and two children...to believe truth...told by an old man in a fix deserving pity and belief, to someone capable of the pity even when none of them really believed him" (p. 126). Once this new relationship with Chick has been established, Gavin delivers his reflections on the place of the Negro in the South as he drives out to the graveyard with Chick on May 9th.

Gavin's ultimate philosophical conclusion comes at the end of the novel (with an interesting comment on Lucas' crucifixion, especially in light of the Christ-motif Faulkner was developing in *A Fable*):

> ...Lucas' life the breathing and eating and sleeping is of no importance just as yours and mine are not but his unchallengeable right to it in peace and security and in fact this earth would be much more comfortable with a good deal fewer Beauchamps and Stevenses and Mallisons of all colors in it if there were only some painless way to efface not the clumsy room-devouring carcasses which can be done but the Memory which cannot—that inevictible immortal memory awareness of having once been alive which exists forever still ten thousand years afterward in ten thousand recollections of injustice and suffering, too many of us not because of the room we take up but because we are willing to sell liberty short at any tawdry price for the sake of what we call our own which is a constitutional statutory license to pursue each his private postulate of happiness and contentment regardless of grief and cost even to the crucifixion of someone whose nose or pigment we dont like and even these can be coped with provided that few of others who believe that a human life is valuable simply because it has a right to keep on breathing no matter what pigment its lungs distend or nose inhales the air and are willing to defend that right at any price, it doesn't take many three were enough last Sunday night even one can be enough and with enough ones willing to be more than grieved and shamed Lucas will no longer run the risk of needing without warning to be saved....(pp. 243–244)

Just as Gavin is convinced that solipsism and extreme forms of personal solitude will not advance the cause of civil rights, he knows that three people are enough to start the process of justice and restore belief in the dignity of human life. Unfortunately, Gavin does not sustain his philosophical mood, but resumes by treating Lucas in a much lighter vein, almost, many critics believe, as if he were a stereotype. To seek a resolution, one where the emotional and psychological energies can be submerged for a while, Gavin mockingly meets Lucas half-way and puts the emphasis on the correct amount that Lucas owes him—in a final scene that is more charade than a genuine reckoning between two individuals of different races (though, in fact, Lucas is a mulatto). Lucas had taught Chick that one does not pay for hospitality and here Lucas teaches Gavin and Chick that one does attempt to pay his legitimate debts especially when the concerned parties have entered into a contractual relationship. Thus, this novel points to a type of resolution, even if perfunctory and inconclusive, hinting that in microcosm race problems can be dealt with, something that Faulkner had not achieved in his earlier novels.

Though Gavin presents a rather persuasive conclusion to his argument concerning the future of the civil rights movement in the South, he has an unfortunate start by characterizing Lucas and the other blacks in the South as "Sambo"—at the least, a slur, at most, denying individuality and humanity. But Gavin's choice of language betrays him, even though he seemingly never speaks in a derogatory manner about Sambo; though he would like to be one who helps to build a solid interracial society based partly on the positive qualities and attributes Negroes have exhibited over the decades, he cannot extricate himself from a high-sounding linguistic construct of his own making. The main problem is not Gavin's Sambo-slur, but his level of abstraction rooted neither in first principles nor in the immediate experience of Chick or the other characters in the novel. He makes no effort to seek a common denominator in attempting to communicate his views with others, and this vitiates the effectiveness of his pronouncements.

In general, Gavin's views are centered on his contention that New England and the South are the two regions in this country where homogeneous people live. The Negro, he adds, possesses this homogeneity, too, though Gavin does not predicate this initially. At least in the South, the blacks and whites need to confederate—the white man should swap with the Negro "the rest of the economic and political and cultural privileges which are his right, for the reversion of his capacity to wait and endure and survive" (p. 156). In addition the South should continue to defend its homogeneity from any interference by the federal government because only in homogeneity is there anything of lasting value. The South must defend the ultimate privilege of setting Sambo (not the emerging black men and women in 1948) free. The chronicle of man's immortality is deep within his capacity to suffer and endure and reach out toward the stars. Integration will take time and the white Southerners will have to ask the blacks to exercise more patience until it is achieved. Once a more comprehensive homogeneity exists, then "we would dominate the United States," Gavin believes (p. 156). Gavin leaves the exact nature of this homogeneity unspecified both in the original draft and the setting copy. Likewise, he fails to develop the specific bonds of unity or the values that will be shared by the blacks and the whites in both the North and the South. This sweep of language sets an abstract goal, but fails to show, alas, how this can be implemented.

The key concept in Gavin's philosophy is his belief in "the divinity of his continuity as Man" (p. 202). The human race must continue to explore its own dynamic and spiritual resources in order to move intelligently into the future. Gavin, however, actually advocates the opposite of what he proposes, when the townsfolk repudiate Crawford Gowrie and deprive him of the full extent of his citizenship in the human race. Gavin is committed to defend Sambo from "the outlanders who will fling him decades back not merely to injustice but into grief and agony and violence too by forcing on us laws based on the idea that man's injustice to man can be abolished overnight by police" (pp. 203–204). The South, in his mind, must expiate the injustice it has caused and this is something due the blacks whether they want it or not. Gavin instructs Chick that there are some things he must always be unable to bear, such as injustice, outrage, dishonor, and shame—concepts that are hollow coming from his mouth. Though Chick responds to Gavin's instructions by saying that he has not been a Tenderfoot scout for four years, Gavin remonstrates with a highly ambiguous, "But just regret it, dont be ashamed" (p. 206). According to

Gavin, the Southerners are in the position like the Germans after 1933 who were either a Jew or a Nazi or like the Russians who are either a Communist or dead; like true soldiers they must defend the Lucas-Sambos even if their numbers are small. Just as there might not be one in a thousand who would grieve for Sambo nor, on the other hand, be the first to lynch him either, yet all thousand would stop outside interference. Gavin's view of Sambo is not limited to the South; Sambo exists in Chicago, Detroit, Los Angeles and is the recipient of many forms of racial prejudice. As is clear, Gavin's solipsistic wisdom borders, at times, on impressionistic opacity; yet, in the novel, he serves Chick's mentor and provides a definite personality against which Chick can appreciate his own nascent philosophical positions.

The novel, however, does not originate from Gavin or his beliefs; its main concern is the interaction of the characters as they help to solve Lucas' problem and bring about a viable awareness of justice in Jefferson. Gavin's philosophy does not save Lucas; it is the courageous act of an old woman and two boys that does this. Aleck Sander, as Chick's companion, provides Chick with a friend who shares with him his childhood experiences, not unsimilar to the Miss Habersham-Molly Beauchamp relationship. Chick is not entering into a racial situation totally unprepared; he has eaten at Paralee's house and is familiar with the Ephraim story, which made a deep impression on him and which becomes a recurring refrain from the novel's hidden chorus, one of the cohesive leitmotifs within the novel. Part of the growth that Chick goes through is to understand Old Ephraim's words: "Young folks and womens, they aint cluttered. They can listen. But a middle-year man like your paw and your uncle, they cant listen. They aint got time. They're too busy with facks" (p. 71). While Lucas can be regarded, from one perspective, as a representative black man of the new South, Aleck Sander is definitely a stereotyped black boy, an interpretation made clear by Clarence Brown in the film of this novel, especially in the grave digging scene where Aleck Sander's eyes pop wide open with marvelous fear. Yet Aleck Sander is credited as being one of the detectives by Sheriff Hampton and is praised for what he does; he admits that no one forced him to go though, ironically, he was not quite sure of the purpose of the mission. Aleck Sander's presence, therefore, makes Chick's action more plausible because Chick not only has grown up with blacks but he is accompanied by a black friend out to the graveyard.

The two women in the novel, Mrs. Mallison and Miss Habersham, take a more active part in the novel than does Aleck Sander. Mrs. Mallison (can one find a typical Faulknerian mother?) is over-protective and unduly concerned with family routines. While she constantly nags Gavin about his driving abilities and argues with her husband about whether Chick should drink coffee or not at his age, Chick regards her as "a hundred times less noisy than his father and a thousand times more valuable..." (p. 208). Chick focuses his attention on his mother at those times when he is tired and near sleep and is particularly sensitive to his mother's touch: "He had had it long enough, even rolling his head but about as much chance to escape that one frail narrow inevitible palm as to roll your forehead out from under a birthmark..." (p. 191). When Chick tries to interpret the meaning of the expedition to the graveyard, in terms of his past experience, he thinks both of the time two years before when he went to Mottstown and secretly his mother came to take him home in a hired car after he had hurt his arm, and the time when he jumped Highboy over a concrete water trough. Mrs. Mallison does not lament these past situations nor complain of imaginary ailments like Mrs. Compson in *The Sound and the Fury*; rather she is outspoken in her solicitude for Chick and does not hamper his growth. She supports him in a way that Gavin or Lucas really cannot. Mrs. Mallison is a more competent parent than her husband and is even willing to encounter a certain risk by joining Miss Habersham at the jail.

Miss Habersham, on the other hand, is a far more interesting character because her actions are so atypical of a woman over sixty (Faulkner at various times in the original draft and setting copy placed her age from sixty to eighty). She comes from an old family: Doctor Habersham and two companions came to Jefferson when it was a Chickasaw trading post. Kenneth Richardson believes Miss Habersham has "the insights of a matriarch who is willing to cross mores in order to reveal the truth."[12]

Faulkner treats her sympathetically, even when he renders her invisible; she reflects something he once said, that he liked to think of a young man as having an aunt or neighbor to listen to because they were often more sensible than men.[13] In her Sears Roebuck catalogue dresses and her expensive New York shoes, Miss Habersham apparently leads a very ordinary life selling chickens and vegetables which she raises and peddles about town in her pickup truck. Faulkner had originally contemplated using a farmer to visit Gavin on Sunday evening, but he changed to Miss Habersham, perhaps to bring out the ironic contrasts between old/young, black man/white woman, expected behavior/ unusual behavior. Miss Habersham, the prime instigator in helping Lucas, is more than willing to risk ostracism by the town even though she does not know fully the events surrounding Vinson Gowrie's death. Yet she is fully aware that her age and sex are in her favor and that if the whole enterprise proves to be a mistake, she would be excused as a dottering old woman—a situation the sheriff understands when he allows her to guard the jail.

Miss Habersham's wisdom is not wrapped in abstract thought or propositions though she can make penetrating distinctions as, for example, when she tells Chick, "Of course. Naturally he wouldn't tell your uncle. He's a Negro and your uncle's a man" (p. 89). Chick knows, too, that it is not the paucity of Miss Habersham's vocabulary that causes her to say this, but that in her own way she is paraphrasing simple truth, something that Lucas and Ephraim, each in his own way, had realized too. Miss Habersham organizes the trip to the cemetery with dispatch and once there she has no qualms about opening up the grave. Her focus is on essentials. When the three detectives hasten to the sheriff's house to tell him the body-switch, she reminds the sheriff that they should remember Lucas in everything they do, even though he is not physically present.

She also suggests that they call the District Attorney in Harrisburg for permission to exhume Montgomery's body and that they should do everything quickly, not waiting for daylight. When Chick envisions Miss Habersham returning home a half-mile from town to her house, he sees her in motion, as venturing into Crossman, Mott, and Okatoba counties, knowing that the best way to go around an obstruction is to just go around it, just as she knew that the most logical way to recover a corpse is to dig up the grave. In his discussion of the oral tradition in Mississippi, Calvin Brown sees this projection of Miss Habersham riding around the country with restless energy as having the ingredients of a tall tale.[14] Like an insect caught on a spinning record, Miss Habersham gathers imagined momentum in her journey until she finally admits to a man in a nightshirt, *"I had to detour around an arrogant insufferable old nigger who got the whole county upset trying to pretend he murdered a white man"* (p. 189). In all, Miss Habersham—who remains on the periphery of society—adds a touch of practical gentility, as if she stepped out of an old English murder mystery that Faulkner had read. She is effective without being overbearing and perceptive without being pedantic. At the end of the novel Gavin appreciates what she has done and cajoles a reluctant Lucas into taking flowers to her to show his gratitude.

The individuals in this novel such as Gavin and Miss Habersham are contrasted with the Gowries, the townsfolk, and the inhabitants of the various beats who have come to witness what happens to Lucas. As a backward, country family, the Gowries are close-knit, unreflective, and in their own way as much a part of the mentality of Yoknapatawpha as are the McCaslins. They represent the clannish, ultra-conservative position in the South and are willing to convict Lucas without due process of law because their law is more basic and swifter. The six sons, described in some detail with the eldest being named after General Nathan Bedford Forrest and the twins, Bilbo and Vardaman, named after famous Mississippi politicians, just by their numbers show the power they hold in this story.[15] Yet, Faulkner portrays the twins as moving and looking like clothing store dummies. Though the Gowries as a unit outnumber any of the other families mentioned, their presence is summed up in the person of their father, Nub, who retains sole power and is considered by Faulkner to be a judge in making family decisions. Though physically impaired, Nub has the independence and strength one would expect of a descendent of the Scottish highlands. As Elmo

Howell notes, the Gowries represent an ambivalent feeling in Faulkner's attitude towards his county: "He loves it in spite of its faults, recognizing even in Gowrie's violence an element of character, of manhood, which seems to be disappearing in mass society...."[16] As men move into the South and the natives are forced into the outer reaches of Mississippi, some of the frontier ideal is lost, and the verbose Gavins tend to replace the rugged Nubs.

Nub Gowrie obstinately refuses to permit the exhumation of his son, but once he is convinced of the plausibility of foul play, he quickly orders the grave to be reopened. During these moments of decision, Chick notices that Nub is grieving, as Lucas had done after Molly died,, thus establishing a sympathetic bond between these two men and their mutual problems. It is at this point, and not necessarily at the end of the novel, that the reader realizes the possibility of an integrated society based on a common humanity. Later, once Montgomery's body had been discovered in a shallow grave, Nub goes berserk and jumps on Vinson's body, now hidden beneath some quicksand. The moment of truth has come: Lucas did not kill Montgomery because he was in jail at the time of Montgomery's death. A third party is involved, one who knew both Vinson and Jake Montgomery and who also possesses a gun. Nub Gowrie realizes the fallacy of continuing to maintain Lucas' guilt and orders his sons to take Vinson's body home.

At this point, the clues begin to mount up—but, in the final analysis, they seem to indicate that the author has lost sight of the finer dimensions of crafting a detective story. The reader knows that Crawford has an automatic German pistol and that he had been dealing in lumber. Crawford is the only real suspect. Before long Gavin manages to pull together the various threads of the murders, mainly with Lucas' help. Jake Montgomery had been buying lumber from Crawford, who, with his brother, was under contract to Mr. Sudley. Because Crawford was stealing lumber and there was a possibility Vinson would learn this, Crawford killed Vinson. To indict Crawford, Montgomery dug up Vinson's body with the idea of taking it to the sheriff. But Crawford intervened, killed Jake, put his body in Vinson's grave instead, and finally took Vinson's body down to the quicksand. He is seen in the dark by Miss Habersham and the two boys in the process. Once Chick and his two companions discover Jake's body, Crawford, having also observed the three detectives, digs up Jake's body and places it in a shallow grave. Because he is never really seen, except obscurely at night, Crawford takes on a symbolic identity; he is never developed as a full character. The reader does not dramatically understand the problems he faces nor appreciate his motive for killing two men.

As Miss Habersham instinctively knows, the primary focus of the novel is not on the Gowries but on Lucas, though in the drama of the story he remains relatively passive. Because of this, his character takes on a different perspective. While Lucas remains the catalyst, the focal point is really on the Chick-Lucas relationship and the growth in Chick as he attempts to understand the fullness of this relationship. Viewed this way, the novel can be divided into three segments. Chapters One-Three concern establishing the Chick-Lucas relationship and providing sufficient motivation for Chick to help Lucas; Chapters Four-Eight concern the mystery plot of going out to the cemetery and discovering that Lucas is innocent, at least of killing Montgomery; Chapters Nine-Eleven concern Gavin's philosophical beliefs in the civil rights movement in the South and Chick's further realization of his own commitment to his community and country, especially when he sees the town's reaction to fratricide. The middle five chapters have little stylistic complexity, unlike the flashbacks of the first few chapters and the reveries and philosophical interludes of the last three chapters. It is particularly in the first three and last three chapters that the Lucas-Chick relationship is important.

Because Lucas knows that he is related to the white side of the McCaslin family (his mannerism and speech constantly remind the townsfolk of Jefferson of this), he does not have the identity problems of a Charles Bon or a Joe Christmas because he is proud of his mixed blood. When a townsman in a fit of rage calls, "You goddamn biggity stiffnecked stinking burrheaded Edmonds sonofabitch," Lucas immediately isolates the operative word, "I belongs to the old lot. I'm a McCaslin" (p. 19). As a forthright man, Lucas will not let others stereotype him or lessen his own self-image. Dorothy Greer says in Faulkner's works it is the Negro's attitude, based on many influences, plus the antagonism and prejudices of the white man that make him what he is and give him his ability to withstand circumstances beyond his own making: "The [Negro] race is a Lucas Beauchamp on trial for its life defended by law, and rising with courage and dignity better than the white man in the same situation could muster, calm, stoical, independent."[17] Other blacks do not really associate with Lucas; even Aleck Sander does not have that personal relationship that might be expected of a black boy helping a black man. The other blacks remain behind closed doors afraid to venture an opinion or show Lucas some sign of support. Graphically, Lucas, in jail, is surrounded by whites who flow in and out of town; the blacks are there, they are just not visible. Indifferent to the established town customs, Lucas has thus incurred the wrath and hatred of the town; he threatens the very roots of Jefferson's society and though he has not done something like rape a white woman, the townsfolk and inhabitants of Beat Four overact because of their hatred for him.

Though Robert Jacobs maintains that the Lucas-Chick relationship is based on family ties, there is no real evidence for this.[18] Rather Faulkner has been sympathetic to Negroes in his writings as he himself admitted: "He [the Negro] does more with less than anybody else."[19] In 1955 at Nagano, Faulkner said that Lucas was doomed because of his black blood but there was a chance he could be saved: "Anyone can save anyone from injustice if he just will, if he just tries, just raises his voice."[20] With Lucas in the limelight, Faulkner reveals the tensions within this Southern community, not recording in a morbid way its demise, but through references to baptism (Chick falling into the creek, for example) and crucifixion he dramatizes a story of potential civic regeneration and resurrection, motifs that were definitely on his mind while writing *A Fable*.[21]

Though Joseph Blotner mentions three possible men who might have served as models, Lucas seems to transcend any biographical figure because most of the time he is sitting in jail and not interacting with others.[22] He lives on the ten acres of land ("like a postage stamp in the center of an envelope" [p. 8]) he has inherited.[23] Lucas suggests a quasi-tragic, isolated figure in a Greek tragedy; his house on the hill resembles the carven ailanthus leaves of the capital of a column. There is also something essentially primitive and antediluvian about this domestic scene; the cryptic three-toed prints of the chickens are out of the age of the great lizards. Thus Lucas is no ordinary person; he bridges the past and the present and, in terms of the drama of this story, looks forward to a future age—though where is he going, and with whom? When Chick sees Lucas, in the first part of the story, he looks at him as he emerges from the icy creek and sees Lucas' face manifesting "no pigment at all, not even the white man's lack of it, not arrogant, not even scornful: just intractable and composed" (p. 7). Chick does not hesitate at first to follow Lucas to Lucas' house though he feels an impulse to turn into Edmonds' house. As a gracious host, Lucas offers both food and warmth by the hearth and when Lucas orders Chick to take off his clothes in order for them to dry, Chick—presenting a telling image—stands naked in Lucas's house, enveloped by an "unmistakable odor of Negroes," an odor which represents in his mind "a condition: an idea: a belief: an acceptance..." (p. 11). He accepts the odor as he accepts Lucas' food—the collard greens, sidemeat fried in flour, biscuits, and buttermilk. Since this scene is a flashback, Chick tries to analyze its meaning in the present; he thinks, perhaps, it was the food that threw him off because when be tried to pay Lucas, Lucas merely looked at him as the coins fell to the floor. Chick violated the unwritten laws of hospitality. He was condescending. He treated Lucas without thinking of the consequences of his action. Lucas, in return, merely orders Chick's companions to pick up the coins and return them to him; he does not lecture or scold because his demeanor conveys how he feels.

Because Chick's relationship with Lucas is unresolved and in the form of a debt, William Sowder observes that much of "*Intruder in the Dust* is devoted to the attempt on the part of Lucas and Chick each to dominate the other: the compositional center of the book is the account of the ruses each used in an effort to prove the other an object."[24] While

Lucas and Chick do not become intimate companions or confidants, Lucas' situation provides an environment in which Chick can see the important values in society, in his family, and in himself. Chick's first encounter with Gavin, not chronologically speaking, but in terms of the drama of the novel, occurs Sunday noon. The beginning of the first and the end of the third chapters present the same scene with the intervening material giving background as to why Chick would go to the jail on Sunday in the first place. By using his cyclic imagination, a mode he had previously used in *Absalom, Absalom!*, Faulkner has achieved at the end of the third chapter what the reader could hardly surmise at the beginning of the first chapter.

Initially Chick's attitudes reflect those of his community; his gradual realization is not to proceed in trying to pay off a jejune financial debt, but to respond adequately to the demands made on him by the individuals he knows, as the Corporal did in *A Fable*. His growth is not linear, but zig-zags through the on-going relationship with Lucas, which is confusing to him at first because he has no maps or guidelines to determine the course this relationship will take. As he learns what constitutes the fabric of Lucas' life, he gains an appreciation of Lucas' behavior. Chick would like to clear the debt immediately through gifts—substitute gestures for the complex reactions he feels. Michael Millgate notes the changes in Chick's attitude:

> Charles, it is true, has an acute awareness of Lucas's individuality. But he is aware primarily of Lucas's sheer impenetrability, and certainly it is no commitment to individualism or to the idea of human dignity which first impels him to act on Lucas's behalf. His principal motivation, it appears, is his irritated recollection of an indebtedness to Lucas which his white pride insists that he discharge, but which Lucas's even more stubborn, and more resourceful, pride has consistently frustrated him from discharging. The progress of Charles's initiation is charted very largely in terms of his rejection of his original

> motive, which derived in large measure from the racial difference between Lucas and himself, in favour of a positive and even passionate awareness of the need to preserve human dignity and avert the shame of mob-violence....This utter atypicality of Lucas, his invincible independence and impenetrability, is what finally undermines any conception of *Intruder in the Dust* as a straightforward moral fable.[25]

Both Chick and Lucas are involved that Sunday noon in a relationship that took four years to establish; the nature of the relationship changed during this time period as Chick recorded it mentally during Lucas' visit to town to pay his taxes. To maintain that Chick comprehended the illusive quality of reality as well as the shifting quality of what appears solid is to overlook the vacillations in his mind as he tried to understand this relationship with Lucas.

The nuances of the Chick-Lucas relationships are complex and can be approached from a number of perspectives. Thomas Connolly incorrectly views that the factor that enables Chick to grow is the same messianic urge which prompted Ike McCaslin; rather Chick is politically, not theologically, motivated: "The messianic urge, interestingly enough, is a deterministic force over which Chick has very little volitional control."[26] Chick does not allow a boyhood hurt to sway him because he intellectually knows that he must not be part of the "injustice and outrage and dishonor and shame" that would result from Lucas' death at the hands of some intransigent men from the outlying beats. Irving Howe believes "the union of the old and patient Negro with the young and innocent white boy not yet corrupted in the ways of his fathers, Faulkner seems to be saying, will cleanse the land of its bloody and evil heritage."[27] Though the conclusion of the novel points to an undefined future, it does not mean that Lucas' ownership of land or his gold toothpick bear sufficient testimony that the rehabilitation of the Negro, at least in this novel, is an economic proposition or that racial identity and social responsibility begin with economic independence. Both

Andrew Lytle and Robert Penn Warren see the importance of Chick's growth, and Lytle suggests this is why the story does not end with the murder scene and its solution:

> Instead of leading up to the murder as a final release to the tensions of involvement, by putting it into the past Faulkner uses the act as a compulsive force to catalyze the disparate fragments of appearance into reality, for the story is not about violence at all. It is about a sixteen-year-old boy's education in good and evil and his effort to preserve his spiritual integrity.[28]

Edmund Wilson's contention that the book contains a kind of counterblast to the anti-lynching bill and to the civil rights plank in the Democratic platform has merit and gives the novel an apperceptive political dimension that warrants investigation.[29] Though Chick does not control the events, because the story has a definite communal dimension, nevertheless he consciously modifies his relationship to Lucas, not with the intention of enslaving him, but of providing an expanding freedom for the both of them.

It is after the experience at Lucas' house that Chick feels the import of the community's sentiments: "*We got to make him be a nigger first. He's got to admit he's a nigger. Then maybe we will accept him as he seems to intend to be accepted*" (p. 18). Lucas' house provides Chick with a place for discovery. As a result of that initial encounter, Chick became more and more observant: "He didn't hear it: he learned it..." (p. 18). He learns for example, that three years before, Lucas went to the crossroads store in his fine hat, watch-chain, and toothpick and Chick surmises that it was Lucas' mannerisms that caused a ruckus in the store. The half-dollar (actually seventy cents) which Chick had tried to give to Lucas begins to weigh heavy with Chick until it "swelled to its gigantic maximum" (p. 21). Chick even worked for his uncle trying to earn some money with which he could buy gifts for Lucas. Unlike the story of a boy who got into an endless cycle of lifting his calf over the pasture fence and still did it as a grown man, Chick refuses to get into this type of routine. Chick "deserted his calf" (p. 21). Even a present of four cigars, snuff, and a flowered imitation silk dress for Molly could not discharge the weight of his debt, as Lucas constantly thwarts Chick's efforts to gain the upper hand. Soon Chick knows "whatever would or could set him free was beyond not merely his reach but even his ken; he could not wait for it if it came and do without it if it didn't" (p. 23). Life has few clear-cut victories and Faulkner knows that a young man must learn to endure a number of unpleasant moments with grace and resolve.

Gradually Chick begins to widen his vision. He learns that Molly had died and that Lucas' daughter had moved away to Detroit. When encountering Lucas in town (each of the meetings being disturbing as he tried to decipher the tenor of their relationship), Chick reflects, *"You dont have to not be a nigger in order to grieve…"* (p. 25). The third time Lucas and Chick meet in town, Lucas looks directly into Chick's eyes, but Chick says Lucas does not recognize him at all: *"He hasn't even bothered to forget me."* (pp. 25–26). After this, Faulkner emphasizes an important theme in this novel: Chick is apparently free because his relationship with Lucas has been terminated. By drifting physically apart from Lucas, Chick thinks he has no obligation toward him and he hopes he can carry "into manhood only the fading legend of that old once-frantic shame and anguish and need not for revenge, vengeance but simply for reequalization, reaffirmation of his masculinity and his white blood" (p. 26). In his own mind he had turned the other cheek: "He was free" (p. 27). After this statement about Chick's illusory, undetermined freedom, Faulkner had originally brought to a conclusion a short story, as indicated on page 26 of the setting copy typescripts, Faulkner conceived of this part of the novel as a conclusion of Chick's growth; though Chick has not paid his debt to Lucas. Thus the first twenty-six pages of this novel set up a situation in which Chick can grow, it will take another chapter and a half before Faulkner brings the story back into the present time at noon on Sunday to give a fuller indication of the direction that growth will take.

At this point in the novel, Chick still shares the beliefs of the community as he learns of the events near Fraser's store from those who were there. Faulkner seems to emphasize constantly Chick's growth towards freedom as he mentions, at least six times after the conclusion of the short story mentioned above, that Chick is a free individual. When Chick visited Gavin's office the Saturday of the murder, he remembers something very important that subconsciously bothers him: the one man, Carothers Edmonds, who could help the situation was in a New Orleans' hospital. After dinner, during which Gavin implies Lucas is guilty, Chick's thoughts are on Lucas chained to a bedpost at the constable's house. Chick realizes that he alone is a key person in this story as Edmonds is out of town. As he returns home he tells Gavin, "It's all right with me. Lucas didn't have to work this hard not to be a nigger just on my account" (p. 34). That evening in bed Chick goes to sleep in "an almost unbearable excruciation of outrage and fury" as he thinks of what Lucas supposedly did, though he remembers that Crawford had served time in a federal penitentiary for armed resistance as an army deserter. Chick is aware of the Gowries and what they represent as they had "translated and transmogrified that whole region of lonely pine hills dotted meagrely with small tilted farms and peripatetic sawmills and contraband whiskey-kettles..." (p. 35). Where few outsiders venture to go, Chick mentally explores what is there.

The murder story is told a number of times in this novel; with each retelling something is added. Chick considers what the murder scene was like and the subsequent apprehension of Lucas by Fraser and his confinement in Skipworth's house, projecting what Sunday morning would be like devoid of Negroes and filled with outraged townsfolk. Chick tries to weigh the possibilities that face him: "Lucas was no longer his responsibility, he was no longer Lucas' keeper; Lucas himself had discharged him" (p. 42). But once Chick sees Lucas in person on Sunday and realizes that Lucas remembers him and needs his personal help, he begins slowly to change his attitude. Lucas has not changed as he gets out of the car in front of the jail; he is still "detached, impersonal, almost musing, intractable and composed..." (p. 44). This scene at the end of the third chapter returns the time scheme of the novel back to the first scene of the first chapter and forms an *inclusio* with it.

Except for the scene inside the jail cell where Chick again encounters Lucas and is further motivated to assist Lucas because he knows now that Gavin will not help, Chick does not see Lucas during the middle five chapters of the book when he and Miss Habersham and Aleck Sander are trying to solve the murders. Thus Faulkner puts great emphasis on this jail scene, recounting a sympathetic description of the jail itself, the story of the young girl scratching her name onto the glass in 1864, and the views of Will Legate and Mr. Tubbs who reluctantly guard Lucas. The jail is replete with the "smell of creosote and excrement and stale vomit and incorrigibility and defiance and repudiation..." (p. 56); a smell far different from that which Chick observed at Lucas' house. Throughout, Gavin dominates the conversation and will not let Lucas tell all that he knows uninterrupted. Lucas' reluctance to trust Gavin is well-founded and he says, with a degree of cautiously hopeful insouciance at the conclusion of their meeting, "I'll try to wait." Their exit from the cell is marked by an echoing sound of extraordinary magnitude: "...the last carborundum-grooved door upon their own progenitorless apotheosis behind one clockless lock responsive only to the last stroke of eternity..." (p. 65). When Gavin leaves, Chick mentions only the formless "black silhouette" of his uncle, an image he is to use again when he falls asleep (p. 196). At this point, Chick feels that full weight of responsibility. He chokes up with "Me? *Me?*" and as he remembers the Ephraim story of the lost half-dollar (reminiscent of the half-dollar he wanted to give Lucas and also the half-dollar which Lucas shot at in the woods in front of Crawford), he finally achieves a further insight into Lucas: *"He's not only beat me, he never for one second had any doubt about it"* (p. 73). With this, Chick has little doubt that he would help Lucas, especially after Lucas' direct appeal when Chick returned with the tobacco.

The actual story of the exhumation of the bodies is perhaps unduly protracted (as is the screen play of "The Big Sleep" which Faulkner helped to write), though upon reflection Gavin realizes the facts are clear enough. Thus when Nub Gowrie and his sons arrive to meet the sheriff, Gavin, and their crew, the grave is empty, and Lucas' innocence in the murder of Montgomery is definitely established. Faulkner had little trouble composing this section in the original draft and then revising it in the setting copy; the most notable change concerns some additions to Gavin's philosophical statements. Most of the murder story is straightforward and involves the least amount of complication of any of the novel's three parts. Once Vinson Gowrie's body has been discovered at the end of Chapter Eight (an easy chapter for Faulkner to write), Faulkner then started with almost totally new material since he had no original draft to follow as he wrote what was to become Chapter Nine. Since the three detectives had been working Sunday evening and into the early hours of Monday morning, the story continues from 2 P. M. on Monday, keeping at this point an essentially chronological time scheme. When Montgomery's body is brought into the undertaker's, the murder mystery is over and Faulkner merely fills in the details. The emphasis shifts from Chick's awareness of Lucas' situation to his awareness of the town's attitude and how he has changed from agreeing with their position, at least as reflected in Gavin's statements.

Since the town is too large and amorphous to be portrayed by developing individual characters, Faulkner collectively represents them in Chick's mind as being one corporate "Face." To show the fluidity of the crowd's ideas and movements, Faulkner uses two images to try to capture their identity. First, the crowd ebbs and flows, and secondly, it stages the Battle of San Juan Hill with "the faces in invincible profile not amazed not aghast but in a sort of irrevocable repudiation..." (p. 185). Chick fuses the experiences of pity, shame, grief, and justice that were part of his experience; dreamily he wants "to leave his mark too on his time in man but only that, no more than that, some mark on his part in earth but humbly, waiting wanting humbly even, not really hoping even, nothing (which of course was everything) except his own one anonymous chance too to perform something passionate and brave and austere not just in but into man's enduring chronicle worthy of a place in it...in gratitude for the gift of his time in it..." (p. 193), a sequence embodying the heart of Chick's self-realization, the ultimate reaches of the growth that has taken place so far. Faulkner said that he wanted to leave his mark, too, like Kilroy, on this world and perhaps he is sharing some of his desires with Chick. Thus, all history is summed up in the present; the mystery surrounding Lucas is paradigmatic: "Yesterday won't be over until tomorrow and tomorrow began ten thousand years ago" (p. 194). Aiding Lucas is like repeating Pickett's disastrous charge in 1863 or like reliving Columbus' landing in the New World in 1492, because life demands that one commit oneself to new battles and explore new lands whatever the risks or whatever the cost.

Contrasted to Chick's experience of commitment is the experience of avoiding the situation by fleeing. Observing the citizens of Yoknapatawpha, Chick says almost to the point of tedium (at least ten times) that "they ran." These people are not running from Lucas because by now they had forgotten him, they are running from the horrendous act of fratricide committed by Crawford Gowrie. They did not want to have to contemplate the notion of having to lynch Crawford as they had once contemplated lynching Lucas for the exact same crime. Ironically, Lucas will be revered and even become the tyrant over the whole country's white conscience. Chick has gone beyond any of the Boy Scout ranks and entered into adulthood because he is able now to compare his actions with those of his fellow townsmen.

Reflecting to a certain extent the cast of Gavin's mind, Chick, having faced the meaning of death and fratricide (how easily the community accepts fratricide!), contemplates the meaning of life and birth. It is by the act of eating that man enters the world, perhaps a reflection on the meal at Lucas' house: "By the act of eating and maybe only by that did he [man] actually enter the world..." (p. 207). When one is born and reborn through life's experiences, he proclaims his "I-Am into that vast teeming anonymous solidarity of the world from beneath which the ephemeral rock would cool and spin away to dust..." (p. 207). Chick has prepared himself to enter into the community he lives with and will hopefully transform it. What is this community like? Faulkner, in a long phrase on page 209, tries to define the essential dynamism of this community by mentioning fifteen times the general word "it"—"that fierce desire that they should be perfect because they were his and he was theirs, that furious intolerance of any one single jot or tittle less than absolute perfection." It has been a long twenty-two hours since Chick and Gavin met the town representative, Mr. Lilley, and learned about the town's values. Chick realizes far more than Gavin that a person who is determined to seek freedom is likewise determined to root this freedom in living with and among other people.

Though the murder mystery has been solved with the help of Lucas, there is the job of catching Crawford and having him face the legal system. To this end, a ploy is devised to take Lucas to Hollymount by way of the Whiteleaf cutoff where Crawford would certainly come to attack Lucas, once Willy Ingrum shared this privileged information with everyone he knew. In all of this, Miss Habersham is not worried because she knows the resourcefulness of Lucas to escape danger. The following Saturday, one week later, the town is back in full swing; it is a busy "Saturday among Saturdays" (p. 236); throughout the novel Faulkner has given a rhythm to the novel by describing the town streets, whether they are empty or full. Almost casually, the reader discovers that Crawford had committed suicide in jail with a German Luger and that Lucas is in town wearing a flashy shirt and a pair of zoot pants. Gavin appears to be back to normal and making snap judgments, suggesting, perhaps, that the preoccupation of thinking about Lucas is just about over:[30]

> So we have to divorce our wife today in order to remove from our mistress the odium of mistress in order to divorce our wife tomorrow in order to remove from our mistress and so on. As a result of which the American woman has become cold and undersexed; she has projected her libido onto the automobile not only because its glitter and gadgets and mobility pander to her vanity and incapacity (because of the dress decreed upon her by the national retailers association) to walk but because

it will not maul her and tousle her, get her all sweaty and disarranged. (p. 239)

Gavin can relax a little, talk about other topics, and learn to live with (or suppress) what has happened without being obsessed by it.

When Lucas appears for the final confrontation with Chick and Gavin, he seems, unlike Chick, to have changed little: "the same face which he had seen for the first time when he climbed dripping up out of that icy creek that morning four years ago, unchanged, to which nothing had happened since not even age…" (pp. 240–41). Gavin encourages Lucas to take some flowers to Miss Habersham to thank her for her help and insists that Chick not stop making progress in his attempt to do what is right. After Gavin refuses to accept payment, he is finally persuaded and with a bit of fumbling Lucas manages to give him two dollars, a scene that is more complicated in the uncorrected setting copy as Lucas arranges and rearranges his coins. The conclusion though comic, as Cleanth Brooks suggests, nevertheless does put Lucas in a demeaning light; on the surface, all the emotions and conflict of the past week are submerged and the three now greet each other in a more relaxed way ("without embarrassing sentimentality, the deepest kind of understanding"), though there is no genuine acceptance of one another on a deeply personal level.[31]

It seems clear that a good deal of Chapter Ten is an effort to tie together the elements of the murder story as expeditiously as possible. Faulkner enjoyed the middle five chapters, but since he had not reached an ultimate conclusion once the two bodies were found, he still had some more explanation to include. Because of the weaknesses in the murder mystery section of the novel (particularly the fact that it takes up about five of the novel's eleven chapters), I think there is room for some psychological reflections on the novel's meaning. In any murder story, whether the actual murder takes place before or during the story, the reader must understand something about the murderer, the victim, and the motive for the murder. Sufficient clues must also exist for the reader to make up his own mind somewhere along the way as to the pattern of the story and the direction it is taking; these clues are often couched in subtleties and the reader must be able to hold in his mind many items until he finds or discovers the discernible pattern. If he is able to enter into the mind of the detective, then the experience becomes all the more enjoyable because he is matching his wits against those of a supposed expert.[32] C. Hugh Holman in his discussion of Faulkner and the detective story says "the detective story is much more concerned with understanding the past through interpretation; it is almost epistemological in its concern."[33] Certainly, Chick in *Intruder* is concerned with understanding the past. The question ultimately is whether the structure of the detective story is sustained and integrated in the overall plot of the novel. Here, *Intruder* is in trouble. Gavin himself has trouble with some primary motivation: "Why did Crawford have to kill Vinson in order to obliterate the witness of his thieving?" (p. 224). Part of Gavin's, and the reader's, inability to answer this is that we do not have a clear picture of the exact nature of the lumber deal that both Vinson and Crawford are engaged in. In addition, the detective story becomes too involved (both Vinson and Jake are exhumed twice); we have no character development of either Vinson or Crawford, nor do we understand fully the reasons for Crawford burying Jake in Vinson's grave. If Vinson's body simply disappeared, then this would cast suspicion on the three detectives rather than throwing the blame on some unspecified third party. Also, the reason for burying Crawford in a shallow grave and not in the quicksand does not make much sense, as it would obviously be easier to find the body in a shallow grave. Finally, why would Lucas put himself in a position where he would be framed and then not really speak out to the proper authorities? These deficiencies in the novel are serious, and while they cannot be excused on one level, perhaps on another level, they can have some significance.

Since a number of the finer points of mystery story writing are missing or underdeveloped in this novel, particularly in the portrayal of the Gowrie family, Faulkner is pointing, as Chick realizes, to some areas of concern within the human conscience. In his own way, Gavin tries to articulate how the Southerner feels about the problem of racial responsibility and civil rights, but as has been indicated, he does not present the most coherent possible picture. If the interlocking relationships among Crawford, Vinson, Chick, and Lucas are seen as being symbolic of some tensions within the Southern mentality, then perhaps the novel makes a bit more sense. Joseph Gold maintains this view:

> The actual digging, the examination of the past reveals the extent to which the present is living in the blind acceptance of falsehood. It turns out that the body in the grave is not that of a murdered man. This discovery leads to the realization that there are two murdered men. Symbolically, it indicates a greater evil in the past than the present wants to admit. The simple judgments and crude prejudices of society turn out to be baseless, and reason and examination lead to an understanding of the underlying complexities of an apparently obvious situation.[34]

Though Faulkner never read any Freud while he was writing *Intruder*, the mystery in this story is part of a far deeper psychological mystery within the Southern psyche.[35] In this view, as developed by Aaron Steinberg, Lucas is seen as an intruder into the white world and also as being a step-child or sibling (the term "boy" has often been used to refer to elderly Negroes) in the unconscious white world.[36] When Lucas is suspected and accused of killing a white man (he is the least likely to prove his innocence), his manner and disposition seem to betray him. Chick breaks a community taboo and defends Lucas because of the guilt feelings he has towards Lucas; by digging up the graves, Chick is probing the white consciousness to find out its secrets. Gavin, as an older member of the white community, tries to delay this process and Chick rejects Gavin's views and acts with the aid of two companions. Gavin's rationalizations are later accepted as being effective for solving the black-white tensions, though this is not really demonstrated in the plot. Basically, "In *Intruder in the Dust*, the unconscious death-wish against the younger child is objectified as Chick, digging up the grave, discovers that the actual murderer was the victim's older brother. In this sense, Chick parallels the psychiatrist in that he probes the unconscious (digs up the grave) to expose the repressed (buried) fratricidal act."[37] The repression of the whites in this murderous act is projected onto Lucas, who stands for the younger brother in society. Once the grave is opened, Faulkner shifts the mystery plot to a presentation of the conscious Southern attitude toward Negroes. Thus Lucas is a device, a catalyst and not really a full character in himself. Steinberg believes "the plot of *Intruder in the Dust* reduces the desperate problem of lynching in the South to the fairy-tale or the comic-strip level," and sees Lucas' request for his receipt as a comic, paternalistic belittling presentation of this black man.[38] Yet the last three chapters do not focus on Lucas, but on Chick's growth to maturity.

One dimension of a psychological appreciation that Steinberg does not develop concerns Chick's dreams which are from a Freudian viewpoint, a reservoir in his unconscious and embody a suppressed renunciation of the concerns of the external world.[39] Just as Gavin finds an expression of the American libido (and perhaps his own?) in the American car, so too, Chick's dreams express wishes which oppose the conscious world (in this case of discrimination) because the mind's censor is relaxed. A dream represents a disguised fulfillment of an unconscious wish and often explains in a fluid way the deeper connections one feels but does not express in everyday conversation. Freud, though opposed by Jung on this, saw phylogenetic references in dreams; that is, they refer not only to the individual's background and desires but to those of the human race as well. As is true with the inhabitants of Yoknapatawpha, they seek free gratification and flee from the realities of the fratricide in order to protect their long-standing beliefs which help them survive. Chick tries to discuss his dreams and discover for himself what they mean: "Besides, it's all right. I dreamed through all that; I dreamed through them too, dreamed them away too; let them stay in bed or milking their cows before dark or chopping wood before dark or by lanterns or not lanterns either. Because they were not the dream; I just passed them to get to the dream—" (p. 205). Chick is probing; what he is trying to express is (somebody or) something about which it is too much to expect for people just sixteen or going on eighty to do. Chick remembers in his dream Gavin's story about English boys his own age who led troops and flew scout airplanes in France in 1918. He identifies very much with these soldiers as he has previously identified with the Civil War soldiers. The deepest recesses of his mind reveal images of conflict (football game) and warfare (Civil War, Battles of San Juan, and World War I) as he attempts to determine subconsciously the nature of his relationship with Lucas.

The vacillation in Chick as revealed in his dreams and reveries is an important part of the perspective of the novel since Faulkner has chosen to tell the story with Chick as a third-person narrator.[40] In his state of exhaustion, Chick reveals the connections and relationships he feels linking the past to the present and the present to the future to give a sense of continuity in his life. Chick's mind encompasses the people around him, especially Lucas, Gavin, Nub Gowrie, his mother, and the townsfolk, as he perceives what is happening. He tests the values of others as they enter his subconscious and filter through this week of crisis. Andrew Lytle sees the novel comprising narrow physical limits, "but the physical action, while performing at its own level, releases the flow of reverie and comment which becomes the embodiment of the intrinsic meaning. Since within this area lies the realm of truth, where all is timeless, the dual consciousness moves through past, present, and even into the future according to the needs of the particular stage of the story's development."[41] In this way, Chick interiorizes the experience of his encounter with Lucas and the murders in Jefferson, achieving for himself an entrance into the realms of universal truth, which go far beyond being just another character in a whodunit.

Perhaps Edmund Wilson overreacted to *Intruder* when he stated that there "has been nothing so exhilarating in its way since the triumphs of the Communist-led workers in the early Soviet films; we are thrilled by the same kind of emotion that one got from some of the better dramatizations of the career of Abraham Lincoln."[42] And even Everett Carter rhapsodizes when he says *Intruder* is a poem of superb craftsmanship and total structure using metaphor, character, and plot.[43] While *Intruder* is not one of Faulkner's more highly rated works, nevertheless it deals with a very important theme: a young man's growth in his civic responsibilities as perceived over a period of four years, but culminating in one crucial week; the emphasis is on action to creatively bring about justice and not a reliance on abstract thoughts and good feelings. While Chick has not reconciled the Jefferson community or offered Lucas a new sense of security, he has grown with the help of some friends and relatives. As Faulkner suggests in this novel, the solution for the South's problems will come from a recognition of its problems, an investigation of the dimensions of the problem and the personalities involved, and a willingness to do something about the inherent injustices. As he said in reference to the civil rights problems dramatized in this novel: "Yes, people have got to do it, not theories. People have got to say: 'No matter how weak I am, I myself, Smith, will not put up with this.'"[44] But what of Lucas at the end of the novel? Where is he going? Back to an empty house? Back into a community that has no regard whatsoever for him and would like to see him banished or imprisoned forever? If anything, this ending is a trap for meditation, in which all the novel's Vocabulary needs to be evaluated and tested.

NOTES

I am grateful to Mrs. Paul D. Summers, Jr., Faulkner's daughter, for allowing me to quote from the typescripts of *Intruder in the Dust* and to the Alderman Library, University of Virginia, for allowing me access to the Faulkner Collection.

1. Cf. *Lion in the Garden*, eds. James B. Meriwether and Michael Millgate (New York: Random House, 1968), p. 177.
2. *Lion in the Garden*, p. 202.
3. James Baldwin, "Faulkner and Desegregation," *Partisan Review*, 23 (Fall 1956), 570.
4. *Lion in the Garden*, p. 184.
5. Cf. Essays, *Speeches and Public Letters*, ed. James B. Meriwether (New York: Random House, 1965), p. 88.
6. *Essays, Speeches and Public Letters*, pp. 102–103.
7. *Essays, Speeches and Public Letters*, p. 111.
8. *Essays, Speeches and Public Letters*, p. 186. For a further look at Faulkner's views

on civil rights, cf. *Faulkner in the University*, eds. Frederick L. Gwynn and Joseph L. Blotner (New York: Vintage, 1959), pp. 209-227; *Essays, Speeches and Public Letters*, pp. 92-112.
9. Malcolm Cowley, *The Faulkner-Cowley File* (New York: Viking, 1966), p. 18.
10. Olga Vickery, *The Novels of William Faulkner* (Baton Rouge: Louisiana State University Press, 1964), p. 142.
11. William Faulkner, *Intruder in the Dust* (New York: Random House, 1948), p. 48. All future references to this novel will be to this edition.
12. Kenneth Richardson, *Force and Faith in the Novels of William Faulkner* (The Hague: Mouton Press, 1967), p. 107.
13. *Lion in the Garden*, pp. 126-127.
14. Calvin Brown, "Faulkner's Use of the Oral Tradition," *Georgia Review*, 22 (Summer 1968), 163.
15. Theodore Gilmore Bilbo (1877-1947) was State Senator from 1908-1912, Governor of Mississippi from 1916-1920 and from 1928-1932, and was U. S. Senator elected in 1934, 1940, and 1946, but did not take the oath to serve in the 80th Congress because of sickness. James Kimble Vardaman served in the State House of Representatives from 1890-1896, was Governor of Mississippi from 1904-1908, and served in the U. S. Senate from 1913-1919. Both men were outspoken politicians often involved in lively debates. In May 1911, John Falkner, Jr., William Faulkner's uncle, was President of the Central Vardaman Club of Oxford.
16. Elmo Howell, "William Faulkner's Caledonia: A Note on *Intruder in the Dust*," *Studies in Scottish Literature*, 3 (April 1966), 252.
17. Dorothy Greer, "Dilsey and Lucas: Faulkner's Use of the Negroes as Gauge of Moral Character," *Emporia State Research Studies*, 11 (September 1962), 59.
18. Robert Jacobs, "Faulkner's Tragedy of Isolation," in *Southern Renascence*, eds. Louis D. Rubin, Jr. and Robert Jacobs (Baltimore: Johns Hopkins University Press, 1966), p. 186.
19. *Lion in the Garden*, p. 79.
20. *Lion in the Garden*, p. 130.
21. Irving Malin, *William Faulkner: An Interpretation* (Stanford: Stanford University Press, 1957), p. 89, discusses the event of Chick's falling in the creek as a baptism.
22. Joseph L. Blotner, *Faulkner: A Biography* (New York: Random House, 1974) II, 1246.
23. Cf. *Lion in the Garden*, p. 255, for a discussion of the significance in Faulkner's mind of the postage stamp.
24. William Sowder, "Lucas Beauchamp as Existential Hero," *College English*, 25 (November 1963), 117.
25. Cf. *The Achievement of William Faulkner*, (New York: Random House, 1966), pp. 219-220.
26. Thomas Connolly, "Fate and 'the Agony of the Will': Determinism in Some Works of William Faulkner," in *Essays on Determinism in American Literature*, ed. Sidney Krause (Kent, Ohio: Kent State University Press, 1964), p. 49.
27. Irving Howe, "The South and Current Literature," *American Mercury*, 67

(October 1948), 497.
28. Cf. Robert Penn Warren, "Faulkner: The South and the Negro," *Faulkner: A Collection of Critical Essays* (Englewood Cliffs, New Jersey: Prentice Hall, 1966), p. 78. This quote is taken from Andrew Lytle's *The Hero With the Private Parts* (Baton Rouge: Louisiana State University Press, 1966), p. 131.
29. In 1948, the Republican Party actually had a stronger plank on civil rights than the Democrats. The Republican Party wrote: "Lynching or any other form of mob violence anywhere is a disgrace to any civilized state, and we favor the prompt enactment of legislation to end this infamy. One of the basic principles of this republic is the equality of all individuals to their right to life, liberty, and the pursuit of happiness." They maintained that these rights should not be denied to anyone because of race, religion, color, or country of origin. The Democratic Party wrote: "The Democratic Party commits itself to continuing its efforts to eradicate all racial, religious, and economic discrimination." *National Party Platforms: 1840–1968*, comp. Kirk Porter and Donald Johnson (Urbana: University of Illinois Press, 1970), pp. 452, 453.
30. Wayne Booth has made a valuable observation about Gavin's intrusion on the meaning of the American automobile: "One's attitude toward the much debated theorizing of Gavin Stevens at the end of Faulkner's *Intruder in the Dust* is not affected markedly by the fact that the ideas are not given directly by Faulkner. The question is whether Gavin's elaborate commentary is essentially related to the nephew's experience of a near-lynching and his consequent growth toward maturity. In any 'truth-discovery' novel, and especially in novels which try to lead young people to the hard truths of adulthood, the problem is to make the discovery a convincing outcome of the experience. In *Intruder*, as in many such works, the attitude toward which Faulkner wants his young hero to grow is so complex that neither the boy nor the reader is likely to infer it from the experience itself. They both must therefore be preached at by the wise uncle, sometimes with little direct relevance to the drama....If we choose to join the chorus of protests against these pages, we must be very clear that we are not objecting to authorial commentary but rather to a particular kind of disharmony between idea and dramatized object. Even if Stevens' views could be shown to differ from Faulkner's, the discovery of irony would not save the work; the disharmony would remain. What is more, our objections would not be stronger if these opinions had been given in Faulkner's own name." *The Rhetoric of Fiction* (Chicago: University of Chicago Press, 1970), pp. 181–182.
31. Cleanth Brooks, *William Faulkner: The Yoknapatawpha Country* (New Haven: Yale University Press, 1963), p. 294.
32. Cf. William Van O'Connor's *The Tangled Fire of William Faulkner*, pp. 135–145, for a discussion of Faulkner and the detective story. O'Connor looks to the Lucas-white citizens of Jefferson as the center of the story.
33. C. Hugh Holman, *The Roots of Southern Writing* (Athens: University of Georgia Press, 1972), p. 170.
34. Joseph Gold, *William Faulkner: A Study in Humanism from Metaphor to Discourse* (Norman: University of Oklahoma Press, 1966), p. 88.

35. *Lion in the Garden*, p. 251.
36. For a full and detailed development of this Freudian interpretation, cf. Aaron Steinberg's dissertation, "Faulkner and the Negro" (New York University, 1963), pp. 294-338. Steinberg relies on the psychological views of one of Freud's pupils, Richard Sterba, particularly the material found as Sterba's essay "Some Psychological Factors in Negro Race Hatred and in Anti-Negro Riots," *Psychoanalysis and Social Sciences*, 1 (1947), 412-415.
37. Aaron Steinberg, "'Intruder in the Dust': Faulkner as a Psychologist of the Southern Psyche," *Literature and Psychology*, 15 (Spring 1965), 122.
38. Aaron Steinberg, "Faulkner and the Negro," p. 331.
39. A complete analysis of dreams in Faulkner's works has not been done. Important references for such a study might include the following: Ruel Foster, "Dream as Symbolic Act in Faulkner," *Perspective*, 2 (Summer 1949), 179-194. Unfortunately, Professor Foster does not deal with this problem in *Intruder*. Sigmund Freud, *The Interpretation of Dreams*, trans. A. A. Brill (New York: Modern Library, 1913); Frederick Hoffman, *Freudianism and the Literary Mind* (Baton Rouge: Louisiana State University, 1957); Ernest Jones, *The Life and Word of Sigmund Freud*, eds. Lionel Trilling and Steven Marcus (New York: Basic Books, 1961); Carl Jung, *Modern Man in Search of a Soul* (New York: 1934); Ernst Kris, *Psychoanalytic Explorations in Art* (New York: International University Press, 1952); Lionel Trilling, *Freud and the Crisis of our Culture* (Boston: Beacon Press, 1955); Philip Wheelwright, *The Burning Fountain* (Bloomington: Indiana University Press, 1954).
40. For an extended development of Chick as narrator, cf. John Hart's "That Not Impossible He: Faulkner's Third-Person Narrator," in *Studies in Faulkner*, ed. Neal Woodruff (Pittsburgh: Carnegie Institute of Technology, 1961), pp. 29-42.
41. *The Hero With the Private Parts*, p.133.
42. Edmund Wilson, "William Faulkner's Reply to the Civil Rights Program," *New Yorker*, 23 October 1948, p. 234.
43. Everett Carter, "The Meaning of, and in, Realism," *Antioch Review* 12 (March 1952), 92.
44. *Lion in the Garden*, p. 142.

Faulkner and the Post-Confederate

Neil Schmitz

Think of Ken Burns's 1990 PBS documentary, *The Civil War*, eleven hours long, nine episodes, shown on five consecutive nights in September 1990, coming at us like the Army of the Potomac, richly funded, beautifully equipped, with its own anthem, Jay Ungar's 1984 composition for three fiddles and two guitars, "Ashokan Farewell." GM, NEH, CPB, the Arthur Vining Davis Foundation, the MacArthur Foundation are up front, announcing their support, as the first and longest episode, "The Cause," begins. At the end, credits almost interminable, long supply trains going on and on, section after section: a stellar cast of readers, Archival Materials, Special Thanks, to many individuals and agencies.

The first word is "We," Oliver Wendell Holmes Jr. speaking. "We have shared," he says, "the incommunicable experience of war." An officer in the Union Army, seriously wounded first at Balls Bluff, then at Antietam, later Chief Justice, of that resonant New England name, Holmes is as Federal blue as one can get. He speaks in the epigraph. First word of text-proper is "American," and it is heavily stressed, repeated. "American homes became headquarters, American churches and schoolhouses sheltered the dying," says the principal narrator (David McCullough), who is never identified or seen. "In two days at Shiloh, on the banks of the Tennessee River, more American men fell than in all previous American wars combined." The repetition insists on closure, on completion, the resolution of the issue.

"American," this is the Unionist designation, and it is stamped on everything we see.

Ohio's Geoffrey C. Ward, sometime editor of *American Heritage* magazine, author of *Lincoln's Thought and the Present* (1978) and *A First Class Temperament: The Emergence of Franklin Roosevelt* (1989), is the principal writer. Pennsylvania's David McCullough, longtime editor and writer at Time magazine, longtime contributing editor at *American Heritage*, then at work on *Truman, A Biography* (1993), is the primary narrator. McCullough's trans-Allegheny/Pittsburghian is the Voice of this History, not Shelby Foote's softly drawling Greenville, Mississippi, voice, though we see a lot of Foote, epic "American" historian of *The Civil War, A Narrative* (1954–1974), in Burns's film, representing the Confederate position, delivering a certain post-Confederate narrative. McCullough's unseen narration is collective, connective, seemingly sideless. Experts, who never converse, argue, or confront each other in the film over the direction of the narrative, singly address its camera eye, report to it. We accept immediately that Foote is the minor historian, that he represents a side, a Southern reading that is incomplete, partial. He won't speak for Frederick Douglass. Barbara J. Fields, the African American historian featured in Burns's documentary, doesn't do battles and leaders, won't represent Bedford Forrest. Everyone is exactly in his or her Civil War place, Northerners, Southerners, whites, blacks.

Talking about battles and leaders, about Lee and Stuart, Lee and Longstreet, in that sad ironically resigned Southern voice, Foote does an elegant post-Confederate, plays his nonthreatening part in this celebratory Unionist text. He does in fact a kind of Faulknerian performance, is a sort of rueful Gavin Stevens, the patriot attorney in William Faulkner's embattled *Intruder in the Dust* (1948), but disciplined, restrained. No danger here of racisms, of embarrassing usages, of inadvertent revelations, of sudden defiances. In 1990, in this major Unionist Civil War documentary, Foote represents the Southern narrative, and he everywhere summons the Southern narrative's great genius, invokes his statement and feeling, often questionably.

In Episode 3, "Gettysburg," wanting to essentialize Confederate

Southern feeling, Foote cites Faulkner's now classical Gettysburgian speech in *Intruder in the Dust*, "For every Southern boy fourteen years old," a speech strongly established in Gettysburg literature. Foote reads it straight, as perhaps we should, in some sense. "For every Southern boy fourteen years old," that passage reads, tacitly excluding Chick Mallison's African American comrade, Aleck Sander, "not once but whenever he wants it, there is the instant when it's still not yet two oclock on that July afternoon in 1863, the brigades are in position behind the rail fence, the guns are laid and ready in the woods and the furled flags are already loosened to break out and Pickett himself with his long oiled ringlets and his hat in one hand probably and his sword in the other looking up the hill waiting for Longstreet to give the word and it's all in the balance, it hasn't happened yet, it hasn't even begun yet, it not only hasn't begun yet but there is still time for it not to begin."[1] Foote does not read the entire passage. He assumes we know it as we know the final passage in F. Scott Fitzgerald's *The Great Gatsby* (1925), and therefore briefly refers to it. He points to the speech, acknowledges its statement. It memorializes this moment of intense Confederate nationality, all the Southern states there, valiant in the cause. All Anglo-Southern boys, Mississippian, Alabamian, Georgian, know the order of battle, where its divisions stood. This is the Confederate thing they share, the glory of this fatal charge, the fantasy of victory.

Faulkner, of course, ironically records this post-Confederate feeling. In the vault of the hyperbole, a suspension of reality, a delay of historical truth, an echo of John Wilkes Booth, a glimpse of Tom Sawyer. Chick Mallison, the boy, and Gavin Stevens, the man, can both enjoy this exaltation of nationality, this outcome, only by rigorously denying sociopolitical actualities, by excluding the issue of slavery, of all that is at stake for Aleck Sander.

Gettysburg is indeed a difficult subject for the post-Confederate, Southern writing in Unionist discourse, early and late. In Barry Hannah's 1993 story, "Bats Out of Hell Division," the Army of the Potomac, unable to endure any more Confederate Southern reliving of the grand suspended Gettysburgian moment, surrenders. Raggedy Confederate specters invest the Federal works. Hannah's story at once answers Gavin Stevens's Gettysburg address and seeks its own escape from the field, memorial Southern writing centered by the Confederate thing. For post-Civil War Southern writers, the issue of repudiation, of relinquishment, required tough delicate thinking, balancing statement, feats of logical and lexical engineering, of circumlocution and ellipsis. How to enjoy at Gettysburg the greatness of this military Confederate moment, when the post-Confederate had always fundamentally to swear: "We understand that when Lincoln signed the emancipation proclamation, your victory was assured, for he then committed you to the cause of human liberty, against which the arms of man cannot prevail—while those of our statemen who trusted to make slavery the cornerstone of our Confederacy doomed us to defeat as far as they could, committing us to a cause that reason could not defend or the sword maintain in the sight of advancing civilization."[2] Henry Woodfin Grady speaks here, delivering his celebrated 1886 banquet speech, "The New South," at a formal dinner of the New England Society in New York, General Sherman seated among the glittering array of Northern bankers and capitalists, his gaze fixed on Grady. Grady let Sherman have it. "I want to say to General Sherman," he said, "who is considered an able man in our parts, though some people think he is kind of careless about fire, that from the ashes he left us in 1864 we have raised a brave and beautiful city."[3] The New South, he told his Yankee auditors, "had nothing for which to apologize."[4] Post-Confederate Southern statement, even as it finds its place in Unionist discourse, is, barbed and bristly.

I want to rethink the post-Confederate narrative Faulkner presents in *Intruder in the Dust*, to observe, as it were, his struggle with it, focusing in particular on the usage "Sambo," this blatant racism, a racism constantly calling Gavin Stevens's version of the post-Confederate into question. It is a usage the younger Chick Mallison scrupulously evades. "Lucas Beauchamp, Sambo," as Stevens so awkwardly and ambiguously has it, recalls Huck Finn's trials with his usage, "Nigger," in referring to

Jim. *Intruder in the Dust* everywhere refers to the *Adventures of Huckleberry Finn*. Lucas gives Chick the gaze. "Jim won't ever forgit you, Huck; you's de bes' fren' Jim's ever had; en you's de only fren' ole Jim's got now."[5] *Intruder in the Dust* takes up the question Mark Twain engages in *Huckleberry Finn*: how to set Jim free, and it, too, addresses the resources of the language, listens to Pap Finn, listens to Gavin Stevens, is unlikely, screwed into a Tom Sawyer plot. How to set Southern writing free, this, too, was Mark Twain's question.

Post-Confederate, as I see it, exactly names the discursive pact Mark Twain, Joel Chandler Harris, Thomas Nelson Page, George Washington Cable, and other Southern writers, in the 1870s and '80s, differently negotiated and signed with William Dean Howells, Richard Watson Gilder, Robert Underwood Johnson, Thomas Bailey Aldrich, Charles Dudley Warner, with *The Atlantic*, *Harper's*, *The Forum*, *Scribner's/The Century*, *The Critic*, the pact that enabled these young Southern writers to have access to the new bicoastal national literary market, to have national careers, to figure in the new postwar American literature. They produce a remarkable set of texts: Cable's *The Grandissimes* (1880), Harris's *The Songs and Sayings of Uncle Remus* (1881), Mark Twain's *The Adventures of Huckleberry Finn* (1884) and *Life on the Mississippi* (1885), which theorizes the post-Confederate, Page's *In Ole Virginia* (1887), parts of which appear in the *Century* as it commences *Battles and Leaders of the Civil War*, the first mounting of Unionist Civil War documentary. Readers of the series could turn from the bitter jangling of Confederate generals, the likes of Joseph E. Johnston and P. G. T. Beauregard, that old South, to the sweetness and light of Harris and Mark Twain, to stories of white lads and black uncles, the New South.

It was understood that this reconstructed Southern writing repudiated the principal articles of Confederate discourse, abjured its Confederate nationality, repudiated the political Confederate Father, though it might still relish the glory of the military Confederate Father. It was understood that this Southern writing accepted the dictate of the new Unionist Republican Federal Constitution, accepted the dictate of the Gettysburg Address: be in, and of, and for, the new nation, that it couldn't advocate racial injustice, that it had to answer, at some point, the Unionist question always there, waiting, the question Grady reached midway through his 1886 speech to the New England Society. "But what of the negro? Have we solved the problem he presents, or progressed in honor and equity toward solution?"[6] It was understood that this Southern writing might present African American experience as its special knowledge, as its cultural capital, report African American narratives, construct scenes of racial amity, produce work that served racial healing.

Post-Confederate, of course, is not a term these Southern writers used. Grady's "New South" was in general usage. Post-Confederate nonetheless better describes the activity of this writing, more accurately positions it, this Southern writing which appears after conquest, during and after occupation, relocated, part of the Unionist discursive work of phrasal consensus, doing the work, along with African American writing, of refiguring plots and characters, yet always in relation to the Confederate moment, the one celebrated by Gavin Stevens in *Intruder in the Dust*, a relation that necessarily excluded Southern African-American writing. In *Life on the Mississippi* Mark Twain puts three writers into it, himself, Cable, and Harris, the Cable of *The Grandissimes*, of the controversial *Century* articles: "The Freedman's Case in Equity," "The Silent South." These few Southern writers are modern, Mark Twain argues, in the world, beyond the dead Confederate thing, Scott (Robert E. Lee), outside its language. The success of the postwar Unionist national narrative, whose mission it was to integrate races and regions, contain their interests, depended on this distinctive Southern articulation, had its first important justification in the transsectional popularity of Harris and Mark Twain. In his wonderfully possessive final tribute, *My Mark Twain* (1910), Howells would call Mark Twain the Lincoln of our literature. Howells's Mark Twain was our Mark Twain.

With the prompt encouragement of Unionist media, post-Confederate writing took up the reconciliatory project of Harriet Beecher Stowe in *Uncle Tom's Cabin* (1851), the first Anglo-American novelist to write biracial fiction, to sentimentalize African American subjectivity. Harris's immensely popular *Uncle Remus: His Songs and His Sayings* (1880) begins with this *mise-en-scène*: Miss Sally, looking for her seven-year-old boy, "heard the sound of voices in the old man's cabin, and looking through the window, saw the child sitting by Uncle Remus. His head rested against the old man's arm, and he was gazing with an expression of the most intense interest into the rough, weather-beaten face that beamed so kindly upon him."[7] The post-Confederate reading of *Uncle Tom's Cabin* effectively cut out everything between young George Shelby's tearful farewell to sold Uncle Tom, the gift of young George's precious silver dollar as a redemptive token, his promise of rescue, their mutual gaze, and that final gorgeous scene where young George Shelby "appeared among them with a bundle of papers in his hand, containing a certificate of freedom to every one on the place, which he read successively, and presented, amid the sobs and tears and shouts of all present."[8] Harris generously acknowledged his debt: "I owe a great deal to…the author of Uncle Tom's Cabin."[9] In its brilliant opening scene, as we shall see, *Intruder in the Dust* recalls the foundational instance in Stowe's novel—the cabin, the gift of money, the gaze—ironically altering the elements, redoing the feeling. "What of the negro?" Responding to this question was a major operation in post-Confederate discourse.

To appear in diverse Unionist publications, this early post-Confederate had therefore to revise its tropes, redo its characters, let go the Pym plots of Edgar Allan Poe, the racist invective of George Washington Harris, yet still define, assert, a recalcitrant sense of nationality, of cultural difference, which was, after all, its principal literary interest. There are tolerances and tensions in the early post-Confederate, partisans left, right, and center. William H. Andrews has recently returned William Wells Brown's *My Southern Home* (1880), a strangely voiced, insidiously subversive African American memoir, to the archive he labels "New South writing." Just as Brown tropes the post-Confederate, his possessive pronoun compact with ironies, Charles Chesnutt's *The Conjure Woman* (1899) is certainly in an ironic play with post-Confederate discourse, with all its fabulous uncles, critically revising Harris's *Uncle Remus* (1880). Northern Unionist, Radical Republican, Albion Tourgée, of *A Fool's Errand* (1879), *Bricks Without Straw* (1880), and *The Invisible Empire* (1883), is also contentiously here, though he saw himself as excluded from Southern literature and scorned its racist mythologizing.

Retro, crypto, and neo-Confederate writing surrounds post-Confederate discourse in the Reconstruction and Redemption period, disagrees with it, writes angry letters to it, has its own fiction and poetry. Thomas Dixon, of *The Clansman* (1905) and *The Leopard's Spots* (1906), is definitely retro. Page begins his career publishing sketches in the *Century*, begins with *In Ole Virginia* (1887), begins in the post-Confederate, but is soon defining a neo-Confederate. Uncles are his primary narrators, the Uncle Sam of "Marse Chan" and the Uncle Billy of "Meh Lady." They are choric figures. Page could not break from Scott's heroic nationalist romance into a new conception of race relations in his fiction. There are no Jims to free in his fiction, no Lucases to save. His uncles never want freedom. Telling their stories of Marse and Mistis, these uncles bask in the glory of their masters. His uncles set Marse free, save Mistis. When Faulkner begins the Yoknapatawpha chronicle in 1928–29 with *Flags in the Dust*, Page informs his racial writing. There are instances where Faulkner's Uncle Simon nearly repeats the lines Page gives to Uncle Sam in "Marse Chan." Here is Simon: "Yessuh, de olden times comin' back again, sho'. Like in Marse John's time, when de Cunnel wuz de young marster en de niggers f'um de quawtuhs gethered on de front lawn, wishin' Mistis en de little Marster well."[10] Even the militant Caspey, home from the war in France, is comical. "I dont take nothin' f'um no white folks no mo'. War done changed all dat."[11] *Flags in the Dust* has its neo-Confederate turns, as Faulkner ventures into racial writing, yet there are also scenes—Bayard Sartoris seeking refuge in a black sharecropper's barn, sharing a meal with the family, entering their cabin, coming in upon their interiority—that turn the novel toward *Intruder in the Dust*, Mark Twain's racialized territory, the cabin Jim builds on the raft, Lucas's house.

Huckleberry Finn is indeed the telling post-Confederate text, a demonstration of the options, an irony of the fictional means, a painstaking setting forth of the available narratives, the possible resolutions. Mark Twain begins with a Unionist decree nailed to a Southern Courthouse door, asserts his mastery of Southern speech, then promptly denounces *Tom Sawyer*, Tom Sawyer's St. Petersburg. What are the lies Mr. Mark Twain tells in *Tom Sawyer*? No matter which way Huck turns in his text, and there are diversions, the race question is before him. How to set Jim free? There is Huck's way, which is to fold, reluctantly, but decently, into the major narrative, Jim's, the slave narrative, or Tom's, which is to write Jim's liberation script, deciding the time, determining the conditions, of said liberation. Ultimately, of course, in the post-Confederate, there is only Tom's white supremacist way, but his version is exposed, his narration discredited, the raft will not move at his command, and we turn back to Huck's failure, to his interrupted text, to the issue of his tortured identification with Jim, his recognition of the integrity of Jim's narrative.

In the gaze that beholds this horrific tableau of relapse, Tom's triumph, Jim's debased gratitude, we get to see an outside, the end of this particular cultural adventure. Huck won't go back. Beyond this, another kind of Southern writing, but what it is, in that new territory, who can suppose it? The ending of *Intruder in the Dust* also declares such an impasse, the enmeshment of Gavin and Lucas in racist routines, their ongoing contestation, Chick witnessing, the narrator giving Lucas the last word, receipt, letting us ponder the true extent of debt and payment in American race matters.

Edmund Wilson's 1948 *New Yorker* review of *Intruder in the Dust*, at once beautifully High Unionist and High Modernist, memorably grieved over Faulkner's prose style, its arrest, its atrophy. It was, finally, Wilson argued, too rhetorically Southern, too provincial, to sustain a serious High Modernist attention. Wilson worked in close on Faulkner's syntax and grammar, parsing sentences, checking off Faulkner's "mismanagement of relatives," his improper punctuation, his confusion of pronouns, his incorrect usages. Wilson acknowledged the novel's humanities, its "reconditioned Southern chivalry," the greatness of

Faulkner's previous fiction, and then abruptly interrogated the politics of *Intruder in the Dust*, took it up as a tract, as a public message, Faulkner doing a Confederate Gettysburg Address, reasserting a contraposed Anglo Southern nationality, the old familiar one, even as the novel exactly performed the post-Confederate's major operation, set Lucas free. It was an anti-lynching novel, Wilson argued, that was also "a counterblast to the anti-lynching bill and to the civil rights plank in the Democratic platform."[12] He underlined "Sambo," exposed the novel's intrinsic racism, rejected its answer to the Unionist question, *what of the negro*, rejected it in this contemptuous high Unionist phrasing, sounding very much like Charles Sumner in the 1850s. "So the Southerners must be allowed, on their own initiative, in their own way, with no intervention by others, to grant the Negro his citizenship. Otherwise— / Otherwise, what?"[13]

Wilson's dismissive reading remains, to a very large extent, the definitive reading. Walter Taylor, James A. Snead, Eric Sundquist, and others, have incisively extended and elaborated Wilson's *New Yorker* critique. Faulkner's contrived plotting in *Intruder in the Dust*, Taylor writes, only works to "justify Gavin's polemics." These "manipulations bordered on the ridiculous, and they were there for all to see."[14] Sundquist similarly regards *Intruder in the Dust* as a "ludicrous novel and a depressing social document." He especially derides Faulkner's application of *Huckleberry Finn*. Mark Twain's "painfully convoluted" ending is "tragically exacting," profoundly ironic. "In Faulkner's new vision there is almost no irony at all, and the burden of shame that is lifted from Charles's shoulders therefore leaves too little of the resonant ambiguity and fully realized moral complicity of Huck's struggle with his conscience."[15]

This is, I think, an exhausted reading, not necessarily a wrong reading, just a concluded reading, and I want to look elsewhere in the text, to retrieve Cleanth Brooks's insistence that Faulkner is not Gavin Stevens. *Intruder in the Dust* certainly marks a crisis in the post-Confederate, marks it succinctly in the foregrounded usage, "Sambo," interactively moves within the complex of the post-Confederate, reworking its practices, always addressing, especially through the usage, "Sambo," Unionist media, Unionist discourse, the editors at Random House, Malcolm Cowley of the 1946 Viking *Portable William Faulkner*, Edmund Wilson in the *New Yorker*. It humorously defends its position, that it does not participate in the subjection of Uncle Tom, and its prerogatives, that it speaks for Jim, that it frees Lucas. It recalls the discursive pact that reconstructed Southern writing signed with the *Atlantic* and the *Century* in the 1870s and '80s, refurbishes its terms, reviews its project, what it repudiates (racism), what it won't relinquish (nationality), delicately distinguishing an older post-Confederate from a younger. A lot of heavy work is done in this text, and all it has for transport is Chick's horse, Highboy, and Miss Habersham's old truck.

The biggest load is the racism, Sambo, constantly before us, either in actual or virtual parenthesis, always glaring in its wrongness. It is a softening euphemism, a pseudoaffectionate idiomatic usage, that Gavin Stevens tries to manage in his post-Confederate speeches, mixing into it a certain irony. He wants at once to recapture Lucas's transgressive character with it and to distance himself from the worse usages of the retro-Confederate, the racist invective one might find in the political speeches of James K. Vardaman and Theodore Bilbo. Finally his Sambo transforms into Booker T. Washington, the honorific Gavin Stevens humorously gives to Lucas at the end of the novel. The text itself gives Stevens no warrant for its usage, shows him immediately as obtuse (his first utterance is racist, names Aleck Sander as Chick's "boy"), so the usage isn't tied down, isn't managed, is loose in the text, always a sore point, a stoppage. Stevens's own distance from it is too shaky. He seems at times to be drawn into it, stuck to it. It is a kind of tarbaby term, Sambo, and of course Stevens doesn't shake it loose with Booker T. Washington.

Should anyone who can't control the racism, Sambo, be trusted to articulate Lucas's case? *Intruder in the Dust* raises the question of entitlement, the question Martin Delany promptly framed in his 1852 reading of *Uncle Tom's Cabin:* can Anglo-American writers do faithful justice to African American experience? What is Faulkner's answer to James

Baldwin's 1956 *Partisan Review* article, "Faulkner and Desegregation," to Baldwin's charge that Faulkner's fictional Negroes are always "tied up in his mind with his grandfather's slaves?"[16] He can't speak. He's in the prison-house of male Anglo-Southern race writing, Uncle Tom's cabin. In the fifties, Faulkner would consistently avoid public discussion with African American writers, who, for their part, continually addressed him. In 1956 W. E. B. DuBois wanted to stage a public debate. Faulkner promptly mailed Du Bois a concession speech, playing Cass to DuBois's Ike. "We both agree in advance that the position you will take is right morally legally ethically. If it is not evident to you that the position I take in asking for moderation and patience is right practically then we will both waste our breath in debate."[17] In 1966, for Random House (Faulkner's publisher), can William Styron, in the first person, *The Confessions of Nat Turner*, present a lubricious Nat lusting after the white Southern belle, Margaret Whitehead?

Faulkner's "Sambo" in *Intruder in the Dust* marks an evacuation, declares an end to a certain kind of post-Confederate writing, reinscribed here, responding to the present crisis, Unionist invasion, Confederate secession. History crunches in on the novel. In 1946 the CIO was intrusively organizing in Mississippi. In 1947 a prestigious federal commission called for an end to segregation. In 1948 President Harry S. Truman sent an ambitious civil rights package to Congress. In 1948 Mississippi Democrats left the national party to form the Dixiecrat party, giving us Strom Thurmond as its first presidential candidate. Says a wiseacre citizen in *Intruder in the Dust:* "Aint you heard about that new lynch law the Yankees passed? the folks that lynches the nigger is supposed to dig the grave?"[18] Here it is, that reconciliatory post-Confederate discourse, Gavin Stevens's version, stuck to Sambo, besmirched, invalidated, as it strives to inform Charles Mallison's understanding, to establish a position for him.

If Faulkner's public statement on civil rights is conflicted in the fifties, his discourse in interviews, letters to the editor, at conferences, leaking racisms, his grip on racist usage in the besieged 1948 *Intruder in the Dust* seems fairly secure. The narrator, virtually some older Charles

Mallison, though never identified as such, presents himself as someone who appreciates and affirms the older Chick's raised consciousness. In his supportive critical language, we observe Chick's thinking through the grips and seizures of elemental racisms seemingly visceral in their truth, racisms of the senses, racisms of odor, racisms of taste. *Intruder in the Dust* begins with this exchange, Roth Edmonds and Gavin Stevens, linking the history told in *Go Down, Moses* (1942), and all its rich ironies, to *Intruder in the Dust*. Bachelor Roth Edmonds, whose big house in *Intruder* is womanless, had once a woman in *Go Down, Moses*, has in fact, elsewhere, unrecognized, a son who is just the sort of boy he names in this exchange. Gavin Stevens is right there in Roth's oblivious language, peer patrician.

> "Come out home with me tomorrow and go rabbit hunting:" and then to his mother: "I'll send him back in tomorrow afternoon. I'll send a boy along with him while he's out with his gun:" and then to him again: "He's got a good dog."
> "He's got a boy," his uncle said and Edmonds said: "Does his boy run rabbits too?" and his uncle said: "We'll promise he wont interfere with yours."[19]

These boys, in a category with dogs, are "one of Edmonds' tenant's sons," thereafter referred to, with a certain remote irony, as "Edmonds' boy," whom Lucas calls "Joe," and Aleck Sander, Chick's best friend. "Edmonds' boy" is older; both "boys" are larger than Chick, skilled hunters who can nail a fleeting rabbit with a tapstick, who would not tumble from a log bridge. Every racism in this first chapter is carefully marked and promptly disvalued, even the most personal racism, given up to a *reductio*: "he could smell that smell which he had accepted without question all his life as being the smell always of the places where people with any trace of Negro blood live as he had that all people named Mallison are Methodists."[20]

In this first order of racisms cluttering everyday discourse, damaging conversational discourse, Faulkner is still astute in his hearing and seeing, immediately showing us Joe and Aleck Sander, older, larger, competent black youths, constrained in the racism, "boy," immediately presenting the majesty of Lucas's stature, Lucas's patriarchal authority unquestionably sounding in his commands: "Get the pole out of his way," "Come on to my house," "Tote his gun," "Strip off," Lucas as the absolute transcendent negation of "boy." Here he is, not only not, but actually an ireful castrating (axe on the shoulder) Grandfather Patriarch, who has you naked, at his mercy, who stands over you, looming. Chick must nonetheless fit him into a racism, regain the security of that designation, give this ominous figure coins, a tip, and this is the dark humor of the first section, his act a futility, the coins (racisms) spurned, spilled to the floor.

A reconstructed confident narrator drives the engine of this antiracist surveillance. When Gavin Stevens, in full rhetorical stride, says: "Lucas Beauchamp, Sambo," there it is, a glaring exposure, a stupidity, a racism pressed too far as an ironic euphemism, a stupidity, and ridiculous, too. The narrator's attentive bracketing of all such instances asks that we acknowledge what he repudiates, a benighted racist language, indeed asks that we respect his privileged sensitivity, his privileged knowledge. Lucas Beauchamp, after all, especially the Lucas Beauchamp in *Go Down, Moses*, might very well be Faulkner's response to the challenge that he lacked the "necessities" to do "black" experience. "*You say (with sneer),*" says Gavin Stevens, anticipating Edmund Wilson's supercilious reading, "*You must know Sambo well to arrogate to yourself such calm assumption of his passivity and I reply I dont know him at all and in my opinion no white man does,*"[21] speaking only for himself, not for the narrator, not for the novel, and certainly not for Faulkner.

It is at the next order of racism, the literary racism of plots and narratives, of situations and characters, of fantasies and resolutions, that the text is problematic. At the level of utterance, of everyday speech, a scrupulous discovery of racisms, constantly operating, always reassuring us. At the level of story the curious return of racisms, of antiracisms as racism, of counterracisms, Lucas's own racism, racism reentering as constitutive, racism the construction of this world: "the house and the ten acres of land it sat in—an oblong of earth set forever in the middle of the two-thousand acre plantation like a postage stamp in the center of an envelope,"[22] racism the already-there of the *mise-en-scène*, the turn in the road. Here we recognize that Lucas has only two sites in the novel, Uncle Tom's cabin and Jim's shed, that Faulkner's exemplary deconstruction of everyday racist discourse circulates within the paradigms and plots of the post-Confederate, takes place within its limitation.

After *Light in August* (1932), after *Absalom, Absalom!* (1936), after *Go Down, Moses* (1942), the abject failures of Gail Hightower and Gavin Stevens to save Joe Christmas from lynching, the challenges of Charles Bon ("I'm the nigger that's going to sleep with your sister."),[23] the racist relapse of old Isaac McCaslin in "Delta Autumn," what is Faulkner's relation to the post-Confederate, to its project, its primordial scenes, its appropriate figures, and what, in 1948, does he seek to gain with this recourse to its narrative strategies, its specific language games? He means certainly to engage Harriet Beecher Stowe and Mark Twain, to engage their fundamental moves, restage their classic presentations, as answer to Malcolm Cowley and Edmund Wilson, as response to a new intrusively judging Unionist discourse, Truman's civil rights legislation. Here is Lucas, axe-bearing Grandfather, as anti-Tom; Lucas with his antique wallet, his dollars and cents, as non-Jim, the Jim who gladly takes his forty dollars from Tom Sawyer at the end of *Huckleberry Finn*, and here, too, is a restoration of Sir Walter Scott in the Gowrie tragedy, the Gowries as Highlanders along with the Ingrums and the Workitts and the Frasers, Beat Four the center of their Southern nationality, their sovereignty. The pleasures of Scott factored through these distinctive Southern things—family, place, Protestant church in piney woods—Gavin Stevens gets high on this nationalism as he drives up into the hills toward Caledonia Church, talking excitedly, sailing off into his convoluted paradoxes, and we see absolutely the misery of its blindspots, its double binds, the constraints of Stevens's post-Confederate. His New South upholds "the postulate that Sambo is a human being living in a free country and hence must be free," declares itself in Unionist discourse, "what the outland calls (and we too) progress and enlightenment," even as it asserts, evoking Confederate discourse: "we must resist the North," defend "our homogeneity from a federal government to which in simple desperation the rest of this country has had to surrender voluntarily more and more of its personal and private liberty in order to continue to afford the United States."[24]

Up, up, into these formulas, and what holds the two priorities together (Sambo must be free, Anglo-American Southerners must be free) in a single coherent emancipatory narrative, is a dependence on, the need for, an Uncle Tom. Just as we reach Caledonia Church, epitome of Confederate nationality, "intractable and independent, asking nothing of any, making compromise with none,"[25] Gavin Stevens reaches this final point in his post-Confederate discourse, describing the necessary Sambo as the one who "loved the old few simple things...a little of music (his own), a hearth, not his child but any child, a God a heaven which a man may avail himself a little of at any time without having to wait to die, a little earth for his own sweat to fall on among his own green shoots and plants,"[26] a Sambo prized from the person of Lucas Beauchamp, the figure who sets this final passage into motion. Chick's thought is close to his uncle's as they make their ascent to Caledonia Church, especially at those verges where the prospect discloses Yoknapatawpha spread mapwise below, county as country, his "whole native land." Confederate feeling, state nationality, *Maryland! My Maryland!*, these are the surges, but Chick's anthem differs, swirls around the intractable figure of Lucas Beauchamp. Chick is still smarting from his first traumatic encounter with Lucas, this "damned highnosed impudent Negro,"[27] he calls him, in the midst of his anthem, so there are rifts and rents in his discourse. He doesn't have the ready usage of his uncle's Sambo, can't postulate him.

Uncle Tom, Uncle Remus, Uncle Lucas. Christina Zwarg has already admirably catalogued and described the decor of Uncle Tom's cabin, read the symbolic import of all its objects, the "brilliant scriptural prints" over the fireplace, the portrait of a colored George Washington, shown us how Stowe uncles this space, makes us rethink the foundational father. It is all there, the flowers, the bedstead, the carpet, table and table cloth, cups and saucers, these objects on the mantel. Zwarg's Stowe is supersophisticated in her discursive racializing. Working through Uncle Tom and his political alter-ego on the Shelby plantation, Sam, doing their different discourses, Zwarg's Stowe invents new subject-positions for patriarchal men, "uncles," creates a space and a speech that escapes the traditional binaries of race and gender. Zwarg's Stowe playfully gets into the dialectical play of Sam's lecturing, Sam's philosophizing, is doing minstrel Emerson in blackface, ironically using blackface in a wily feminist way.

This is not the cabin Faulkner reads in *Intruder in the Dust*, though the objects he sees are the same: furniture, a print over the mantel and by the bed a portrait on an easel. The print, a calendar lithograph "in which Pocahontas in the quilled fringed buckskins of a Sioux or Chippewa chief stood against a balustrade of Italian marble above a garden of formal cypresses," specifically indicates the racism of Stowe's idealization of Uncle Tom as it exposes generally the appropriative racism of all Anglo-American racial representation. Everything is wrong here, costume and setting. Opposite it, Faulkner's portrait, the wedding portrait of Lucas Beauchamp and Molly Worsham, singularities, actual persons. Here, too, something is wrong. A racism mars this wedding portrait. When Chick finally scrutinizes it, he sees, with a shock, the same "calm intolerant face" he confronts in the present pressing Lucas.[28] Everything in Uncle Tom's cabin operates to dispel the uncanny racist horrors of sameness/difference, to calm racist anxieties. Everything in Lucas's cabin works oppositely, to upset the conceit of the sentimental, to heighten racist anxieties. No boyish George Shelby is comfortably at home in this cabin. Showing the grassless way to Lucas's cabin, Faulkner defoliates Stowe's embowering flowers, the garden greenery, and what is for dinner, what wonderful thing from Aunt Molly's oven?

It is a crisis, Chick's innocent racism, his failure to recognize the young hair-styled Molly Worsham in the wedding portrait. He only knows her as wearing a headrag. His apparent confusion at the easel stirs up in the observing Molly ancient race-caused griefs in her marriage, causes her to speak, to distance herself from the falsified person in the portrait, and brings Lucas necessarily into the logic of this discussion. We are already in Lucas's doings, she says, as she explains the portrait. "That's some more of Lucas's doings."[29] She exposes Lucas in this very racism, the present tense situation, the forced intrusion of Chick, the awkwardness of his being there, Lucas's inappropriate, possibly mean, transgression of racial codes, Chick just a boy and obviously disconcerted, shaken. More of his doings, this grand hospitality that catches Molly unprepared, without enough food in the house to feed the guests. It is Lucas's worst moment in the section, this expression of his internalized racism, his intolerance, his sexist disdain of Molly. He has to justify the act, and first fibs, displaces responsibility, says the photographer made Molly take her headrag off. He must say it finally, admit his own racism, his own derogation of Molly: "I told him to....I didn't want no field nigger picture in the house."[30]

Aunt Chloe and Uncle Tom, here redone. It is also a warning, Lucas's disclosure, a complex admonition: *and there ain't no field nigger in this house*, direction as to how Chick is to treat Lucas, and therefore weak. Molly has forced Lucas from the chain of his imperatives. Clutching his coins, already himself defeated, unable to deal directly with Lucas, Chick turns toward Molly, establishing social ties, to give her Lucas's payment, and she would charitably take the payment, receive it inside the racism, which neither Chick nor Molly herein hurtfully designates. It is a sort of refuge in racism, this racism as a brief haven, this racism as an anti-Lucas measure. Lucas's defiance of white racism, always prompt, is itself racist, therefore vulnerable, open to irony. Still, for all its peremptory treatment of Molly, Lucas's rough usage is a shock therapy, a disabling of white racist descriptives, *boy, uncle, Sambo,* and the like. There is indeed no field nigger in this house. Lucas's challenge ultimately sets Chick relatively free of such racisms, allows the instance of a nonverbal communicative gaze, gives us the antiracist wit and wisdom of our narrator, a skillful operator in advanced post-Confederate.

In *Huckleberry Finn*, after Cairo is missed, Jim's experience has only two representational sites: Huck's ongoing escape narrative, which has only a limited space for him, as accomplice, as caregiver and storyteller, as social dependent, a life somewhere between the *Je suis* of Aunt Chloe and the *Ich bin* of Uncle Tom, and Tom's surreal prison-break scripts, Jim in whiteface writing: "Here's a captive heart busted."[31] The king and the duke paint Jim blue, put him in "King Leer's outfit," placard him: "Sick Arab." Tom's scripts take from Alexander Dumas, prefigure Ralph Ellison, weirdly evoke scenes and situations from classic slave narratives: chains sawn off, secret notes exchanged, disguises, messages of betrayal, work like Hollywood movies in the thirties and forties, dehistoricizing the manacle, emptying the secret note of its socio-political meaning. Subject-categories in advanced post-Confederate, these two suspect Jim. Huck's discourse is privileged because it can partially admit Jim's narrative, see him, hear him, outside the clutter of racisms, and it can regard Tom's plotting, report, and sometimes protest, its demands, its dangers. In Huck's narrative there is a thin outside, a documentary gaze, which lets us see, enacted, the complicity of the versions, the limitation of the one, the brutality of the other.

Some such gaze is surely operating at the end of *Intruder in the Dust*, positioning the three persons, giving the final word to Lucas Beauchamp, "receipt," Lucas's racism. White folks lie, cheat, break their promises. Get it in writing. Get a receipt. "If you aint stealing the lumber," Lucas says to Crawford Gowrie, "get me Uncle Sudley Workitt's receipt." What do you want, Stevens asks, seeing that the dismissed Lucas is not going, but standing there, looking at them. "My receipt," says Lucas, out-patronizing Stevens, out-ironizing him, the last move his. Isn't this final scene necessarily a valedictory, Faulkner's effective withdrawal from the field of African American representation? Lucas pushes that pile of pennies across Gavin Stevens's desk, thanks for "representing my case," two dollars worth of help for the due process and the habeas corpus. What, after all, is Stevens's reputation in doing such legal work? Joe Christmas, Nancy Mannigoe. Receipt is closure. Surely this ending reflects Faulkner's tacit understanding of what is about to happen, African American writing evicting Anglo-American writing, post-Confederate and High Unionist alike (Joel Chandler Harris, Mark Twain, Gertrude Stein, Carl Van Vechten, Faulkner, Styron) from the field of African American representation. The beginning of *Intruder in the Dust* an exorcism in the post-Confederate, confronting Uncle Tom in his cabin, the ending a post-Confederate valedictory. There is, of course, a reprise in *The Reivers* (1962). Uncles return, Ned and Parsham, one wily, the other noble, acting out their post-Confederate parts, but with a certain signal attached: "Ned said; he wasn't being Uncle Remus or smart or cute or anything now!"[32]

Lucas enters the final scene addressing Stevens and Chick Mallison with a forbidden usage, one declaring Lucas's parity, Lucas's true social position. "Gentle-men," he says, and it brings immediately into play Jim's great line in *Huckleberry Finn*: "Dah you goes, de ole true Huck; de on'y white genlman dat ever kep' his promise to ole Jim." Between Lucas's "Gentlemen," and Lucas's "My receipt," a dumb-show from the post-Confederate. Like Tom Sawyer, Stevens insists on the formality of Lucas Beauchamp taking flowers and gratitude to Miss Habersham. Like Huck, Chick worries that Stevens might have put Lucas in harm's way, out there on the street, where lynch-minded white racists are still moving about, some maybe angry at Miss Habersham for coming to the assistance of a "damned highnosed impudent Negro," lurking in her bushes. Like Tom, Stevens airily brushes these considerations aside. Lucas does not do the grateful Sambo that Jim does at the end of *Huckleberry Finn*, but he is archaic in his McCaslin clothes, that "old-time white waistcoat," his cocked beaver hat, a comic figure.

Faulkner's advanced post-Confederate in *Intruder in the Dust* achieves this surveillance. By insisting on a bill, "within reason," on payment and receipt; on the routine of this exchange, Lucas sets up the situation where racism must routinely occur, be foregrounded, and immediately takes charge of it, captures it, enters its routines, its language game. He has come to pay the defense lawyer who presumed him guilty. This is, as it were, more of Lucas's doings, his kind of signifying, the McCaslin outfit, counting out the pennies. There is no other language for Lucas, or for Gavin Stevens, just this one, routine, prescriptive, limited, and for all that, complex, hurtful, heavy. Though truces may be struck, and escapes engineered, it goes on.

What happens to Chick's advanced post-Confederate discourse in the fifties and sixties? Hard discursive demands are put on Chick, as hard as those put on Huck out there on the water dealing with the slave-catchers, to say whose side he is on, whose story he must privilege. What kind of beautifully racialized antiracist Southern writing exists outside the conditions and protocols of the post-Confederate, intermediate and advanced? Faulkner doesn't get there. Historical time in Faulkner's fiction stops in 1947. *Intruder in the Dust* everywhere marks boundaries, the Beats, the county, the highlands and bottomlands, marks the distinctive place of Southern writing in American literature, just as, in some other sense, in its action, its patriotic speeches, the novel anticipates, prefigures, in the distant dust of travelled roads, intruders, transgressions, boundaries crossed, the end of Southern writing, as the novel knew it.

Notes

1. William Faulkner, *Intruder in the Dust* (New York: Vintage International Edition, 1991), 190–91.
2. Henry Woodfin Grady, "The New South," in the *New York Daily Tribune*, 23 December 1886.
3. Ibid., 312.
4. Ibid., 320.
5. Mark Twain, *Adventures of Huckleberry Finn*, eds. Walter Blair and Victor Fischer (Berkeley: University of California Press, 1985), 125.
6. Grady, "The New South."
7. Joel Chandler Harris, *Uncle Remus: His Songs and His Sayings* (New York: Schocken Books, 1974), 3–4.
8. Harriet Beecher Stowe, *Uncle Tom's Cabin*, ed. Elizabeth Ammons (New York: W. W. Norton & Company), 379.
9. Quoted in Jay Hubbell, *The South in American Literature, 1607-1900* (Durham: Duke University Press, 1954), 786.
10. William Faulkner, *Flags in the Dust* (New York: Random House, 1973), 359.
11. Ibid., 53.
12. Edmund Wilson, *Cannibals and Christians* (New York: Farrar, Straus and Company, 1958), 465.
13. Ibid., 476–78.

14. Walter Taylor, *Faulkner's Search for a South* (Urbana: University of Illinois Press, 1983), 163.
15. Eric J. Sundquist, *Faulkner, The House Divided* (Baltimore: Johns Hopkins University Press, 1983), 149.
16. James Baldwin, *Nobody Knows My Name* (New York: Dell Publishing Company, 1961), 108.
17. *Selected Letters of William Faulkner*, ed. Joseph Blotner (New York: Random House, 1977), 262.
18. *Intruder in the Dust*, 137.
19. Ibid., 3-4.
20. Ibid., 9-10.
21. Ibid., 210.
22. Ibid., 8.
23. William Faulkner, *Absalom, Absalom! The Corrected Text* (New York: Vintage Books, 1987), 446.
24. *Intruder in the Dust*, 150-51.
25. Ibid., 154.
26. Ibid., 153.
27. Ibid., 148.
28. Ibid., 10, 14.
29. Ibid., 14.
30. Ibid., 15.
31. *Huckleberry Finn*, 322.
32. William Faulkner, *The Reivers* (New York: Random House, 1962), 261.

"THE SUM OF YOUR ANCESTRY": CULTURAL CONTEXT AND *INTRUDER IN THE DUST*

Evelyn Jaffe Schreiber

Although Faulkner claims to have written *Intruder in the Dust* as a potboiler detective story, the novel nevertheless exemplifies the concern with race and its impact on community and individual identity evident in Faulkner's other works. To contextualize the exploration of racial issues, I teach the text's cultural ideology, that is, the text's representation of racist constructs and the social structures that create/maintain them. For example, Faulkner's work struggles with the socially constructed Southern identity of African Americans as inferior to whites. Specifically, in *Intruder*, Charles (Chick) Mallison grapples with understanding his heritage of bigotry while desiring to escape it. Thus, as Faulkner's work explores issues of race and social structures, a useful approach to teaching *Intruder* is to analyze the novel by way of cultural theory. To enable students to engage in a cultural analysis of the text, I begin our discussion by introducing theoretical frameworks that explain interpersonal dynamics. I outline how the writings of Mikhail Bakhtin describe layers of social segments in a culture's language. Next, I explore the way the work of V. N. Volosinov delineates how ideology is imbedded in language. Then, I consider Lev Vygotsky's research that specifies the impact of this ideology on identity. Finally, I use Kenneth Bruffee's work on collaborative learning to suggest how a culture's ideology alters over time. These cultural theorists can illuminate contextual readings of Faulkner's work.

A brief summary of the novel is useful before continuing. Four years prior to the current events, Chick Mallison fell into a creek while hunting on the Edmonds estate. Lucas Beauchamp, a black (actually, mulatto) descendant of Old Carothers McCaslin who owns and farms part of this land, rescued Chick from the creek. When Chick accompanied Lucas to his home to dry off and eat, he became aware of his social expectations of Lucas. For the first time, Chick processed a black person as a *person*, not as a socially constructed idea. Chick erred by trying to pay Lucas for his kindness, and so began a four-year relationship during which Chick has never able to get the better of Lucas. Currently Lucas, aware that he can call in his debt, summons Chick to the jail when he is arrested on circumstantial evidence for the murder of a white man.

To begin the study of the impact of socially constructed beliefs on members of society, I introduce the idea of multiple layers of inflection in the text—of the voices of the text as differing from each other—by discussing Bakhtin's "'languages' of heteroglossia" (291). In *The Dialogic Imagination*, Bakhtin posits that the novel form captures social nuances by being "ever evolving and in process of renewal represented precisely as a living mix of varied and opposing voices....Language in the novel not only represents, but itself serves as the object of representation" (47, 49). Novelistic language characterizes a culture's socio-ideological history and explains individual development. Bakhtin concludes that the "ideological becoming of a human being...is the process of selectively assimilating the words of others" (341). My students use this premise to investigate character formation and social interactions in the novel. For example, in an opening scene at the jail, three voices resonate with the community's ideology. The jailer, Mr. Tubbs, voices the "mob" mentality that clings to its racist views. He protests to Will Legate (the sharpshooter hired to protect Lucas), "'Me get in the way of them Gowries and Ingrums for seventy-five dollars a month? Just for one nigger? And if you aint a fool, you wont neither.' 'Oh I got to,' Legate said in his easy pleasant voice. 'I got to resist. Mr. Hampton's paying me five dollars for it'" (52). Although he says that it is his job to guard Lucas, Legate has the option of refusing that position. The fact that he accepts that responsibility indicates a choice against mass thinking. Gavin Stevens, lawyer to Lucas and uncle to Chick, reinforces the stance of doing what they can to resist the crowd. He tells Tubbs and Legate that the townspeople "either will or they wont [attack] and if they dont it will be all right and if they do we will do the best we can…what we have to do, what we can do" (53). This dialogue illustrates the tension between prevailing cultural norms and personal conscience.

Other examples of voices in the text also reveal the culture's ideology. For example, even though he chooses to protect Lucas, Gavin believes he is guilty, thinking, "He's just a nigger after all" (57). Later, Gavin explodes when Lucas calmly tells of the events that led to his framing. Having discovered that Crawford Gowrie was stealing lumber from his brother, Lucas confronted Crawford as a white man would have done. Gavin tries to comprehend how Lucas could stray so far beyond social boundaries: "And you, a Negro, were going up to a white man and tell him his niece's sons were stealing from him—and a Beat Four white man on top of that. Dont you know what would have happened to you?" (220). Even the most seemingly liberal elements in this culture have difficulty processing shifting roles. Lucas's awareness of Gavin's reservations causes him to confide in Chick, rather than in his lawyer. Further, Lucas voices the rules of white society by insisting on paying for Chick's detective services as well as for Gavin's legal representation. Examples such as these help clarify the heteroglossic aspect of the text. Thus, Bakhtin's philosophy of the intersubjective aspect of language in a text organizes our early discussions.

Next, we consider how multi-voiced language transmits ideology. To examine how Faulkner's text embodies and dramatizes the influence of past ideology on the current voices of society, I also introduce V. N. Volosinov's theory of the ideological aspects of language. According to Volosinov, "[C]onsciousness itself can arise and become a viable fact only in the material embodiment of signs.…Signs emerge, after all, only in the process of interaction between one individual consciousness and another" (11, Volosinov's italics). Further, social interactions define the individual: "The processes that basically define the content of the psyche occur not inside but outside the individual" (25). Finally, "the content of the 'individual' psyche is ideological, historical, and wholly conditioned by sociological factors" (34). It is this attention to the ideological, historical, and social components of individual consciousness that forms a basis for examining the interpersonal dynamics in *Intruder*. Specifically, Southern ideology regarding race and a hierarchy of power controls the events and characters in the novel, as we will see in the following discussion.

After clarifying Volosinov's idea that a culture's language embodies its ideology, we look at the work of Lev Vygotsky and its emphasis on the impact of social expectations on individual development. According to Vygotsky, "the true direction of the development of thinking is not from the individual to the socialized, but from the social to the individual" (20). This social aspect of thought carries significant consequences for society. For if "[v]erbal thought is not an innate, natural form of behavior but is determined by a historical-cultural process and has specific properties and laws that cannot be found in the natural forms of thought and speech," then altering ideology involves an intricate negotiation between the individual, history, and culture (Vygotsky 51). In *Intruder* Chick's development exemplifies how this negotiation plays out to modify community thinking.

This altering of ideology serves as a focal point for social-constructionist educators who build on the social character of language to work toward the development of a more democratic society. The work of Kenneth Bruffee proposes that all knowledge is socially constructed. In his studies, collaborative learning moves individuals towards an understanding of socially constructed knowledge and their part in shaping such knowledge. For Bruffee, a switch in the context of learning by means of a decentered classroom enables students to work through problems together, become part of a larger social conversation, and ultimately, contribute to the reshaping of that social fabric. I use Bruffee's educational theory, in combination with multicultural educational approaches, to assist students in perceiving how social changes come about in practice. For instance, multicultural educators seek to provide all members of society with access to political and economic power. Specifically, differing ethnic groups in society struggle to gain recognition despite hegemonic thinking. This process raises issues of pluralism, tolerance, and assimilation. Defining the nuances of these terms and their application to the students' own experiences illuminates Chick Mallison's dilemma in *Intruder*. Chick's encounters with Lucas alter his socially constructed Southern identity so that he is able to consider blacks from a perspective unlike that of his society. His problem rests in whether (and how) he will use his awareness to create social change, or whether he will "approve the violent enforcement of the community's racial norms" (Karaganis 69).

A brief exposition of these cultural paradigms provides an explanatory framework of how cultures evolve and helps students understand the two main characters—Lucas Beauchamp and Chick Mallison—in *Intruder*. Both characters struggle to separate from their culture and internalized norms. Chick recognizes his town's small-mindedness, thinking of himself, "you really were the sum of your ancestry" (92). His racist society derives from a white patriarchy born of a slave culture. According to Charles Hannon, the ideological structure of the South involves "white Southern men…[in] a position of superiority" as well as "an obsession…with the power of whites to remove the town's black presence" (264, 268). Chick inherits generations of a social hierarchy that separates black from white and prohibits any informal, easy relationship between the races. For white Yoknapatawpha County, blacks remain inferior and suspect, vulnerable to the whims of white power structures. With little access to the political and economic core of their community, blacks have assumed their assigned role. Racist thinking keeps blacks on an almost subhuman level, exemplified in Chick's thinking about a dog while hunting: "a nigger dog which it took but one glance to see had an affinity a rapport with rabbits such as people said Negroes had with mules"(5). Chick recognizes his community's need for hierarchy, thinking they "got to make [Lucas] a nigger first" (18). Thus, ideology, permeated with issues of politics and power, has ancestral roots for its influence on the community.

However, Lucas Beauchamp refuses this role, identifying instead with his white, landowning grandfather. He is an enigma for his community because he refuses to be "black" or to assume any designated position. To separate himself from both the black and white communities, Lucas remains proud, self-reliant, and financially independent. He moves beyond unwritten codes of behavior by coming to town on weekdays as a white man would and dressing up on Saturdays with his grandfather's coat, hat, gold toothpick, and gun, by paying his taxes and addressing white people as equals. It is his long-time resistance to his community's expectations and his flaunting (through the beaver hat, gold toothpick, and revolver) his heritage of miscegenation that make Lucas a target of white hatred. For example, when Lucas enters a local store, a townsman—set off by the attitude evident in his walk, his avoidance of others, his purchase, and his toothpick—verbally attacks Lucas: "You goddamn biggity stiffnecked stinking burrheaded Edmonds sonofabitch.... Keep on walking around here with that look on your face and what you'll be is crowbait" (19). Lucas responds by looking "at the white man with a calm speculative detachment" (19). The shop owner intervenes to prevent violence and asks Lucas to leave, but the desire for Lucas's downfall has been set. As Gavin Stevens puts it when he visits Lucas in his cell, "Has it ever occurred to you that if you just said mister to white people and said it like you meant it, you might not be sitting here now?" (60). He voices the "ideological, historical, and wholly conditioned" Southern cultural response to Lucas (Volosinov 34).

This social conditioning reaches all members of society. However, Chick's chance encounter with Lucas as a child forces him to comprehend and challenge the socially constructed notions of race embedded in his society. Prior to this meeting, Chick was barely aware of race "as a social artifact" (Karaganis 67). As a guest in Lucas's home, he recognizes Lucas as a man, equal or superior to himself. The accoutrements of race—Molly's headrag, Lucas's dinner, the smell of the quilt—come into focus. When Chick attempts to pay Lucas for his hospitality, the boy realizes that he has insulted Lucas's humanity. Chick will spend the next few years trying to erase his own shame by evening the score with Lucas. Chick's inability to best Lucas, combined with his recognition of Lucas's grief at Molly's death, causes him to see Lucas as a human being rather than as a member of a specific race. Thus, when Lucas is accused of a murder that Chick knows he could not have committed, Chick must choose between Lucas's humanity and his society's mass perception. The text, reveals Chick's transition to this role through his constant denial that he can succeed: "I'll have to get out there and dig him up and get back to town before midnight....I dont see how I can do it. I cant do it" (72). But Lucas's response confirms the possibility for success: "I'll try to wait" (72). The bond that Chick and Lucas have formed becomes what Volosinov terms an "interacting consciousness" that moves them beyond current social norms and puts Chick into action.

The perceived crime, the murder of a white man by a black one, calls for mob rule and a lynching, compelling the people of Beat Four—the "brawlers and farmers and foxhunters and stock-and-timber-traders"—to demand their own justice (35). It is understood that the lynching will be postponed until after the Sabbath, but the retaliation, while defiant of the law, is expected. Thus, the social drama unfolds. Blacks go into hiding and a white racist mentality takes over. "Who in this county or state either is going to help [the sheriff] protect a nigger that shoots white men in the back?" (39–40). When Gavin Stevens arrives to defend Lucas, someone in the crowd yells, "Lawyer hell. He wont even need an undertaker when them Gowries get through with him tonight" (44). Even Legate, paid to guard the jail entryway, knows that the mob could overtake him: "I don't expect to stop them. If enough folks get their minds made up and keep them made up, aint anything likely to stop them from what they think they want to do" (52). In short, ingrained social structures sanction the lynching, with "the nigger acting like a nigger and the white folks acting like white folks and no real hard feelings on either side...once the fury is over" (48).

Yet the link forged between Lucas and Chick invades this drama. Lucas will rely on Chick's debt of honor to pursue the truth and the evidence that can free him. Chick realizes that "he alone of all the white people Lucas would have a chance to speak to between now and the moment when he might be dragged out of the cell and down the steps at the end of a rope, would hear the mute unhoping urgency of the eyes" (67). Even his uncle Gavin, hired to represent Lucas, believes from the circumstantial evidence that Lucas is guilty. Lucas's understanding of Gavin's mindset bars him from confiding in the lawyer, leaving Chick his mainstay of support. Chick processes the external social thinking that would demand Lucas to "die not because he was a murderer but because his skin was black" (70–71). Yet his experiences with Lucas equip him to reject this ideology.

In addition to Chick, Lucas has other allies who will buck the group mentality. The sheriff, Hope Hampton, chooses to uphold his sworn duty. He disperses the crowd firmly, saying "I told you folks once to get out of here. I aint going to tell you again" (44). Likewise, Legate performs his job out of moral obligation as well as for pay. The jailer Tubbs, who would like to remove himself from the conflict, saying that Lucas is not worth sacrificing his life and leaving behind his wife and children to fend for themselves, nonetheless acquiesces to his conscience: "[H]ow am I going to live with myself if I let a passel of nogood sonabitches take a prisoner away from me?" (53). He does, however, go so far as to take the blanket off the cot to assure the separation of white and black. In addition, Miss Habersham (based on her intimate connections with Molly and her family) and Aleck Sander take up Lucas's cause. By accompanying Chick to the grave, they serve as catalysts in securing Lucas's freedom.

Despite their reasons for assisting Lucas—whether moral obligation or prior close association with him—these townspeople counter socially constructed roles. It is useful to look at specific collaborative moments that help reshape the community. When Chick struggles to figure out a way to get to and from the grave, he has an imagined conversation with Lucas in which he tries to justify what he fears will be his ultimate failure:

> *We have to use the horse...:* and Lucas:
> *You could have axed him for the car:* and he:

> He would have refused....He wouldn't only have refused, he would have locked me up where I couldn't even have walked out them let alone had a horse: and Lucas:
> All right, all right....After all, it aint you them Gowries is fixing to set afire....(83)

Through this dialogue, Chick works through the obstacles only to arrive at the ultimate horror of what is at stake. In this collaborative moment, Chick realizes that despite the impediments, he must act. By doing so, he achieves a perspective on himself: "a provincial Mississippian...still a swaddled unwitting infant in the long tradition of his native land" (95). But his collaboration with Lucas transforms Chick and he muses (in the still-ingrained racist language of his culture) that he does not know what had forced him to befriend "a damned highnosed impudent Negro who even if he wasn't a murderer had been about to get...exactly what he had spent the sixty-odd years of his life asking for" (148). And his change influences his uncle Gavin, who asks, "When did you really begin to believe him?...I want to know, you see. Maybe, I'm not too old to learn either" (124).

Thus, the effect of collaborative partners grows. Lucas recruits Chick, who drafts Aleck Sander and Miss Habersham, who convince Hope Hampton and Gavin Stevens, who sway Chick's mother. Their cooperative efforts reshape individual consciousness, a prelude to renegotiating social constructions of identity. By the close of the novel, Lucas's plight has permeated the conscience of the entire county, causing the mob or "Face" to run (178). This confrontation with socially constructed racial being reverses the prevailing mindset that blacks kill whites and brothers do not kill brothers. Innocence can no longer be sacrificed for the sake of accepted stereotypes.

And yet, this movement is slow. Despite their belief in Lucas's innocence, the sheriff, Chick, Miss Habersham, and Gavin all leave Aleck Sander to eat his breakfast in the kitchen while they have theirs in the dining room, thereby perpetuating separation. Likewise, Hope Hampton brings black prisoners to dig up the graves, designating a racial quality to the work. The social shifts so sorely needed will take time, and Gavin's controversial musings on the South's right to change without the intervention of Northern or federal authorities speak to the complexity of the process.[1] The collaboration of Lucas and Chick attest to the charge that change must come from within the South, an alteration "which we [the South] will have to do for the reason that nobody else can" (151). That the South must "abolish [injustice] ourselves, alone and without help" points to the initiatives that individuals must undertake (199). As Karaganis has stated, "[N]ational redemption isn't really a collective movement at all...but rather a liberation in series of individuals such as Chick, who thus both represents the process *and begins it*" (78). In his reflections about his society, Gavin summarizes the goals of multicultural education that strive for equal access to economic, political, and social power: "We—he and us—should confederate: swap him the rest of the economic and political and cultural privileges which are his right, for the reversion of his capacity to wait and endure and survive. Then we would prevail" (153). This cooperative working together suggests a path for social change. At the novel's close, Lucas issues an invitation to Chick to visit him without a fall in the creek: "You'll be welcome without waiting for a freeze" (235). In doing so, he acknowledges how their bond has taken them outside accepted social protocol.

Cultural identity, like individual subjectivity, requires alteration of internal codes. Cultural change will surface, but resistance by current thinking slows the process. Gavin describes this process when he tells Chick that the South is "defending not actually our politics or beliefs or even our way of life, but simply our homogeneity from a federal government to which in simple desperation the rest of this country has had to surrender voluntarily more and more of its personal and private liberty" (150). He also echoes current arguments for states' rights and less government control. Perhaps because my students are in Washington, D.C., they are attuned to these social and political issues. As a result, *Intruder* lends itself to discussions of politics. Ongoing controversies regarding Confederate monuments, gun registration, immigrant policies, and state sovereignty reinforce the fact that many states continue to be at odds with government regulations.

This cultural approach illuminates Faulkner's treatment of race in *Intruder* and explores how "[t]he novel's readers, like its characters, then and now, are defined by their histories and contexts" (Moreland 67). On another level, while the plot drives *Intruder* in a more chronological fashion than some of Faulkner's other works, students still encounter misunderstandings in the text. References to "he" sometimes indicate Chick and sometimes Lucas, causing confusion as to whom the text refers. Therefore, the intricacies of the plot itself—the identities of the Gowrie brothers, the different visits to the grave, the actual murder weapon, what Lucas knew and when—all need to be addressed. Prior to their reading of the novel, I hand out a "Who's Who" sheet to identify the main characters. However, I usually cover plot on the second discussion day, when I know everyone has finished the book. The first day we discuss the social constructions at work and what the text reveals about Southern culture.

A cultural framework allows students to examine how cultural codes pervade Faulkner's text. The magnitude of Chick's dilemma and what he must overcome to rescue Lucas comes into focus. Ironically, Miss Habersham (like Rosa Millard in *The Unvanquished*) relies on the cultural codes that overprotect women to aid her as she works to free Lucas. Both characters address the problem of altering a fixed way of thinking. Finally, *Intruder* is a novel about community awareness of the anachronistic ideology of white society. The text reveals the heteroglossic voices that break down established codes and express the recognition that an altered ideology, though distant, is foreseeable and long overdue.

NOTES

1. See Neil Schmitz for a discussion of Gavin's racism and Faulkner's post-Confederate writing in "Faulkner and the Post-Confederate," *Faulkner in Cultural Context. Faulkner and Yoknapatawpha, 1995*, eds. Donald M. Kartiganer and Ann J. Abadie (Jackson: University Press of Mississippi, 1997), 241–62.

BIBLIOGRAPHY

Bakhtin, Mikhail. *The Dialogic Imagination.* Ed. Michael Holquist. Trans. Caryl Emerson and Michael Holquist. Austin: University of Texas Press, 1990.

Bruffee, Kenneth A. "Collaborative Learning and the 'Conversation of Mankind.'" *College English* 46.7 (1984): 635–52.

Faulkner, William. *Intruder in the Dust.* 1948. New York: Vintage International, 1991.

Hannon, Charles. "Race Fantasies: The Filming of *Intruder in the Dust.*" In Kartiganer and Abadie, *Faulkner in Cultural Context,* 263–83.

Karaganis, Joe. "Negotiating the National Voice in Faulkner's Late Work." *Arizona Quarterly* 54.4 (1998): 53–81.

Kartiganer, Donald M., and Ann J. Abadie, eds. *Faulkner in Cultural Context: Faulkner and Yoknapatawpha, 1995.* Jackson: University Press of Mississippi, 1997.

Moreland, Richard C. "Contextualizing Faulkner's *Intruder in the Dust.* Sherlock Holmes, Chick Mallison, Decolonization, and Change." *Faulkner Journal* 12.2 (1997): 57–68.

Schmitz, Neil. "Faulkner and the Post-Confederate." In Kartiganer and Abadie, *Faulkner in Cultural Context,* 241–62.

Volosinov, V. N. *Marxism and the Philosophy of Language.* Trans. Ladislav Matejka and I. R. Titunik. Cambridge: Harvard University Press, 1973.

Vygotsky, Lev Semenovich. *Thought and Language.* Eds. and trans. Eugenia Hanfmann and Gertrude Vakar. Cambridge: Massachusetts Institute of Technology Press, 1962.

Permissions

"The Community in Action," Cleanth Brooks. From *William Faulkner: The Yoknapatawpha Country*, by Cleanth Brooks (Baton Rouge: Louisiana State University Press, 1963). Copyright 1963 by Cleanth Brooks. Reprinted by permission of Louisiana State University Press.

"Man on the Margin: Lucas Beauchamp and the Limitations of Space," Keith Clark. From *The Faulkner Journal* (Fall 1990), pp. 67-79. Copyright 1990 by the University of Akron. Reprinted by permission of the University of Central Florida.

"Eunice Habersham's Lessons in *Intruder in the Dust*," Ikuko Fujihira. Printed by permission of the author.

"Teaching *Intruder in the Dust* Through Its Political and Historical Context," Robert W. Hamblin. From *Teaching Faulkner: Approaches and Methods*, edited by Stephen Hahn and Robert W. Hamblin (Westport, CT: Greenwood Press, 2001), pp. 151-62. Reprinted by permission of the Greenwood Publishing Group.

"Race Fantasies: The Filming of *Intruder in the Dust*," Charles Hannon. From *Faulkner in Cultural Context: Faulkner and Yoknapatawpha, 1995*, edited by Donald M. Kartiganer and Ann J. Abadie (Jackson: University Press of Mississippi, 1997), pp. 263-83. Reprinted by permission of the University Press of Mississippi.

"Negotiating the National Voice in Faulkner's Late Work," Joe Karaganis. From *Arizona Quarterly* (Winter 1998), pp. 53-81. Reprinted by permission of *Arizona Quarterly*.

"Faulkner's Comic Narrative of Community," Donald M. Kartiganer. Printed by permission of the author.

"Contextualizing Faulkner's *Intruder in the Dust*: Sherlock Holmes, Chick Mallison, Decolonization, and Change," Richard C. Moreland. From *The Faulkner Journal* (Spring 1997), pp. 57-68. Copyright 1997 by the University of Akron. Reprinted by permission of the University of Central Florida.

"Man in the Middle: Faulkner and the Southern White Moderate," Noel Polk. From *Faulkner and Race: Faulkner and Yoknapatawpha, 1986*, edited by Doreen Fowler and Ann J. Abadie (Jackson: University Press of Mississippi, 1987), pp. 130-51. Reprinted by permission of the University Press of Mississippi.

"*Intruder in the Dust*: A Re-evaluation," Patrick Samway, S.J. From *Faulkner: The Unappeased Imagination*, edited by Glenn O. Carey (Troy, NY: The Whitston Publishing Company, 1980), pp. 83-113. Reprinted by permission of the author.

"Faulkner and the Post-Confederate," Neil Schmitz. From *Faulkner in Cultural Context: Faulkner and Yoknapatawpha, 1995*, edited by Donald M. Kartiganer and Ann J. Abadie (Jackson: University Press of Mississippi, 1997), pp. 241-63. Reprinted by permission of the University Press of Mississippi.

"'The Sum of Your Ancestry': Cultural Context and *Intruder in the Dust*," Evelyn Jaffe Schreiber. From *Teaching Faulkner: Approaches and Methods*, edited by Stephen Hahn and Robert W. Hamblin (Westport, CT: Greenwood Press, 2001), pp. 163-70. Reprinted by permission of the Greenwood Publishing Group.